PRINCE'S
MANUAL OF
ROSES

BOOKS IN THE

OLD ROSE SERIES

THE BOOK OF ROSES OR,
THE ROSE FANCIER'S MANUAL
by Catherine Frances Gore

HISTORY OF THE ROSE
by Roy E. Shepherd

OLD GARDEN ROSES
by Edward A. Bunyard

OLD ROSES
by Ethelyn Emery Keays

PARSONS ON THE ROSE
by Samuel B. Parsons

PRINCE'S MANUAL OF ROSES
by William Robert Prince

ROSARUM MONOGRAPHIA OR,
A BOTANICAL HISTORY OF ROSES
by John Lindley

THE ROSE
by H. B. Ellwanger

THE ROSE AMATEUR'S GUIDE
by Thomas Rivers

THE ROSE GARDEN
by William Paul

THE ROSE MANUAL
by Robert Buist

PRINCE'S
MANUAL OF
ROSES

William Robert Prince

New Foreword by
Léonie Bell

Earl M. Coleman, Publisher

Stanfordville, New York   1979

Library of Congress Cataloging in Publication Data

Prince, William Robert, 1795-1869.
  Prince's Manual of roses.

  (Old roses series)
  Reprint of the 1846 ed. published by the author, New York.
  1. Roses.   2. Roses—Varieties.   3. Rose culture.   I. Title.   II. Title: Manual of roses.   III. Series.
SB411.P69   1979   635.9'33'372   79-20719
ISBN 0-930576-18-7

This Earl M. Coleman edition of PRINCE'S MANUAL OF ROSES is a faithful facsimile reproduction of the edition published in New York in 1846. It includes a new foreword prepared for this edition.

FOREWORD TO THE 1979 EDITION

The story of William Robert Prince and his *Manual of Roses* remains something of a mystery to me. Even after learning as much as possible about the man, who was part of the first great horticultural family in America, I can only conjecture why he chose to proceed as he did.

Of the first Prince, Robert, there is no record of his arrival in North America except that he settled his family along the north shore of Long Island, across the Sound from what was then New Amsterdam, early in the 1700s. The Huguenots who had already discovered the felicitous climate there had brought from France many of their fruits, and so began the local interest in growing things that was to dominate the area for many generations.

By 1737 Robert Prince had entered the plant trade; with the help of his son William, the "Old American Nursery" gradually became the largest supplier of fruit trees and grape vines in the New World. The War of the Revolution slowed business only temporarily; afterward there was greater demand for fruit trees than ever. The catalogue of 1794 offered such variety that a modern nursery might blanch at the work involved.

The second proprietor, William, was the first to see the advantage of growing the native pecan commercially. This he accomplished by sowing thirty nuts brought by fur traders from the South; ten grew to young trees, most of which he shipped to England for ten guineas each, an enormous sum in those days. Pecans were a specialty of the nursery from that time on.

In his advanced years he divided the nursery between two sons, Benjamin and William. The second, William Prince, decided to purchase additional acreage nearby, and so, in 1793, was begun "The Linnaean Botanic Garden", as he was fond of calling it, soon to be known internationally as the primary source of not only fruits but fine native trees and shrubs and every kind of ornamental.

Into this milieu was born the fourth generation and the third William, William Robert Prince, in 1795. As a young man he accompanied such renowned botanists as John Torrey and Thomas Nuttall on botanical forays and plant collecting expeditions throughout the Eastern States. He absorbed so much experience and knowledge of grape culture from his father's nursery practices that in 1830, he published his first book, *A Treatise on the Vine*, a work that was the standard reference for decades to come and earned him a reputation as "one of the three geniuses of American grape growing", according to U. P. Hedrick in *A History of Horticulture in America.*

The following year William Robert did the same for apples with *A Pomological Manual.* Ten years later, according to Hedrick, the 1841 catalogue of the Prince Nursery offered for sale 272 kinds of apples, 420 pears, 109 cherries, 156 plums, 116 grapes, 147 gooseberries, as well as every other kind of berry in equally generous assortment. Of ornamentals there were 196 deciduous species and varieties of trees, 273 shrubs, 111 evergreens, 73 vines, 680 roses, 85 herbs, and more than 800 garden perennials. Even the great Kohankie Nursery in Ohio could not touch such a list in its prime.

The shared aim of father and son, William and William Robert, was to propagate and grow every known plant of merit from the United States and England, not so much for profit as from a deep-rooted love of botany and the disciplines of horticulture itself. The Prince catalogues from 1815 through 1850 became standard texts among plantsmen, and in a period of great horticultural ferment when botanical expeditions were turning up plants of great commercial potential all over the world, the Prince Nursery could claim its share of memorable introductions. Among those familiar to most of us were Tree of Heaven *(Ailanthus)*, Hardy Mimosa *(Albizzia)*, Cedar of Lebanon, Japanese Scholar Tree *(Sophora)*, Saucer Magnolia, pineapple, coconut, mango and coffee.

One would think these accomplishments enough to satisfy any professional plantsman in his lifetime. Apparently they were not.

Understandably, William Robert worshipped his father. When the elder Prince died in 1842 at 76, the age all the Prince men seemed destined to reach, his son was sick with grief. He could not have sought the distraction of putting together another manuscript at that time for his *Manual of Roses* was not published until four years later, but he did use the book then as a podium for announcing his keen sense of loss in a stirring dedication.

Questions arise. Would he have considered a book about roses had his father lived? We know he was an extremely proud man, perhaps even choleric, from his letters to local newspapers that have survived. Besides the loss of a beloved parent, what other events occurred that might have spurred him to action?

Within a mile of his fields another nursery sprang up in 1838 as Samuel Bowne Parsons offered an assortment of plants essentially the same as those of the Princes, but specializing in roses. Probably because Parsons was "old family", Prince didn't seem to mind. What went on down in Philadelphia was another story.

There, a young Scot trained in Edinburgh, Robert Buist, and a partner, florist Thomas Hibbert, opened a nursery in 1830 that specialized not only in roses but in camellias, the first flower of fashion in those days. Two years later, the pair collaborated on a book, *The American Flower Garden Dictionary,* that, in its later revisions made by Buist, was to become the accepted authority on gardening. Soon the gregarious younger man (he was born in 1805), had attracted to him others of similar interests and enthusiasm. In time he introduced such of their finds as the *pointsettia* and proceeded to popularize that bright exotic as a greenhouse plant.

Did Buist's activities and success appear some sort of threat? For Prince the last straw must have come in 1844 when Buist published *The Rose Manual*, the first book about roses in the United States. Modeled on the first edition of a small volume by his fellow Britain Thomas Rivers, Buist's work was nevertheless completely original and an instant best seller.

Prince was forty-nine at the time, ten years' Buist's senior. Age, pride, and an overwhelming sense of heritage must have combined to infuriate him. Because he owned the largest collection of roses in the country, the privilege of having written the first book about them should have been his. To him, Buist was not only younger and over-educated; worse, he was foreign (as comes out later). He would show the upstart how the job should be done.

For years his mentor on roses had been Thomas Rivers (also younger than Prince, by the way), who conducted in England a large experimental nursery very like that of the Prince family. His *Rose Amateur's Guide* of 1837 proved such a success as rose development picked up momentum that he had to enlarge it twice by 1843. Prince must have thought that Rivers' work could not be improved upon because he decided that his book would "combine in its pages every item that is comprised in that estimable work, and to extract from every other source whatever additional information was available, thus forming a concentration of all the information existing in Europe." Strange, that European knowledge was acceptable while the European person was not.

He could not quote others yet because in 1846 there were none to quote. Instead, he did indeed use Rivers' "every item", but he presented it as his own. Rivers' sensible theories, his imaginative suggestions for further hybridizing, his inspired predictions were a hat that suited Prince, so he put it on. Three-quarters of the text is Rivers' own. Whether his permission was asked is not told. How Rivers felt about this later, we find no hint.

Ever since Mrs. Catherine Frances Gore published her translation of M. Boitard's work in her *Rose Fancier's Manual* in 1838, she has been accused of plagiarism, the most virulent attack as recent as 1970. The fact that the first eighty pages of introduction to that were her personal research, or that she gave credit to Boitard (and other botanists) there, or that Boitard's great work measured all of three by five inches, composed of tissue-thin pages on which the typeface is so small as to be illegible without a lens, is not told. I like to see things put into perspective. Mrs. Gore deserves our thanks, not our brickbats. As for Prince, there has never been a breath of suggestion that his course of action may have been less than ethical.

He says in his preface, "All details are given with candor, and throughout its pages, the author has cast aside all business prejudices, and discussed the subject as an admiring amateur." First, how could he possibly pass for an amateur when he had "above 700 varieties"? Did that not make him the most professional cultivator of roses in the country?

As for casting aside business prejudice, see what happens. On the very second page of text, he breaks into Rivers for the first time to add, "One can scarcely refrain from a smile at the puerile statement made by an American (not by birth) writer" who had the audacity to be confused, in print, by the French terms *provins* and *provence*. Farther on: "I have already referred to the confusion made by a writer on Roses in this country, who professes to give Americans 'Accurate Description' . . . Here is a triplicate of blunders. In the first place, no writer whatever has been so silly and ignorant as to confuse this Rose. . . " As someone said, "Prince did not act *princely*."

Now for the good news, of which there is plenty. The one-quarter of the text which is his own is very fine indeed. In my working photostatic copies of Prince and Rivers, I have indicated in the Margins of the former who wrote which paragraphs and descriptions to determine what is different. It was a tedious job but to the readers who would mine the gold in this book, I recommend it. Singled out like this, Prince's observations are still querulous, but interesting, as he raves on for a page about the Europeans' proclivity for passing off old roses under new names, for instance.

In fact, you may find as I did that when he interjects descriptions of his own, he is so deft at it, we mind he didn't take complete initiative and compose all the small word-pictures we old-rosers of any era are hungry for. He had plenty of experience at writing, with two important studies to his credit.

Prince made some immediate improvements on Rivers' edition of 1843. (We know he used this from the dates he copied, failing to realize that Rivers had not in every instance of a given year corrected his own statements from the first edition of 1837.)

He lists the roses alphabetically. Rivers started each Class by trying to keep the names in order but inevitably bogged down.

He italicizes the names, a great visual help in small pages of no indentations and fine type.

Instead of lumping all the Gallicas together in one chapter, he devotes one to those of solid color and another to those with stripes, dots and blotches, a sensible arrangement.

He keeps many of the older kinds that Rivers had already begun to drop. This policy alone by a nurseryman on our own shores, makes the Prince work invaluable. Some chapters double Rivers' offerings, in particular those on the Moss Rose, Hybrid Chinas, the Chinas and Teas. These last could not have been too popular in England for they needed intense sunshine and warm dry air to perform well; over here, ten to twenty degrees of latitude farther south, they thrived. Prince had only to fill the demand.

Thanks to this same need for heat, Samuel Feast's hybrids of our Prairie Rose never caught on overseas. Prince proudly gives the group six pages. He also attempts to set the record straight on *Rosa laevigata,* the oriental species that came to North America so long ago it was believed to be a native by early botanists, although, due to similar three-parted foliage, he still has it confused with the Banksian roses.

The chapter on early Hybrid Perpetuals is especially useful because many more varieties had been introduced since 1843. Indeed, Rivers himself had to amend his own work for its fourth edition, also in 1846, to accommodate all the new kinds.

But the peak of Prince's reportage happens in the chapter on the Noisette Rose, which is definitive. Whatever anyone since has written about the origin of this controversial hybrid of Musk and China, if he has not gone back to Prince, he will have it garbled. The truth of the matter is that John Champney of South Carolina, who had corresponded for years with the elder Prince, sent him two tubs of his small repeating rose long before Phillippe Noisette took such intense interest in it that he grew a seedling from it and sent this plus more seeds to his brother in Paris. Noisette was hardly the first to recognize its value.

The list Prince then presents is the lengthiest ever set forth. (Two years later, William Paul tells of 74 of which 19 were really Tea-Noisettes. Prince describes over 50 but offers for sale 83, only 12 of which are the newer Tea-Noisettes.) Included are quite a few of American origin and all of the early true Noisettes, they of the pale colors, small size, and enormous clusters from June to November. These small originals were never permitted to die out in the United States as they were in Europe; each year more of the delicate-looking but tough antiques surface, to tantalize and dare us to identify.

The great glory of Prince's small volume is the catalogue he added at its end. This was no whim of the binder, despite the fact that not every copy has it; he intended it be there, as we read in his preface. Here was the sum total of the Prince roses brought together by father and son, over 1600, at that time the longest list of *actual rose plants,* their prices given, in the entire world of roses.

He produced this at precisely the time, the watershed decade of the 1840s, when the old once-blooming European roses were still held in estime but the hybrids of Chinese species that rebloomed were starting a tidal wave of such impetus that new kinds peaked and were unheard of ten years later. As Prince notes in the catalogue, there was a "total change in the public taste" as more and more roses capable of successive bursts of bloom revealed themselves.

Though the print is fine, don't miss a word of it. Often, his one-line notations here are more revealing, more helpful than what appears in the chapters, whether his own work or Rivers'. Few are the roses known before 1846 not included here. The explanatory paragraph before each Class is so practical and clear, we wonder again why he could not have provided his own text in the book.

Of special usefulness are three categories unique to Prince. (Two are covered in Mrs. Gore but only in the historical sense; her translated descriptions were of roses often only pressed specimens in some herbarium.) See if you are not fascinated by his offerings of *Black Roses*, those of so dark a red or purple to appear somber indeed. Here is where Mrs. Keays found the short list of *Frankfort Roses* that puzzled me for years. Her copy of Prince was entire; my borrowed one was not.

Last are the *Rejected and Superseded Roses*, kinds that Prince offers "for 18 to 25 cents" that year but will throw out the next. In a way it is even more interesting than all that has gone before, because we can infer from the names what had gone out of fashion, what no longer sold. Would that other rose cataloguists had done the same, although we can hardly expect them to have been thoughtful of the needs of readers 130 years into the future.

The Prince policy was to offer the largest plants available for the least price, with generous discounts when ordered in quantity. We wonder if this revered nursery was the first to practice such good merchandising. At printing, the manual was priced at 50 cents; my copy has the "50" crossed through and "75" penciled in. For readers who like to compare costs, it is interesting to note that the more expensive roses, two to three dollars, have not been heard of since.

The publication of this volume will be a great boon to every rose researcher. Prince never produced another edition, for obvious reasons. It has long since disappeared from the lists of used book dealers, and libraries which preserve sound copies in their Rare Book collec-

tions do not make it readily available because it is so frail.
I think it has been caught up just in time.

Léonie Bell
Conshohocken, Pa.
July, 1979

PRINCE'S
MANUAL OF ROSES,

COMPRISING THE MOST COMPLETE

HISTORY OF THE ROSE,

INCLUDING

EVERY CLASS, AND ALL THE MOST ADMIRABLE VARIETIES THAT HAVE APPEARED

IN

EUROPE AND AMERICA;

TOGETHER WITH

AMPLE INFORMATION

ON THEIR

CULTURE AND PROPAGATION.

——————————— "See,
I have cull'd the fairest flowers:
  And where not sure—perplex'd, but pleased,
I guessed at such as seem'd the fairest !"

BY WILLIAM ROBERT PRINCE,

Proprietor of the Linnæan Botanic Garden and Nurseries, at
Flushing, and author of the Treatises on Horticulture, on Fruits, and on the Vine.

NEW-YORK:

PUBLISHED BY THE AUTHOR,

AND

CLARK & AUSTIN, SAXTON & MILES, WILEY & PUTNAM,
AND STANFORD & SWORDS.

1846.

DEDICATION.

THE first work penned by this hand, since that fated hour when thou sankest into the tomb, I now inscribe to thee! thus dedicating the aspirations of the mind to the source whence their power emanated.

To me the encomiums of the living are nought: I seek not their plaudits, which, if received, would pass me by like the idle breeze—heeded not.

But to thee, oh my Father! rises at all times the soul-felt devotion, which the remembrance of thy manifold kindnesses, and of the ever-pervading purity of feeling which stamped thy mind above all other men, is alone capable of inspiring. Rest! Rest, my Father! from the toils of life in the regions of peace; or in the sublimated enjoyment of another transition in the chain of existences, so oft by thee recounted; where—oh! where— the enlarged intelligence and expanded conceptions of a more glorious sphere, are destined to reward the well spent life; by unveiling to the enraptured imagination the perfections of the Deity, and the magnificence of the Universe.

WILLIAM ROBERT PRINCE.

PREFACE.

During the last ten years the acquisitions made to the Family of Roses, have been so remarkable for their splendor, fragrance and other qualities, that the public attention has been awakened to their culture in a degree almost unprecedented in the annals of Floriculture. This general regard has given rise to several publications on the subject, in France, England, Belgium, and America, and it has, at the same time, imparted an increased impetus to the culture of the " Queen of Flowers." The most prominent of the publications referred to, is from the pen of Mr. T. Rivers, Jr., of England ; and it has been the desire of the writer of the present little volume, to combine in its pages, every item of knowledge that is comprised in that estimable work, and to extract from every other source, whatever additional information was attainable ; thus forming a concentration of all the information existing in Europe on this interesting subject, and presenting the *tout ensemble* of European attainment as the starting point for American advancement, adding thereto whatever information was existent here in the present stage of the Rose Culture, and which has been derived more particularly from the labors and experience of his father and self and some few others.

The author regrets exceedingly the destitution under which we labor in regard to Chinese works on this subject, as from the proofs of knowledge presented to us in the plants themselves, which have been derived from that interesting country, they must be most ample, original, scientific, and interesting.

The culture of the Rose is not only becoming general throughout our country, but artificial fertilization is now practised by many amateurs, from which the most happy results will doubtless ensue. For the development of the various classes of the Rose in all their luxuriance of growth, beauty of foliage, expansion of flowers, and maturing of seeds, our climate possesses not only the greatest advantages over that of England, but is unsurpassed by that of Italy, or any other country in the world. The stamp of pre-eminence placed on our mighty country by the Omnipotent hand, and so well known to exist in its natural productions, is extending its influence not only in the bodily development, and intellectual advancement of the progeny of the human race emigrating to our shores, but manifests itself in a surprising degree, in the improvement by seminal reproduction of the exotics belonging to the vegetable kingdom.

In Europe hundreds of acres are now devoted to the Rose Culture, and so assiduous are the Rose Fanciers of France, Belgium and England, that each succeeding year presents the world with numbers of new and unexpected novelties of the most perfect character ; and the popular taste has become so fastidious, that only the most admirable varieties, and unique combinations, can command approbation.

William Prince, Sen., the grandfather of the author, was the first American amateur who formed an extensive collection of Roses by making importations, and his son, the late William Prince, continued to enlarge the collection annually, with the finest varieties obtainable from foreign climes ; and he also formed, in connection with the writer, a most perfect collection of our native species and varieties. At the time of his decease, in 1842, his Rose Garden comprised above 700 varieties, which he had selected with great care, rejecting such as he deemed unworthy of culture.

The Catalogue of the collection now existing in the gardens of the author, is attached to the present volume, and comprises not only the most extensive assortment in America, but being a concentration of the choicest and most splendid varieties that could be culled from the best collections of Europe ; it forms a *tout en semble* unequalled by any one European establishment ; and presents the acme to which the Rose has attained in both hemispheres. The new annual acquisitions will be announced in subsequent periodical publications.

The present little Treatise which has been prepared at leisure moments, may be considered as a general guide to the lovers of the Rose.   All the details are given with candor, and throughout its entire pages, the author has cast aside all business prejudices, and discussed the subject as an admiring amateur.   He trusts, therefore, that the directions given will be found both interesting and useful.

Varieties inserted in the Catalogue, and not noticed here, are, in many cases, equally beautiful with those that are ; but in these instances they perhaps much resemble others, or at least have no particular distinguishing traits.   It may be asked, why are so many varieties enumerated in the catalogue ?   To this I reply, that some roses resemble each other in the form and color of their flowers, yet differ much in the character of their leaves, branches, and general habit, or have other striking peculiarities, so that it is almost indispensable to have plants differing in character, but whose flowers are similar.

Some new roses inserted in the catalogue have only bloomed here one season, and perhaps not in perfection, so that accurate descriptions could not be given of them : the most of these are undoubtedly fine varieties.   In classing the roses, I have retained those that are but slightly hybridized in the division to which they have the nearest affinity ; for instance, if a rose between the French and Provence roses, has more of the character of the former than the latter, it is retained with the French roses, as it will group well with them, though not a pure French rose ; this helps to avoid too numerous subdivisions.

It is a circumstance most gratifying, that all pursuits connected with natural objects, carry with them a charm far transcending every fictitious enjoyment. These pursuits are calculated to soften the asperities of our nature, and to awaken and enliven the noble emotions which are inherent in the mind of man, but which are in a great degree rendered dormant and paralyzed by what are entitled the refinements of civilization ; which is in truth but another term for the annihilation of every natural emotion, and for a most unnatural duplicity and contrariety in all the forms and actions of life ; thus, in a great degree, banishing all that is true and really gratifying in the natural affections, and presenting in their stead only the basest counterfeit of the ennobling original.

He who seeks for unerring truth, and has become sickened at the unmeaning forms and falsities of life, will find it in the charming realm of Flora, for there at least, as in the immutable paths of astronomy and geology, he will find *nature true to herself.* In the earlier days of the writer, it was his frequent response to friends, when the sorrows of life formed the theme, that he " ne'er knew a sorrow, that he could not ramble among flowers and forget ;" and such indeed are the pure and unalloyed sensations that twine around the heart and entrance the mind of the true votary of Flora ; sensations generated with our existence, the unadulterated aspirations of the natural and uncontaminated mind, as it came from the hand of its Maker ; and which can only be neutralized, blighted, or obliterated by the falsities of (so called) civilized society.

The culture of flowers, although now mingled with the numerous and sterner duties of life, is still, to the writer, the medium whence is derived the most soothing and pleasurable mental relaxation ; and as such, he recommends it to his friends in that degree, which they may find consistent with the more serious and arduous duties of life, to which it will serve as a most cheering relief and amelioration.

                                        THE AUTHOR.

SUMMER OR JUNE ROSES.

THE PROVENCE, OR CABBAGE ROSE.

Rosa Centifolia, var. *Provincialis*.

OF all the imported species this was the first introduced
to our hemisphere, and several of its varieties have become
widely disseminated throughout our country and the
British Provinces, but they are seldom met with in Mexico
and South America. It has long and deservedly been the
favorite ornament of English gardens; and if, as seems
very probable, it was the hundred-leaved rose of Pliny,
and the favorite flower of the Romans, contributing in no
small degree to the luxurious enjoyments of that great
people, it claims attention as much for its high antiquity,
as for its intrinsic beauty. 1596 is given by botanists as
the date of its introduction to our gardens. That " prince
of gardeners," Miller, says that it is the prettiest of all roses;
and this idea still prevails to a great extent in the agricultural districts of England, where, in the farm and cottage
gardens, the Cabbage Rose and the Double Wall-Flower
are the most esteemed inmates; forming in their turns,
with a sprig of rosemary, the Sunday *bouquet* of the re-
spectable farm-servant and cottager.

The groves of Mount Caucasus are said, by Berbestein, to

be the location of its natural growth, as are also Languedoc and Provence; but the claims of these latter have been disputed and doubtless extends no farther than the fact, that it there first became naturalized to the soil and climate. The French appellation of "Provins" Rose, applies solely to the Rosa gallica, or French Rose, and it was given to that species in consequence of its being grown very extensively for distilling in the vicinity of the town of that name, 99 miles from Paris, in the department of Seine and Marne. One can scarcely refrain from a smile at the puerile statement made by an American (not by birth) writer, who professes on his title-page to publish "An accurate description of all the finest varieties of Roses," that the "Cabbage Rose" has obtained the name of " Provins" from being cultivated at the town above referred to, when in fact the term of " Provins" has never been applied to any other than the " Rosa gallica." In doing this he commits the gross blunder of adopting the title of the " Provins or Cabbage Rose" for this whole class, and enumerates all the varieties of Provence Roses separately as " Provins" Roses. The results of this unaccountable blunder do not stop here, but has caused him to increase the confusion by another misapplication equally palpable under the head of " Rosa gallica," which I shall notice in its place. A very old rose amateur in France informed Mr. Rivers that the species with single flowers is found in a wild state in the southern provinces ; and it is therefore very probable that it was called the Provence Rose, from growing more abundantly in that locality. It has, however, an additional name in France, it being also called the "Rose à Cent Feuilles," from the botanical name, Rosa centifolia, or Hundred-leaved Rose. Hybrid roses, between this and Rosa gallica, are denominated Provence Roses by the French amateurs of the present day. Mr. Rivers remarks that, when he was a young rose-fancier, this name often misled him, as he was very apt to think that it referred to the Scotch and other small and thickly-leaved roses, and did not for a moment suppose that the term was applied to the petals or flower-leaves.

The Provence, or *Cabbage Rose*, although its fame is contested by numerous modern aspirants, still retains its ancient prerogative of being " a favorite flower," and vies with the most estimable in size, beauty, and fragrance. With us, however, it is a less abiding friend than in Europe. In the humid atmosphere of the British Isles, and of a large portion of continental Europe, the expansion of its flowers continues during six or eight weeks of the Summer months, whereas beneath the vivid and powerful rays of our Columbian sun, some varieties bloom but for a few days and none exceed a fortnight's duration. The French and English Rose fanciers have experienced great difficulty in deciding as to the varieties that legitimately belong to this species, in consequence of the multitude of seminal progeny produced during late years, connected with the natural and artificial hybriding of this with other species. I will now proceed to describe a few of the finest varieties that are deemed to belong to this class, selecting from those that are exceedingly varied in form, and in the disposition of the petals. The term " *Cabbage*" *Provence Rose*, is derived from the form of the old variety and of several others, which are of a round cupped form, very compact before expansion, and never becoming flat. This parent of a countless family has wood of vigorous growth, sparsely studded with thorns, and its flowers are of a clear and delicate pink hue. It flourishes most in a half shady position, the direct rays of our sun being too powerful and often killing the shoots.

The *Dutch*, or *Large Provence*, is very large, bright red, equally fragrant, but less double than the preceding. It is much esteemed for forcing, and unlike the Cabbage Rose, it expands fully. This variety appears to have existed longer, and to be more widely disseminated in our Atlantic gardens than any other. The *Belgic Provence*, or *Belgic Blush*, is totally distinct from the preceding, of a delicate silvery blush color, very double, and blooms in profuse clus- sters. *Anemoniflora* has the central petals imperfect, and partially fimbriated, imparting to it somewhat the appear- ance of a semi-double Anemone, whence its title. It is perhaps more curious than beautiful. *Belle Ruineuse* is of a pale rosy blush hue, very double, and beautifully cupped.

The *Celery-leaved Rose*, or *Rosa Apiifolia*, is also a curious rose, unlike any other : its leaves are, perhaps, as much like imperfectly curled parsley as celery. The *Curled Provence* is as beautiful as curious, having fine globular-shaped flowers, with petals waved in a very pe- culiar manner. *Cricks*, or *Yorkshire Provence*, has great affinity to the old Cabbage Rose, varying only in being a shade darker and in a more free expansion of its flowers. *Crested Provence* will be found among the Moss Roses, which I as well as Mr. Rivers, have deemed its most appro- priate location. *Coligny*, is an extremely beautiful new French variety, of a crimson hue, marbled with white, and very desirable. *Dianthæflora*, *Oiellet*, or the Pink-flowered Rose, is a curious variety, with imperfect laciniated petals, unlike any other rose, and something like a pink. *Duchesne* is slightly hybridized, with very large, finely-shaped, rosy blush flowers. *De Nancy* is a cupped flower, very large, and of a brilliant rose color. *De Rennes* is of a globular form, large, and of a silvery blush hue. *Fenelle de la Chine* is deep rose color, with curious foliage. *Foliacée* is very large, and rose colored ; there is a flesh colored variety of the same name among the Hybrid Provence Roses. *Grand Bercam* is a large flower of a deep rose color, and one of the darkest of its class, but less perfect in form than many others. *Grande Agathe*, also known as the Läcken Provence, is indeed a grand rose, remarkably double, and finely formed. Its flowers are of the palest flesh-color, and like some others of the true Provence Roses, its clusters of bloom are too heavy and pendulous to be seen with effect on dwarf plants. *Glandulosa*, is rose color, the leaves gilded on the margin. *Kingston*, an ancient variety, very small, rose colored, full double and pretty. The *King of Holland* is a very old variety, with immense globular flowers, and curious sepals ; so that the flower-bud seems surrounded with leaves. *Lilacina variegata* is much admired, although somewhat variable ; the color is lilac striped with white.   The *Monstrous Provence, Cabbage-leaved*, or *Centifolia bullata*, has that large and curious inflated foliage, which we have no expressive name for, but which the French call " bullé ;" it is a vigorous-growing plant, with flowers like the Old Provence. *La Reine de Provence* really deserves to be the queen of this division. Its large and finely shaped globular flowers have a good effect when suspended from a standard : these are of a pale lilac rose-color, distinct and beautiful. *Petalless*, or *Sans petales*, a very singular variety. *Pompone*, very small and pretty, rose colored, and full double. *Pompone carné*, or *blanc*, of same size as the preceding, but of a pale incarnate hue. *Rochebardon* is deep rose colored and beautiful. *Royal Welsh Provence* is a very large and beautiful rose, of a fine blush color, and the shoots grow vigorously. *Scarlet Provence* is an old variety, one of those misnomers that in flowers so often lead to disappointment : it was probably the first Provence Rose that made an approach to scarlet ; but the faint carmine of its flowers is very far removed from that rare color among roses. The *Sylvain* is of cupped form, brilliant rose color, and very superb ;

the plant is of vigorous growth. The *Striped Provence* is a delicate variety with flowers of a pale flesh-color, often striped with red. It has smooth glaucous green shoots, and leaves much resembling the Striped Moss, and the Old White Moss.

The Unique, or *White Provence,* is a genuine English rose, which was found by Mr. Grimwood, then of the Kensington Nursery, (England,) in some cottage-garden, growing among plants of the common Cabbage Rose. It is a very double flower, the buds edged with pink, and is very beautiful both before and after expansion. This variety was from the first much esteemed, and plants of it were sold at very high prices. Most probably this was not a seedling from the Old Cabbage Rose, as that is too double to bear seed in the English climate, but was what is called by florists a sporting* branch or sucker. In describing this and the next division, I shall have occasion to notice more of these spontaneous deviations. *The Striped Unique* is one ; for this was not raised from seed, but a flowering branch of the Unique having produced striped flowers, plants were budded from it, and the variety was "fixed," as the French florists term it. However, this is certainly *not fixed ;* for it is a most inconstant rose, in some soils producing flowers beautifully striped, in others entirely red, and in the soil of Mr. Rivers' nursery, most frequently pure white. In Sussex, where it has bloomed finely in its variegated character, it has been honored with a new name, and is there known as " the Maid of the Valley." The *Wellington Provence* is one of the largest of this division,

---

* A term used to denote any portion of a plant departing from the character the entire plant should sustain. Thus, one stem of a carnation will often produce plain-colored flowers, while the remainder of the plant has striped flowers : it is, in such case, said " to sport."

something like Grand Bercam in the color of its flowers,
which are of a beautiful deep rose, very double, nearly as
as much so as those of the Cabbage Provence.   This forms
a splendid standard.   *Triomphe d'Abbeville* is of vigorous
habit, the flower of cupped form, and of a beautiful vivid
crimson hue.   *Vilmorin* is large, incarnate, and full double.

The Superb Striped Unique is very beautiful and constant in its variegation ; it is of less vigorous growth than
the common Striped Unique, its leaves nearly round and
deeply serrated.   This is not the variety mentioned as
grown in Sussex, but a French variety, which was found
among others, and propagated on account of its distinct
character.

New and beautiful varieties are being added by seminal
production, each succeeding year, to this interesting family.

There are but two ways in which Provence Roses can
be employed as ornaments to the flower-garden,—as standards for the lawn, and as dwarfs for beds.   Standards of
some of the varieties, if grown on a strong clayey soil,
form fine objects of ornament, as their large globular flowers are so gracefully pendant.   In this description of soil,
also, if grown as dwarfs, they will not flourish, unless they
are worked on the Dog Rose, or Sweet Briar ; but in light
sandy soils it will be advisable to cultivate them on their
own roots.   The freedom with which they grow in light
sandy soils points out this method of culture on such soils
as the most eligible.   In pruning, they require a free use
of the knife : every shoot should be shortened to three or
four buds in February.   If not pruned in this severe manner, the plants soon become straggling and unsightly.   In
poor soils, they should have annually, in November, a dressing of rotten manure on the surface of the bed, to be
washed in by the rains of winter.

To raise Provence Roses from seed, for which more full directions are given when treating of the Moss Rose, the Wellington should be planted with, and fertilized by, the single Crimson Moss, and the Grand Bercam with the Luxembourg Moss; if seed can be procured from either of these varieties, thus fertilized, some fine crimson, and, what is also very desirable, pure Provence Roses may be raised. As the characters of the true Provence Rose are so desirable, the object ought to be to endeavor to obtain deep crimson varieties, with all the pleasing qualities and perfume of the original. Wilberforce, planted with the single Crimson Moss, might possibly produce seed; but this variety is a hybrid, and like many other hybrid roses, it does not bear seed so freely as those that are pure: but I shall have occasion to notice many exceptions to this, in giving instructions for raising new roses from seed: these instructions and hints, with the names of the best seed-bearing roses, will be given at the end of each article, and they will, I hope, form a valuable addition to this work.

THE MOSS ROSE.

Rosa centifolia muscosa.

THE Moss Rose, or Mossy Provence Rose, is most probably an accidental sport or seminal variety of the common Provence Rose, as the Old Double Provence Rose, which was introduced to England from Holland in 1596, is the only one mentioned by early writers on gardening. If it had any claims to be ranked as a botanical species,* the

---

* Miller says, with a most remarkable simplicity, that he thinks it must be a distinct species, as it is so much more difficult of propagation than the common Provence Rose.

single-flowering Moss Rose would most probably have been the first known and described; but the single Moss, as compared with the Double, is a new variety. The year 1724 is recorded by botanists as the date of its introduction, or rather of its being first noticed in Europe, and Miller mentions it in 1727. Some few years since a traveller in Portugal mentioned that the Moss Rose grew wild in the neighborhood of Cintra; but most likely, the plants were stragglers from some garden, as I have never seen this assertion properly authenticated. The origin of the Double Moss Rose, like that of the Old Double Yellow Rose (Rosa sulphurea) is therefore left to conjecture; for gardeners in those days did not publish to the world the result of their operations and discoveries. As regards the Moss Rose this is a subject of regret, for it would be very interesting to know how and where this general favorite originated. Probably, when first noticed, gardening was of such small consideration, that the discovery of a rose, however remarkable, would not be thought worth registering. That it is merely an accidental sport of the common Provence Rose is strengthend by the fact, that plants produced by the seed of the Moss Rose do not always show moss: perhaps not more than two plants out of three will be mossy, as has been often proved. Those that are not so are most evidently pure Provence Roses, possessing all their characters. To show, also, the singular propensity of the varieties of Rosa centifolia to vary, I may here mention that the common Moss Rose often produces shoots entirely destitute of moss. Mr. Rivers makes mention of his having observed a luxuriant branch of the Crimson or Damask, which is generally more mossy than the Old Moss Rose that presented a remarkable appearance, being almost smooth. The next season it had entirely lost its moss, and had produced semi-double flowers, the exact resemblance of the

1*

Scarlet Provence. The *White Moss* is another instance of this singular quality, for that originated from a sporting branch ; the Mossy de Meaux is also a curious deviation, the history of which will be given under its descriptive enumeration ; and the *Crested Moss, or Provence,* is another case in point. It seems, therefore, very feasible that the Provence Rose, from being cultivated in Italy through so many ages, produced from seed, or more probably from a sporting branch, the Double Moss Rose, that is, a double Cabbage or Provence Rose, covered with that glandular excrescence which we term moss; this branch or plant was propagated, and the variety handed down to us, perhaps, as much or more admired in the present day as when first discovered. These Roses always have been, and I hope always will be, favorites : for what can be more elegant than the bud of the Moss Rose, with its pure rose-colour, peeping through that beautiful and unique envelope ?

The assertion advanced by some writers that this Rose when cultivated in Italy "loses its mossiness almost immediately, through the influence of climate," is puerile, when the fact is so well known to us that it retains this distinctive character at New-Orleans, and at other localities far exceeding Italy in an approach to a tropical climate.

The ancient variety which we have referred to, called the *Common Moss, Mossy Provence,* or *Red Moss Rose,* is of a pure rose-color, and when in bud is surpassingly beautiful. When fully expanded it is a fine rose, but at that period, the moss being concealed beneath the petals, it no longer presents to the eye its distinctive attraction. During nearly a century that this Rose existed in Europe, no new variety was produced, but of late years the greatest attention has been devoted to the production of seminal varieties, and the success has been so triumphant that not less than 70 fine varieties have been produced, including some which bloom several times during the year, and others hybridized with the Bourbon, and other classes of Roses. I have at great expense imported the entire collection.

I will describe a number of them, and will commence with the *Asepala, Sans petales*, or *Rosa muscosa asepala;* a new variety, something like the Provence Dianthæflora, curious, sometimes very pretty. The *Blush Moss* is a most beautiful variety of the color of that well known rose, the Celestial,—so exactly intermediate between the White Moss and the common, that it is quite necessary in a collection. The *Crimson* or *Damask Moss*, sometimes called the Tinwell Moss, was originated in the garden of a clergyman at Tinwell in Rutlandshire. This is a more luxuriant grower than the Old Moss. Its flowers are of a deeper color, its foliage larger, and its branches, leaves, and buds are more mossy. It is an excellent rose for beds; for, if its shoots are pegged to the ground with small hooks, the surface is soon covered with its luxuriant foliage and flowers. For this purpose it is better on its own roots, as worked plants so treated would throw up too many suckers. The *French Crimson Moss* is distinct, deeper in color, and much more double than the preceding, not so luxuriant in growth, but one of the best Moss Roses we have. The *Crested Moss, Crested Provence, Fringed Provence, Rosa cristata*, or *Rose des Peintres*, for it is known by these three names, is said to have been discovered growing from the crevice of a wall at Friburg in Switzerland. No rose can be more singular and beautiful than this. The buds, before expansion, are so clasped by its fringed sepals, that they present a most unique and elegant appearance, totally unlike any other rose. When the flower is fully expanded, this peculiar beauty vanishes, and it has merely the appearance of a superior variety of the Provence Rose. It should here be mentioned, that, if

grown in a poor soil, its buds often lose their crest, and become plain, like the Provence Rose. As a standard, this
rose is very graceful, its large flowers and buds drooping
from their weight. *Veillard* is large and very double, of
a delicate rose color, not differing in this from the Common
Moss; but it seems more dwarf and delicate in its habit, and
more abundantly mossed. It has been confused by one
American writer with the Luxembourg Moss, but it is
quite distinct both in color and form, this being globular
and rose colored, whereas, that is cupped, and crimson,
with a purple tinge. The Luxembourg is also of very
robust habit. *Eclatante* is a variety quite worthy of
notice; for it is so vigorous in its growth, that it soon forms
a fine tree; its color is also remarkably bright.

Moussué Partout or Zoé, is indeed all over moss; its
leaves, branches, and buds being thickly covered. The
flowers of this singular variety are much like the common Moss Rose. *The Miniature Moss* is one which
Mr. Rivers originated from seed in his endeavors to raise a
superior dark variety from the Single Moss Rose. Its
flowers are small, of a bright pink, and pretty, though only
semi-double. *The Prolific Moss* is not the Prolifère of
the French, but a dwarf variety of the common Moss, and
a most abundant bloomer. This is known by the French
florists as the Minor Moss: it is a most excellent variety
to keep in pots for forcing. *Prolifère*, sometimes called
Mottled Moss, is an old French variety of vigorous habit,
producing very large globular flowers, with petals that are
crisp or curled before the expansion of the flower, whence it
derived its name of Mottled Moss. The flowers do not open
well in the humid climate of England, but beneath our powerful sun they develope themselves with great beauty. The
Pompone Moss, or Mossy de Meuax, has for some years
been a great favorite. This rose was found by Mr.

Sweet in a garden at Taunton, England, in 1814. He obtained possession of the plant for five pounds ; and afterwards distributed the young plants at one guinea each. It was most probably an accidental sport from the Old Rose de Meaux, and not from seed, as that rose is too double to bear seed in the English climate. This is one of the prettiest of roses, and one of the first to make its appearance in June, gladdening us with its early clusters of small and finely-shaped flowers. It is not well adapted for a standard; for when grafted or budded, it is but a short-lived plant, at least in the generality of soils ; on its own roots, in light rich soils, it may be grown in great perfection. *The Perpetual White Moss*, or *Quatre saisons mousseux* of the French, is a Damask Rose : it is pretty only in bud; for, when expanded, the flower is ill-formed. It made a great noise in the rose world when it first appeared ; but its reputation for beauty was much overrated. However, if grown luxuriantly, it produces immense clusters of buds, which have a very elegant and unique appearance. This rose is a proof, often occurring, that florists are apt to designate a plant by some name descriptive of *what they wish it to be, rather than what it is*. It is *not perpetual*, but in a rich free soil sufficiently moist, it will usually bloom three or four times during the season. The *Luxembourg Moss, or " Ferrugineuse,"* was raised from seed, within these few years, at the Luxembourg Gardens. It is evidently much tinged with the dark coloring of some variety of Rosa gallica, and *approaches* to that grand desideratum, a dark crimson Moss Rose. This is a superb variety, of great luxuriance of growth, forming a fine standard : it will probably be the parent of a dark Moss Rose still more splendid, as it bears seed freely.

The Scarlet Moss, the Mousseuse de la Flèche of the French, from having originated at the town of la Flèche, is a pretty brilliant rose, with flowers nearly as small as the Pompone Moss, but not so double. *The Old Striped Moss, or Mousseuse Ponctuèe,* is a singular rose, of delicate growth, often producing flower-stems and buds entirely without moss; still its glaucous foliage and striped flowers give to the plant a pretty and original appearance. *The Sage-leaved Moss* is a good double rose, remarkable only for its leaves, which are much like those of the common sage. *The Single Moss* and *Single Lilac Moss* are desirable as being distinct, and capable of bearing seed from which new varieties may be raised. *Rivers' Single Moss* is inclined to be semi-double. This is a remarkably luxuriant grower, as is also the *Single Crimson Moss,* which is quite worth notice, for its beautiful color, and as it is a true Moss Rose, and bears seed abundantly, it will, I hope, be the parent of some first-rate varieties. The *White Bath, or Clifton Moss,* is a favorite and beautiful Rose ; and owes its origin to a sporting branch of the common Moss, which was found in a garden at Clifton, near Bristol, about thirty years since. The *Old White Moss* is perhaps, a French variety, as the French cultivators, when speaking of the Clifton Moss, call it Mousseuse Blanche Anglaise ; and the Old White Moss, M. Blanche Ancienne. This has not so much moss as the Clifton, and is not pure white, but inclining to a pale flesh-color; it is also much more delicate in habit.

To the Moss Roses described in the preceding pages may now be added Lancel, so named from its originator, which has the merit of producing the most beautiful of flower-buds. The moss with which they are enveloped is long and abundant, and of the most lively green; its flowers, when expanded, are of a deep reddish rose, rather irregular in shape: it is in its buds that this rose is interesting. *The Agathe-leaved Moss, "Mousseuse à Feuilles*

d'Agathe," is a new hybrid, between the Rose gallica
Agathe and the Moss Rose : its flowers are of a pale flesh
color, rather irregular in form ; this is interesting from its
singularity, but not by any means beautiful. *Mousseuse
de Metz* proves 'to be a very pretty bright carmine Moss
Rose, with flowers double and finely shaped; in short, a
rose quite worthy of cultivation.

*The Scarlet Pompone, Pompone écarlate, or Mousseuse
Picciola,* is a new variety, something like Mousseuse de la
Flèche in character, but more dwarf, with flowers much
smaller, and nearly or quite double ; it is a very pretty
bright carmine rose, and will probably prove one of the
prettiest of our dwarf Moss Roses.

A new double *White striped Moss Rose, Mousseuse Panachée pleine,* was received two years since from France,
and has proved a very pretty rose ; its flowers are pale
flesh-color striped with pink, and generally constant ; but
sometimes half the flower will be white, and the remaining
petals of a bright rose color.

A Feuilles pourpres, so named from its young leaves
being dark red. This is a pretty brilliant carmine rose,
quite distinct, with flowers rather small, and will probably,
when its character is more developed, prove to be worthy
a place in a good collection. *Alice Leroy,* recently raised
in France, that highly favorable climate for raising roses
from seed, is of a robust habit, giving full-sized double
flowers, rather a deep rose tinged with lilac.

Anemoné is a very distinct variety, with shoots very
slender and graceful ; flowers bright pink, petals incurved,
much like those of some double Anemonies. *Celina* is one
of the very best dark crimson varieties we yet possess: its
foliage has a peculiarly dark glossy-green tint, quite distinct ; its flowers are large and double, but not quite full at
the centre, color very brilliant but deep crimson, in some

seasons slightly tinged with purple ; this will most probably supersede the Luxembourg Moss, which only a few years since, was our only deep-colored moss rose. Its habit is not quite so robust as that of the latter, which in some soils is almost too much so, making here shoots six feet in length in growing seasons. The *Crimson Pompone* or *Oscar Foulard*, raised from seed by M. Foulard of Le Mans, blooms profusely, the flowers, are small, quite double, very mossy, color red, tinged with purple : a pretty and distinct rose, *Helène Mauget* and *Hortensia* are quite new roses, from that prolific parent the Luxembourg : they are pretty, but not enough distinct to be important ; to the collector only they will prove interesting. *Louise Colet* is a remarkable and distinct variety, not so much in the color of its flowers as in its curious leafy sepals, giving the flower, which is of a delicate rose color, a pretty and singular character. *Malvina*, raised by the same cultivator in France, is really a good double rose ; the whole plant distinct in character ; flowers full sized, and very double, of a bright rose-color slightly tinged with lilac. *Pompone Feu* is a dwarf variety, with peculiar brilliant pink flowers, not quite double : this is a pretty dwarf rose, and should be planted with the other Pompone Moss roses. *Princess Royal* was raised from seed by crossing that old variety Mousseuse ponctuée with the Tuscany Rose. This would indeed be the most splendid of moss roses if its flowers were quite double ; they are not so, but still more than semi-double, and the number of its petals seems to increase annually, as in the Single Crimson Moss, which, from being quite single, is now semi-double. Princess Royal is, if possible, still more robust in its habit than the Luxembourg ; it makes shoots five to seven feet in one season ; its leaves and shoots in spring are of a deep red ; it gives a profusion of flowers, which are of a very deep crimson purple, mottled with bright red ; when in bud, or half expanded, they are very beautiful. As this rose bears seed freely, it will most probably be the parent of some unique varieties. We have now also what was at one time thought to be impossible, viz. the Old Rose Unique mossed : this is called *Moss Unique de Provence.* I cannot learn its origin ; if from seed or otherwise ; but I am inclined to think it is a sport from our old favorite, the Unique Rose : its habit is exactly similar, and equally robust ; its flowers of the same pure white, and blooming in similar magnificent clusters. This beautiful white rose offers a fine contrast to Celina, and equally deserves a place in every garden.

Angelique Quetier is of vigorous growth, the flowers medium size, very double, of a delicate rose color, and the foliage of peculiar appearance. *Heloise* is of globular form, rosy crimson, with a full and projecting centre. *Indiana* is of cupped form, rose color, and very double. *Panaget* is a very distinct flower, double purple striped with red, being the only variety yet produced of this character. *Emperor*, a fine, new English variety, of cupped form, and bright crimson color. *Lansezeur* is of deep crimson, veined with Lilac. *Précoce* is an early variety, the flower deep pink, sometimes mottled near the border.

Perpetual Red Moss, or Perpetuelle Mauget, is of large size, expanded form, deep rose color, and full double. This desideratum of its class, which is said to bloom the whole summer, was originated in France by Mr. Mauget. The price there is still about $3, which may serve to indicate its estimation. The plants imported for the first in 1844, being very small, I have not yet been able to decide upon its merits from my own observations ; and we must rely for the present on the great favor with which it has been greeted in France. There is one happy circumstance in our favor as regards Roses of the perpetual character,

which is, that our powerful sun is fully adequate to develope any such characteristic, and even to a greater degree
than in France.

Sans Sepales is a distinct variety, with incarnate flowers of medium size, tinged with pale rose on the edges.
Large fruited Moss, or Mosseuse à gros fruit, is a very
valuable variety, as a stool to obtain seedlings from.   The
flower is large, rose colored, only semi-double, and having
the sexual parts perfect, will produce seeds freely.   *Mrs.
Wood* is of medium size, full double, and of a carmine
purple hue, much admired.   *Lucid leaved,* or *A feuilles
luisantes,* is one of the highest priced new French varieties ; the flower is of medium size, full double, of a delicate
rose color, with a rosette centre.   *Orleans* is a fine rose of
medium size, double, and of a purplish flame color.   *Mauget* is a deep purple rose, of the usual size, and full double.
Eclatante is very robust, with expanded flowers of a brilliant rose color.   *Sablée* is a semi-double French variety,
of a bright roseate hue, often dotted with red, whence its
title.

Charlotte de Sor is an estimable French variety, of medium size, full double and rose color.   Its foliage is what
the French term " à feuilles d'Agathe."   It is one of the
highest priced of its class.

Catharine de Wurtemburg is a new and distinct French
variety, greatly esteemed.   Its growth is very vigorous, the
flowers of a rosy blush color, and double, with stamens.

Etna is a new French variety of the usual size, cupped
form, double, of a purplish flame color, and very beautiful.

Comtesse de Murinais is a fine hybrid damask variety,
with large double white, or pale incarnate flowers.   This
was obtained from seed, but the previous white ones were
merely sportive varieties of the Provence, with the exception of the Perpetual White Moss, which, like the present

one, is a variety of the Damask. This new and highly prized Rose is of the most vigorous growth, and will flourish in soils and locations where the other White Moss varieties will not succeed. It has bloomed but one season in this country, but we may anticipate a rich display during the summer of the present year.

Princess Adelaide is the first variety produced of what will hereafter constitute a new class, to which the French have given the title of *Hybrides de Bourbons Mousseux*, or *Mossy Bourbon Roses.* If the admirable qualities of the two species thus amalgamated are fully developed, this class will be one entitled to our highest admiration. The present variety is of the same vigorous habit as the Bourbon family; the flowers are produced in immense clusters, and are large, full double, and of magnificent appearance. This Rose is one to which they attach the title of " *Une Fleur parfaite*," a perfect flower. The second and only additional variety yet obtained is La Delphinie, with flowers of a small size and brilliant rose color. The seven varieties last described, are yet rare even in France, and have been imported by the author at great expense.

Moss Roses, when grown on their own roots, require a light and rich soil : in such soils, they form fine masses of beauty in beds on lawns. In cold and clayey soils they in general succeed much better worked on the Dog Rose, forming beautiful standards. I have ascertained that they establish themselves much better on short stems, from two to three feet in height, than on taller stems. If short, the stem increases in bulk progressively with the head, and the plants will then live and flourish a great many years.

A very erroneous impression exists in regard to the hardihood of the Moss Rose. It will withstand almost any degree of cold much better than excessive heat. In fact, the old Moss Province Rose, and the white and striped

sportive varieties, and others of delicate growth, flourish
most in a northern exposure, or at least one that is sheltered from the extreme heat of noonday, such as may be
termed a half-shaded position. The new seedling varieties
which are mostly of vigorous growth, do not exact any
such precaution, but appear to flourish with as little attention as the commonest garden varieties.

To insure a succession of bloom, the plants intended to
flower early should be pruned in October, and those for
the second series the beginning of May—shortening their
shoots, as recommended for the Provence Roses. Give
them also an abundant annual dressing of manure on the
surface, in November.

To raise Moss Roses from seed is a most interesting employment for the genuine rose amateur ; such a pleasing
field is open, and so much may yet be done. The following directions will, I hope, assist those who have leisure,
perseverance, and love for this charming flower. A plant
of the Luxembourg Moss and one of the Single Crimson
Moss should be planted against a south wall, close to each
other, so that their branches may be mingled. In bright
calm sunny mornings in June, about ten o'clock, those
flowers that are expanded should be examined by pressing
the fingers on the antlers ; it will then be ascertained if the
pollen is abundant ; if so, a flower of the former should be
shaken over the latter ; or, what perhaps is better, its flow-
er-stalk should be fastened to the wall, so that the flower
will be kept in an erect position. Then cut a flower of
the Luxembourg Moss, clip off its petals with a sharp pair
of scissors, and place the anthers firmly but gently upon a
flower of the Single Crimson, so that the anthers of each
are entangled : they will keep it in its position : a stiff
breeze will then scarcely remove it. The fertilizing will
take place without further trouble, and a fine hep full of

seed will be the result. To obtain seed from the Luxembourg Moss, I need scarcely say that this operation must
be reversed. A wall is not always necessary to ripen
seed; for in dry soils, and airy exposed situations, the
above Moss Roses bear seed in tolerable abundance. The
treatment of the heps, sowing the seed, and the management of the young plants, as applicable to all, is given at
the end of the first part.

HYBRID PROVENCE ROSES.

Rosa Provincialis hybridæ.

These beautiful roses are exactly intermediate between
the French and the Provence Rose, partaking, almost in an
equal degree, of both parents. They have upon the long
and graceful shoots of the Provence the close and more
dense foliage of the French rose; and, in some of the
varieties, the pale and delicate coloring of the first is en-
livened by the rich and deep crimson hues of the latter.
The origin of these roses may be soon attested; for, if the
Single Moss, or Provence Rose, is fertilized with the farina
of Rosa gallica, Hybrid Provence roses will be produced,
agreeing in every respect with the above description.
Among the most superior varieties is *Agnes Sorel*, a delicate flesh-colored rose, very double and finely-shaped;
Alain Blanchard is large, semi-double, crimson violet, and
spotted; *Amelie Guérin* is evidently from the seed of that
good old rose, the Globe Hip, but with smaller and more
double flowers, of the same pure white; a pretty and distinct variety. *Blanchefleur* is of the most delicate flesh
color, or nearly white; very distinct, and even now one of

the finest roses. *Clelie* is a magnificent rose, of the largest dimensions, forming a very fine standard, as its branches are graceful and spreading. *Celinette* is also a very large and fine rose, of the most delicate flesh color, possessing in its habits all the characters of this division.

Duchesse d'Angoulême, or the Wax Rose, is an old but deservedly a favorite variety : its color is so delicate and its form so perfect that it must always be admired ; the habit of the plant is most luxuriant, and rather more erect than most other members of this family. *Enchantress, Grande Henriette*, or *Rose Parmentier*, for these, and I believe some others, are its synonymes, is an old and most beautiful variety, so double and finely shaped that it may be considered a prize-rose of the first character.

Foliacée is large, full double, of a delicate rosy incarnate hue.

Gracilis, or *Shailer's Provence*, is a very old and delicate-growing rose, unlike most other varieties of this family in its habit, as it seems to be between the Boursault and the Provence Rose.

The *Globe Hip*, the " Boule de Neige " of the French, was raised from seed in England, many years since. This is now much surpassed by some of our new white roses, but still is a favorite variety. Its habit is most luxuriant ; and if grafted on the same stem with George the Fourth, or some other vigorous-growing dark variety, the union will have a fine effect. The *Glory of France* is an immense rose, of the most luxuriant habit, having a fine effect grown as a standard, but, like some other very large roses, its flowers are irregularly shaped. *La Ville de Londres*, is a new variety, possessing in its bright vivid rose color, and perfect shape, all that can be wished for in a rose. *La Calaissiene* is a most perfect flower, large, of a roseate color, the habit of the plant very vigorous and robust.

L'Ingénue is most undoubtedly a descendant of the Globe Hip, with flowers of the purest white, the centre of the flower inclining to yellow; this is one of the finest white roses known, and, like the Globe Hip, it is of the most luxuriant habit. *Lycoris* is a new variety, of a fine vivid rose color, marbled and spotted in a very distinct and beautiful manner. *Madame Huet* is a full double incarnate rose, superb and perfect. *Malibran* is a distinct and good rose, with peculiar glossy foliage and shoots; it is not spreading and diffuse in its habit, but very erect, unlike any other rose in this division. *Reine des Belges*, a fine white rose, has been classed in some catalogues among the Hybrid China roses, but it is so evidently a seedling from the Globe Hip, that I have now placed it in this division : this rose, when it blooms in perfection, is one of the most double and beautiful in existence.

To this family we have some interesting additions, particularly to White Roses, of which *Melanie*, or *Melanie de Waldor*, and the *New Double Globe*, or *Boule de Neige à Fleurs pleines*, are very perfect and beautiful varieties : the latter is also called Clarisse Jolivain ; this is an improved variety of the Globe Hip.

To blush roses, *Blanche de Castille*, one of the most elegant delicate-colored roses known, and the *Blush Globe*, a seedling from the Globe Hip fertilized with the Tuscany, are valuable additions as prize roses. *Eliza Leker* is a new deep rose-colored variety, spotted, of much beauty.

Very many beautiful roses have within the last five years been added to this class ; one of the most distinct is *Christine de Pisan*, deep reddish pink, occasionally mottled ; this is a very beautiful rose, and differs much in habit and flowers from all in this family. *Délice de Flandres* is large, of a delicate shaded pink hue, fragrant, and

distinct. *Duc d'Angoulême* slightly departs from the habits
of the true Provence Rose ; it is finely shaped, and of a
vivid rose-color. *Duc de Choiseul ponetué* is a large
and splendid flower, of a roseate hue and spotted. *Donna
Sol* is white tinged with lemon. *Emerance* is also perfectly
unique, and one is inclined to wonder how this peculiar
color could be gained : its flowers are most perfect in shape,
and of a delicate straw color, differing altogether from any
other summer rose. *Illustre Beauté* or *Célestine*, has large
flowers extremely double, and not quite so globular as those
of the true Provence Roses ; it is a most beautiful rose,
and a very abundant bloomer. *Laura*, with flowers very
large, of a fine rosy blush, is a first rate and most beautiful
variety, deserving of all that can be said in its praise.
Madame Huet, and *Rose Devigne* are delicate blush roses
much alike, and both beautiful ; the latter has, perhaps, the
larger flowers of the two. The color of both is very similar, being a delicate blush. *Mathilda de Mondeville* is of
a delicate rosy lilac, varying to blush, and blooms profusely. *Odette de Champ divers* is one of the fine acquisitions of the French cultivators, and is quite distinct, of a
fine rose color, marbled with white. A new white rose,
Princesse Clementine, has within the last season been introduced ; this was raised at Angers, and is reported to be
the finest and largest white rose known. *Nero* is a fine
deep purplish red rose, grouping admirably with the, perhaps, too many pale roses in this family. *Reine Caroline*,
or *Queen Caroline*, is partially hybridized, and blooms ten to
fifteen days later than the other varieties. It is a large
flower, of a deep pink hue, varying to blush, and very beautiful. *Semilasso* is also a deep-colored and finely-shaped
rose, equally worth a place in the rose-garden. The
Spotted is of great beauty with large globular flowers of the
deepest rose color, delicately spotted. This fine rose has

large leaves, and makes upright shoots of great luxuriance and vigor. *Wilberforce* is a new variety, and very splendid. This and *La Simplicité* are slightly hybridized with some dark variety of Rosa gallica, which has greatly added to their beauty, as they both produce flowers approaching to dark crimson, a rare color among Provence Roses. *Hypacia* is a new variety of much beauty ; flowers perfectly cupped, and of the most regular shape ; color deep pink, occasionally mottled : this is a distinct and charming rose.

Hybrid Provence roses are very robust and hardy, useful to the rose amateur, as serving to form a most delicate group of soft colors : they also make admirable standards, as the branches of most of the varieties are inclined to be spreading, diffuse, and of course graceful.

The seed-bearing roses of this family are the Globe Hip, the flowers of which should not be fertilized if pure white roses are desired. Some few years since Mr. Rivers raised a plentiful crop of seedlings from this rose, fertilized with the Tuscany, and nearly all the plants produced semi-double blush and rose-colored flowers ; the Blush Globe forming the only exception. Blanche fleur, with Clélie, would possibly produce seed from which fine shaped and delicate colored roses might be expected. The same course with the Tuscany rose, would most probably originate deep rose colored varieties, with finely shaped cupped flowers.

2

THE FRENCH ROSE.

Rosa gallica.

First Division : Self-colored Flowers.

The French Rose (Rosa Gallica, of botanists) is a native inhabitant of the continent of Europe, growing abundantly in the hedges of France and Italy. In the "Floræ Romanæ" of Sebastiani, published at Rome in 1818, this rose, Rosa sempervirens, and Rosa canina, are said to be the only roses growing naturally in the Papal States. This was one of the roses introduced at the earliest period to our gardens. The year 1596 is given by botanists as the date of its introduction into England ; and owing to its bearing seed freely, it has been the parent of an immense number of varieties, many of the earlier sorts being more remarkable for their expressive French appellations than for any great dissimilarity in their habits or colors. I have already referred to the confusion made by a writer on Roses in this country, who professes to give to Americans "Accurate Descriptions." Under the present head, Rosa Gallica, he says, "Some writers consider it evidently the Hundred-leaved Rose of Pliny, so that it must have been long in cultivation, and it is rather curious that the French should call it Rose de Provins, while the English give it the name of French Rose." Here is a triplicate of blunders. In the first place, no writer whatever has been so silly and ignorant as to confuse this Rose, which is a genuine native of the French soil, with the Hundred-leaved Rose of Pliny, but one and all of them have identified the Rosa centifolia, or Cabbage Rose, with the Rose of Pliny. Secondly, it is not "*rather curious*" that the French should call this "Rose de Provins," when this is the identical species so extensively cultivated at "Provins," but it would indeed be "*rather curious*" if they called the Rosa centifolia, or Cabbage Rose,

"Provins," as the writer states in another chapter, when that rose is not in fact cultivated there at all. Thirdly, the English call it "French Rose," because it is a true native of France, whence its title of Gallica, and by what other name should they call it? The Semi-double Red Rose, or *Officinal Rose*, grown in Surrey for the druggists, is of this family, and a very slight remove from the original species, which is of the same color, with but one range of petals, or single. All the roses of this group are remarkable for their compact and upright growth, and many for the multiplicity of their petals, and tendency to produce variegated flowers. Many of the spotted, variegated, and striped varieties are very singular and beautiful. The formation of the flower, in most of the superior modern varieties of Rosa gallica, is very regular; so that most probably this family will ultimately be the favorite of those florists who show roses for prizes in the manner that dahlias are now exhibited; that is, as full blown flowers, one flower on a stem, as they bear carriage better when fully expanded, than any other roses. In France, this is called the "Provins Rose;" from the circumstance of its extensive culture at the town of Provins, as explained by the previous remarks. Some varieties of it have been classed by Rose fanciers in a separate division, as "Agathe Roses." These have curled foliage, and pale colored, compact flowers, remarkable for their crowded petals.

To describe a selection of these roses is no easy task, as the plants differ so little in their habits; and their flowers, though very dissimilar in appearance, offer nevertheless but few prominent descriptive characteristics. Some of the new varieties lately introduced, and much prized in France, do not bloom well in England, the change of climate being very unfavorable, but in our dry and warm climate they attain a perfect development.

Africaine, or *La Belle Africaine* is a very beautiful rose, one of the darkest, approaching to black. *Amourin* and Aurora are old varieties, now superseded by better ones, the former is blush and the latter pale rosy. *Anarelle* is a large-cupped and finely shaped rose ; its outer petals pale lilac, and its centre of a deep purplish rose color, distinct and good. *Antonine d'Ormois* is of vigorous habit ; the flowers large, delicate blush, and of most splendid form. *Ardoisée* is a new French variety, full double, and slate color. *Asmodée* is large, full double, rosy crimson. *Aspasie* is one of the most delicate and beautiful roses known, its form being quite perfect, a little inclining to globular, like some of the hybrid China roses. *Aurélie Lamarc* is much like the last in color and form, but is delicately spotted with white. *Assemblage des Beautés* is not quite full enough of petals, but deserves its name, for its varied and finely colored crimson and scarlet flowers on one stem are always admired. *Baron de Stael* is large, well formed, of a pale pink hue. *Belle aimable*, and *Bishop*, are obsolete varieties, the former dark red shaded and the other light red or pink. *Belle Esquermoise* large full double, shaded slate color, new and fine.

Boula de Nauteuil, or *Comte de Nauteuil*, is a most splendid flower of perfect form, crimson purple, very large, and none more admired. *Carmine brilliante* is, as its title indicates, of a carmine hue. *Cerise superbe* is one of the most brilliant in color, approaching to scarlet, and in shape perfectly beautiful. *Columella* is a deep, bright pink, shaded with flush on the margin of the petals ; sometimes it produces self-colored flowers, but is always first rate and remarkably distinct. *Champion*—there are two varieties of this name : one is bright red, an old variety now cast aside, although I notice it is called " quite new" by one writer ; the other is a dark mottled, or black variety, and superb. *Cicero* is a very large new French variety, crimson, and full double. *Cordon bleu* (erroneously called "Chardon bleu, or Blue Thistle," in a recent publication,) is a full double flower of a shaded slate color. *Coronation* is one of the older varieties, full double, well formed, brilliant color approximating to scarlet. *Comte Walsh* has not proved true to the European description, as it is not margined, but it is nevertheless a first-rate show rose.* The *Comte de Murinais* is a large flattish rose, of a slate-colored ground, spotted with rose-color ; a very distinct and good variety. *Duc de Trevise* is a most beautiful rose, of first rate form for a show rose, and of robust and distinct habit. *Duchess of Buccleugh* is very large, deep rose colored, and full double, a new variety. *Eclatante* is a rose that may be distinguished in a group, however crowded, being so extremely bright; it perhaps ought not to be called scarlet, yet no other term so well describes its color.

Eclat des Roses is a very double and large rose, of the most perfect form for a show rose ; the plant is also of the most vigorous habit. *Elemensie* and *Eliza* have now given way to the new improved varieties, the former rosy crimson, and the latter blush color. To *Fanny Parissot*, sometimes called *Fanny Bias*, the description of Eclat des Roses may also be applied, only that its color is much more delicate. *Feu brilliant* is large, purplish flame color, and constant; a new and very fine variety. *Fleur d'Amour* is one of the most vivid-colored roses in this group, much like Assemblage des Beautés, but more double. *Franklin* is a deep rose color. *Gloire des jardins* is deep red, now cast aside. *Grandissima* is a most robust-growing and very large carmine rose, likely to prove a show rose of first rate excellence. *Guerin's Gift* is of a brilliant roseate hue, and very perfect in

---

* This term is applied to those varieties that produce very double and perfect flowers, fit to be exhibited singly, as dahlias are.

form. *Hercules,* and *Hortense Beauharnois,* although possessing some valuable properties, have given place before the crowd of more estimable varieties. *Heureuse Surprise,* is a new very large full double crimson variety from France. *Isabella,* or *Prolifère,* and *Julianna,* are pink roses, and *La Favorite* is red, all rather handsome, but now superseded. *Kean* is always a beautiful rose, in size first rate, and in shape quite perfection ; color bright reddish crimson, sometimes approaching to scarlet. *King of Rome, Ponceau parfait,* or *Theodore de Corse,* (they being the same,) is a beautiful double and compact rose, so exactly like a double ranunculus that it might almost be mistaken for one. *L'Ombre superbe,* is an old black rose, (so called) but not so dark colored as many of its class, being only a deep shaded purple. *La Tour d'Auvergne* is a large cupped flower, crimson, and very beautiful. *Lee* is very large, full double, of a bright and beautiful rose color, a new variety. *Leon the* 10*th* is rose colored, of immense size, being one of the largest of roses. *Letitia,* or *La Volupté* is by some ranked as a Hybrid Provence ; it is of a beautiful rose color, prettily veined, and of perfect form. *Leopold* is a fine dark rose, much like that old favorite the Tuscany Rose, but with smaller and more double flowers.

La Moskowa is a large dark rose, not quite double enough for a show rose, but its flowers have a fine effect.

Madame Cottin, or *Sophie Cotton,* is a large and well shaped rose, adapted for a show rose ; as is also *Madame Dubarry,* one of the finest double roses. These are both of the most vigorous habit. *Matilda* is a pretty pink colored rose, and *Mohéléda,* as well as *La Négresse,* both erroneously included in this class by some, are Damask roses. *Narbonne* and *Nonpariel,* the former rosy purple, and the latter pink, are no longer found in select collections. *Ninon de l'Enclos* a new French variety, large full double, deep rose color. *Nouvelle Transparente* is large, full double, of a rosy crimson hue. *Ombrée parfaite* is full double, of medium size, and violet shaded. *Ornement de Parade* is an old variety, fine red color, and possesses the advantage of growing very tall on its own bottom. *Oracle du Siècle* is a most charming rose, perfect in form, and rich and beautiful in its fine crimson and scarlet coloring.

Oriflamme is a fine bright red rose, perhaps scarcely double enough. *Philippe Quatre*, or *Philip IV.*, is an old variety, cherry red, and now superseded, as is also *Pourpré de Vienne* which is rosy purple. *Polivites* is a violet shell rose, of fine form. *Pluto* is a new variety of medium size, full double, and of the deepest violet purple or blackish hue of all this class. *Princess Victoria* is a fine brilliant crimson rose, and generally a good show flower, and regular in its form. *Queen of Violets* is of imbricate form, and violet purple hue, a good ancient variety. The old *Ranunculus* rose, as well as a *Royal Bouquet* and *St. Francis* we placed in our " Rejected" list of roses three years ago. *Shakspeare* is of a fine shaded rosy hue, and usually has a brilliant red centre, which gives it a charming effect. *Superb Tuscany*, is a seedling from the Old Tuscany, with larger and more double flowers, very dark, perhaps more so than its parent, but less brilliant. *Sir Walter Scott* is finely formed, and of that deep purplish rose color that has a very rich appearance ; its shape is generally perfect. *Souvenir de Navarino* is pale pink, and *Susanna* light red, both tolerable flowers, but now cast aside for better ones. *Schoenbrunn* and *Triumphe de Jaussens* are brilliant crimson roses, quite perfect in shape, constant and beautiful. *Triomphe de Rennes* is a very large and finely shaped rose ; the habit is luxuriant and it forms a fine standard. *Tuscany* or *Black Tuscany* is not so dark as several other varieties ; the color is a very dark blackish crimson, very brilliant; it is not full double, and having its parts perfect, it produces abundance of seeds. *Eliza Leker,* and *Duc de Choiseul,* although erroneously placed by some persons in this family, belong in fact to the Hybrid Provence class.

There are yet numerous other self-colored roses in this family, of equal beauty, but of which it is impossible to give descriptions without a sameness, which would be tedious to the reader. In the Catologue which I have attached, short but very accurate descriptions are given of each variety.

Most of the varieties of Rosa gallica are robust and all are hardy, and flourish equally as bushes on their own roots, grafted or budded on short stems, or as standards; but they cannot be recommended for tall standards, as their growth is too compact to be graceful. To grow them fine for exhibition as single blooms, or "show-roses," the clusters of buds should be thinned early in June, taking at least two-thirds from each; manure should also be laid round their stems on the surface, and manured water given to them plentifully in dry weather. With this description of culture, these roses will much surpass any thing we have heretofore seen in this country. To prolong their season of blooming, two plants of each variety should be planted; one plant to be pruned in October and the other in May. These will be found to give a succession of flowers. In winter pruning, shorten the strong shoots to within six or eight buds of the bottom; those that are weak cut down to two or three buds.

To raise self-colored French roses from seed, they should be planted in a warm, dry border, sloping to the south, in an open, airy situation. The shade of trees is very pernicious to seed bearing roses; and, in planting roses for the purpose of bearing seed, it must be borne in mind that it will give great facility to their management if the plants are planted in pairs, close to each other; accident will then often do as much as art in fertilizing them; thus the Woodpigeon Rose may be planted with and fertilized by the Tuscany, La Globuleuse with Comte de Murinais, Oriflamme with Assemblage des Beautés, Vesta with Feu Turc, Jean Bart with Princess Victoria, Superb Tuscany with Leopold, La Majestueuse also with the latter. All these roses bear seed, often without being fertilized, but the crop is almost certain if that operation is performed; and the above unions are likely to produce roses of decided colors and first-rate qualities.

THE FRENCH ROSE.

Rosa Gallica variegata.

Second Division: Striped, Variegated, Mottled, and Marbled varieties.

THE Rosa Mundi, or Garnet striped Rose, is the most ancient of this division, and is a striped sportive variety of the old semi-double red Rosa Gallica, or Officinal Rose. The flowers are large, boldly striped with bright red and white, and it has been frequently confounded with the York and Lancaster, which is a pure Damask, very different in the appearance of its flowers, and entirely distinct in its habit, being a strong growing plant, and attaining to thrice the height of the present variety.

The Rosa Mundi often loses its stripes entirely, and returns to its parent, the semi-double plain Red Officinal rose, and where a bed of them is allowed to remain and expand themselves, perhaps four out of five will change to the red variety. This striped variety may be considered the type of the present class, which, until within a few years, had added to it but two or three varieties; but latterly by the assiduous exertions of the French rose fanciers has been greatly extended, and now comprises variegated and striped roses of every shade.

Some of the spotted roses, more particularly those with a red or crimson ground, look as if they were disfigured by the weather, that is, as if the rain had caused some discoloration, but other varieties are very distinct and pretty. And among the new French varieties which form by far the greater portion of those I shall describe, there are very many of remarkable beauty and interest. The author has taken particular pains to import all these fine French varieties and at great expense, some having cost 20 to 30 francs, or $4 to $6, each.

A Fleurs and Feuilles marbrées, as the name implies, has its flowers and foliage marbled or stained, as are also its branches. It is so double that it has as much the appearance of a Ranunculus as of a rose, and is very beautiful. *Agar* is deep rose color, spotted, with a rosette centre. *Aglæ Adanson* is a fine mottled rose, something like the preceding in color, but much larger, and finely formed. *André Thouin* is a brilliant purplish crimson, spotted with purple. *Arethuse* is small, of a brilliant roseate hue, distinctly spotted with pink or blush, and very pretty, with marble foliage. *Arlequin* is pale red, prettily marbled, and very double. *Belle Herminie,* No. 1, is a semi-double purple spotted rose, remarkable as being the parent of most of the spotted and marble varieties. There are now six spotted and marbled varieties of this rose, which are known as No. 1 to 6, besides a numerous progeny under other titles. *Belle de Fontenay* is quite unique, its margined flowers being peculiar and characteristic. *Berangèr* is small, full double, rose color, spotted with white. *Berlèze* is dark purple, full double, most beautifully mottled with crimson. *Bicolor* is an old semi-double variety, almost scarlet, with white stripes, and suitable to produce seeds. *Bizarre mar-*

bree is very double, large, and well formed, of a bright deep rose color, beautifully shaded and variable. *Camaieu* is a very pretty and distinct striped rose, rather small, full double, of a rosy lilac, with pale incarnate stripes. *Charmante Isidore* is a fine purple, veined with crimson. *Compte de Murinais* is large, full double, slate-color, marbled. *Cosimo Ridolfi* is of the usual size, full double, purplish crimson, spotted. *Cramoisie Picotee* is a distinct and curious slate-colored rose ; delicately spotted, but not so pretty and brilliant as the old Picotee, its spots having a reddish brown appearance. *Cuvier* is full double, rosy crimson, spotted. *Delille* is very prettily spotted on a purple ground. Like most of the roses of this color, it is only to be seen in perfection in the morning if the weather is sultry ; but in cloudy weather, or if partially shaded, it will retain its beauty throughout the day. *Donna Sol* is a vigorous and beautiful new variety; the flowers large, purplish crimson. *Duc de Nemours*, is full double, violet crimson, marbled with red. *Duc d'Orleans* is a fine and brilliant flower, large, beautifully cupped, and distinctly spotted with white, and also of robust and vigorous habits. *Euphrasie* is deep rose colour, very delicately spotted. *Fanny Ellsler* is a new and pretty spotted rose. *Fatime* is of the usual size, rose color, spotted. *Fenelon* is double, purple-spotted. *Fontenelle* is large, rosy crimson, spotted with pink. *Fornarina* is a cupped flower, deep rose color, marbled with white. *General Foy*, a new and high priced French variety of a deep purplish violet color, prettily spotted. *Hersilie* is a fine rose color of imbricated form, full double, and spotted with white. *Insigne Destekles* is full double, rosy marbled. *Isabelle de Lorraine*, very large, full double, rose colored, with a blush. *Jeanne Hachette*, very large, double, red spotted very profusely with crimson. *Kretly* is full double, violet, spotted with purple. *La Capricieuse* is indeed capricious, for some of its flowers are plain and some most beautifully pencilled with white, which on its vivid rose colored ground has a pretty effect.   *Lafayette* is a pencilled rose, quite different from the generality, and much like Nationale Tricolor.   It is shaded with purple and crimson, and varies much with the season.   *L'Hospital* is full double, deep roseate, spotted.   *La Nationale* is a distinct, bright rose colored flower, marbled and striped with crimson, and one of the prettiest of its class.   *Lavoiseur* is deep rose color, prettily spotted and finely formed, with variegated foliage. · *Lucille* is very pretty pink, spotted with white.   *Madelon Frequet* is of perfect shape, rose spotted with blush, and remarkably full of petals like the old Crivalis.   *Malesherbes* is of vigorous growth, apparently a hybrid between this and the Chinese ; the flower is purple, very double, and spotted with white, and soon fades unless sheltered from the sun, as is the case with all roses that are purple and slate color.   *Mazeppa* is bright red, edged and marbled with white, and superb.   *Mecène* is a very beautiful expanded flower, white variegated with rose color. It is one of the newest and highest priced French varieties. *Minos* is of a bright roseate hue, profusely spotted with flesh color.   *Modeste Guerin* has some petals bright rose, some nearly white, and others often bright rose mottled with white, and is very beautiful.   *Monime* is deep rose color, spotted with pale purple.   *Nationale Tricolor* is one of the prettiest of variegated roses, generally shaded red and purple, with a white or yellowish centre, but the central color is not constant.   *Nero* is a new French variety, violet crimson, prettily spotted, and very double. *Oiellet Flamand* is an expanded flower, richly variegated with white and deep rose colored stripes.   *Oiellet parfait* is of globular form, pale blush, beautifully variegated with crimson and lilac, closely resembling a Bizarre Carnation.

It is a hybrid between the Gallica and the Damask and greatly esteemed. *Panachée Semi-double* is deep rose color variegated with lilac, a beautiful and estimable variety to obtain seeds from, suitable for producing valuable varieties. *Perle des Panachées* is very double, white, variegated with lilac and pale violet, exceedingly beautiful. The present price at Paris is $4, it being quite new. *Picotee,* or *Violet Picotee* in some soils produces flowers of a deep violet crimson striped with white, in others it loses its variegation : but under all circumstances is a pretty and very distinct rose. *Porcelaine Royale* is a beautifully shaped mottled rose ; not large, but cupped, and perfect in its form, and adapted for a show rose. *Pourpre striée de blanc* is pale purple, full double, profusely veined with small white stripes. *Prince de Chimay* is of a rosy purple hue, distinctly spotted with blush white. *Pulchra Marmorea* is one of the best of this class, a bright rosy red, marbled with white. *Ranoncule Ponctuée,* or the *Spotted Ranunculus,* is happily named ; for it is much like a ranunculus, both in its form and in the disposition of its colors, and is a peculiar and beautiful variety. *Rouget de Lille,* is a new fine double variety, purple spotted with pale violet. *Sombrieul* is a delicate spotted rose, something like Aurélie Lamarc ; probably having the same origin, as it was raised from seed by the same grower. *Superb Marbled, Superbe Marbrée,* or *General Damremont* is a finely shaped full rose, crimson, sometimes marbled very beautifully with purple ; this is an inconstant flower, but, when perfect, is a very superb rose. *Tibulle* is large full double, rosy lilac, handsomely spotted. *Timarette* is very double, purplish rose color, and neatly mottled or spotted. *Tricolor,* or *La Belle Alliance,* is now a very old variety ; its flowers prettily striped with yellowish white, on a purple ground. *Tricolor Pompone* seems to be merely a variety

of the preceding, with smaller petals, and a greater proportion of white in them; probably it owes its origin to a
sporting branch of the original Tricolor. *Tricolor superba*
is one of the finest of the striped roses; its ground color is
of the darkest crimson, on which its regular stripes of
nearly pure white have a good effect; it also bids fair to
be constant in its variegation. *Tricolor d'Orleans* is very
distinct, the flower of a peculiar vivid and shaded red,
striped with white. *Tricolor de Vazemmes* is of a violet
purple hue, with white lines. Tricolor No. 1, is of medium size, neatly bordered with white. Tricolor No. 2, is
a beautiful variety, crimson, purple and white. *Triomphe
de Beauté* is a dark brilliant violet crimson rose, prettily
striped with red, and is a very neat well shaped rose.
Tullie is a very large rose, of a bright rose colored ground,
distinctly and largely spotted. The *Prince*, bright red,
spotted with blush, is a very remarkable and pretty rose.
Like all the roses of this color, it requires to be kept from
the sun. The *Village Maid*, or *Panachée double*, or *Belle
Rubine* is a well known rose, varying much in color, and
in some situations, has red or carnation colored, in others
slate colored or purple stripes. It combines three colors,
often in full stripes of rose, lilac and white, resembling a
Bizarre Carnation. The *New Village Maid*, or *Panachée
pleine*, is an improved variety of the above, being more
double and compact, but it is not more beautiful, the color
is deep rose striped with pure white. It is better calculated
to exhibit as a prize flower singly than the preceding
variety. *Uniflore Marbrée* has a tendency to produce its
flowers on single footstalks, whence its name. It is a good
shape and very double rose, beautifully marbled.

New varieties of this family are raised with such facility that it would lengthen this little work too much to enu-
merate and describe the crowd of beauties that have been

received, but, as the characters of the variegated roses cannot be given without some adequate description, a few of the most remarkable have received a passing word.

To raise variegated roses the following, which also bear seed freely, should be selected and planted as before directed:—Aglæ Adanson with Anacreon, the Village Maid with Duc d'Orleans, Tricolor and Tricolor Pompon also with the Village Maid. This last union would probably produce some pretty striped roses.

Berlèze may also be planted with Seguier, Duc d'Orleans with André Thouin, and the Leopard Rose with Anacreon; these would most likely give pretty spotted roses. Picotée might be fertilized with the Village Maid, and, if seed could be procured, some fine varieties must be the result; but the central small petals should be removed with a pair of tweezers from the former rose, when its flowers are half expanded, as they are too much crowded to allow it to bear seed. Clear white and crimson striped roses are yet desiderata, as those we possess are inconstant. The Tricolor varieties fertilized with the Globe Hip which abounds in pollen, will be an experiment worth trying. The Tuscany Rose, is a most convenient variety for imparting dark colors, as it abounds with pollen more than any other cultivated rose, and it should be planted in every seminary.

THE DAMASK ROSE.

Rosa Damascena.

THE Damask Rose, is so called from its having been brought originally to Europe from Damascus, in Syria. The variety thus introduced, was the old semi-double light red variety, which, as well as some others, are still grown in the gardens of that city, and the original type of the species with single flowers is said to be a native of Syria. The name of the Damask Rose has been long familiar to every reader of English poetry, as it has been eulogized more than any other species, and its beauties portrayed with a poet's license. In these glowing descriptions, the truth, as is frequently the case in poetry, has been entirely lost sight of, for in plain unvarnished prose, it must be conceded that the original Damask Rose, and the earlier varieties, such as have been the roses of our poets, though peculiarly fragrant, are most uninteresting flowers. However, we must not ungratefully depreciate them, since they are the types of our present new, beautiful and fragrant varieties. The shoots of the Damask rose are green, long, and diffuse in their growth; the leaves large, pale green, serrated, and pubescent, and generally placed far asunder, the prickles on most of the varieties abundant, and the flowers are produced in clusters, and possess a delicate and exquisite perfume. To those old members of this family, the Red and the White monthly Damask, or Quatre saisons, of the French and Dutch, which by some peculiar excitability, often put forth flowers in warm moist autumns, nearly all our perpetual roses owe their origin, and we can now depend upon having roses from these new varieties, in October as fragrant as in June. *The York* and *Lancaster Rose*, with pale striped flowers, is one of the oldest varieties of this division : the flowers are sometimes half red and half white, thus presenting a fair type of the pacific union of the houses of York and Lancaster, whence it derived its title. There is, perhaps, a little too much sameness of character in some of the varieties of the Damask rose ; their gradations of color are sometimes too delicate to be distinct, but the following may be depended upon as fine leading varieties.

Arlinde, a beautifully-formed rose, of a delicate rose-

color, is not a pure damask, as its foliage is less pubescent
than in some other varieties. *Angèle*, is a pretty bright-
colored rose, very double and distinct. *Belladonna* is of
distinct habit, delicate pink color, and blooms profusely.
Blanche d'Avilliers is pure white. *Blanche bordé de Rouge*
is a fine rose when it opens well ; sometimes its flowers are
pure white, at others finely margined with purplish red.
Bachelier, so named from a Belgian amateur, is one of the
finest show-roses in this division, producing large double
compact flowers, of a fine rose-color, and very perfect shape.
Calypso is a large flower, quite double, and rose-colored.
Climene is a new variety of dwarf habit, with rather small
beautifully-shaped flowers, of a very brilliant pink or rose
color. *Couronne Blanche* is a pure Damask rose, distinct
in habit, and a pretty white variety. *Coralie* is a beautifully formed rose, of a pale flesh-color, with rosy centre,
to which several of this family are inclined. *Déesse Flore*
is a first rate variety, with flowers rather larger than Coralie,
and much like it in color : when about half expanded they
are most beautiful. *Grand Triomphe* is full double, of a
pale pink hue, in abundant clusters.

Imperatrice de France is not a pure Damask rose, but
very nearly allied. This is a large compact flower, bright-
rosy, very robust, and distinct in habit. *Imperial blush* is
an old and very indifferent semi-double rose, but the plants
grow tall and vigorous, and the multitude of flowers give it
a showy appearance at a distance. *La Cherie* is a splendid
incarnate rose, with a pink centre. *La Folie de Corse* is
a large flower, full double, of a bright rosy hue. *La Fi-
ancée* seems a hybrid between the Globe Hip and the Damask, a pretty shaded rose, nearly white, with a pale rosy
centre. *La Ville de Bruxelles*, has rose-colored flowers,
very large and double : this is a distinct and fine new variety. *Lady Fitzgerald* is a beautiful rose, very valuable in
this division, as its brilliant rose-colored flowers are so con-

spicuous in a clump of Damask roses.   It is not a pure Damask rose, but very nearly so : its foliage when young is a
little stained with the coloring matter of some variety of
Rosa gallica, which much adds to its beauty. *Marc Aurèle* is a
fine new French variety, full deep rose color, prettily spotted.
Ma Favorite is a very small rose, of a delicate flesh-color,
and exceedingly neat and pretty.   *Madam Hardy* was
raised from seed in the Luxembourg gardens, by Monsieur
Hardy, in 1832.   It is not a pure Damask rose, as its leaves
have scarcely any pubescence ;   but a more magnificent
rose does not exist, for its luxuriant habit and large and finely shaped flowers place it quite first among the white roses.
Madame de Maintenon is a delicate, pretty rose, with deeper coloring towards its centre : this is a new variety, pale
incarnate, with a rosy centre. ˙ *Mohéléda* is a hybrid Damask, with large double rose-colored flowers, prettily marbled.   It is a new and good rose. ˍThe *Painted Damask*,
or *Leda*, will for some time to come be a favorite, as it is
distinct and beautiful ; its large and thick foliage and painted flowers are quite unique, but like most of the variegated
roses, it is inconstant, as its flowers are sometimes pure
white ; in general, however, the outer edge of each petal is
tinged with fine purple.

Some pretty and interesting varieties have lately been
added to these favorites of the poets.   The *Duke of Cam-
bridge,* which was at first thought to be a Hybrid China, will
perhaps be better grouped with the Damask roses, of which
it largely partakes.   It is a very fine rose, quite distinct, of a
vivid rose color, and robust luxuriant growth.   *Belle d'Au-
teuil* is a large and perfect show-rose of great beauty ; the color bright roseate, with fine foliage.   *Bella Donna* is a true
Damask rose, bearing a profusion of delicate pink or bright
rose-colored flowers.   *Adonis,* as a pretty pale blush or
rosy white variety, is quite worth cultivation.

Some new Damask roses, of deeper colors than we have hitherto possessed, now give an increased interest to this elegant family : among these, *Châteaubriand* is remarkable for its brillant red flowers, very perfect and beautiful in shape. *Louis XVI.* has flowers rather deeper in color than the preceding, and is a distinct and good rose. *La Négresse* is by far the darkest Damask rose known ; its flowers are of a deep crimson purple. *Olympe* is a fine French variety, of the usual size, the color crimson purple. The *Tree Pœony* rose produces flowers rivalling in size those of the Pæonia Moutan or Tree Pœony, but as they are flat, irregularly shaped and not very double, it cannot long continue to be a favorite with the amateur. *Pope* is large and distinct, crimson purple, and inclines to bloom in Autumn. *Portland pourpre* is a large flower, of a light purple color. *Pulcherie* is a pure white rose, remarkably beautiful. *Semiramis* is quite novel in color, and a most perfect and beautiful rose : the centre of the flower is of a bright fawn-color, and its marginal petals of a delicate roseate. This fine variety ought to be in every collection. *Penelope* is remarkable for its fine foliage ; the edges of its leaves tinged with red ; the flowers of a very deep rose, globular, large and distinct.

The roses of this neat and elegant family have a pretty effect arranged in a mass, and like the varieties of Rosa alba, they are so beautiful in contrast with the dark roses : they also form fine standards, more particularly Madame Hardy and the Painted Damask, which will grow into magnificent trees, if their culture is attended to. The pruning recommended for Rosa gallica will also do for these roses.

The variety of this family that bears seed most freely is the Purple Damask or Jersey Rose, which should be planted with Imperatrice de France. From this union large and very double roses may be expected, and the Painted Damask, if some of its central petals were removed, would probably bear seed, and if fertilized with the Purple Damask, some fine variegated varieties might possibly be originated. Bella Donna with Lady Fitzgerald would produce some brilliant colored varieties, which are much wanted in this family.

THE WHITE ROSE.

Rosa Alba.

Rosa Alba, or the White Rose, so called because the original species is white, is a native of middle Europe, and was introduced to the English gardens in 1597. In some of the old farm and cottage gardens of Hertfordshire and Essex, (England,) a semi-double variety is frequent; this is but a slight remove from the single flowering original species, and grows luxuriantly without culture in any neglected corner. Both these original types I have in my collection. The roses of this division may be easily distinguished by their green shoots, leaves of a glaucous green, looking as if they were covered with a grayish impalpable powder, and flowers generally of the most delicate colors, graduating from pure white to a bright but delicate pink.

Astrée is a new, large and fine French variety, of a roseate hue. *Attila* is one of the deepest colored varieties of this division, with large and partially cupped flowers of a perfect shape. *Belle Auguste* is incarnate, but becomes almost white; it is full double and of vigorous growth. *Belle Clementine,* an old, but very pretty variety, a hybrid departing in a slight degree from the characters of the group, often produces flowers finely mottled; it is a luxuriant grower, and forms a fine standard. *Blanche Superbe,* or

Blanche de Belgique, is a much older variety than the preceding, with all the characters of this division, and producing very large and double flowers of the purest white. *Blush hip* is a hybrid, possessing more of the characters of this division than of any other, consequently it is placed in it ; this is a fine and free-growing rose, always beautiful. *Bullata* is a curious but pretty variety, with large foliage and tinted white flowers, forming a robust and fine standard. *Camelliæflora*, a small but very pretty pure white rose, with cupped flowers, possesses all the characters of the species, and is quite worthy of cultivation. *Duc de Luxembourg*, a hybrid, is a most beautiful and unique rose, producing globular flowers of the largest size: the exterior of the petals is almost white, the interior of a bright rosy purple, at once singular and pleasing. *Etoile de la Malmaison* is quite new, incarnate and much esteemed in France, but rare here. *Fatime* is a pretty rose, its color not pure white, but tinted with a delicate pink in the centre of the flower; this is peculiar to roses of this family, and in general it is very pleasing. *Fanny Sommerson*, a new and very fine variety, is a most robust grower, producing rose-colored flowers, extremely double, and finely shaped, a little imbricated, but so perfect that this variety may be considered a good show-rose. *Félicité* is also a new, distinct, and beautiful rose; its flowers are exactly like a fine double ranunculus, of a most delicate flesh-colour.

Ferox is a very anomalous variety of this family, as most of its members are thornless, but this is completely covered with those fierce defenders; its flowers are of a pretty tinted white, very double and perfect. *The Globe Hip*, *Princess Clementine*, and *Reine des Belges*, are hybrid Provence roses, and *Madame Hardy* is a Damask rose, and they will be found under their respective heads.

Marie de Bourgogne is double rose colored, spotted with incarnate. *Josephine* and *Josephine Beauharnais* must both be mentioned, as they are so often confounded : the first is a most robust grower, producing in large clusters flowers not very double, of a delicate pink ; the latter has large globular flowers, very double, white, tinted with rosy buff. *La Séduisante* is most appropriately named ; it is not a new variety, but a rose most perfect in shape and beautiful in color. *Madame Campan* is a hybrid departing a little from the characters of the species, but producing flowers of a bright rose finely mottled with white, of first rate excellence. *Petite Cuisse de nymphe* is of small size, full double and incarnate hue. *Pompon bazard* is small, and of a delicate rose color. *Pompon carnée*, often erroneously called Pompon blanc, is of moderate size, full double, and incarnate. *Princesse de Lamballe* is one of the finest in this division, possessing all the characters of the species in its foliage, branches and flowers : these are of the purest white, and of the most perfect and beautiful shape. *Queen of Denmark*, an old but estimable variety, produces flowers of first rate excellence as prize-flowers : so much was this esteemed when first raised from seed, that plants were sent from Germany to England at five guineas each. *Sophie de Bavière* is light purple, and full double. *Sophie de Marsilly*, a new variety, is a most delicate and beautiful mottled rose, with flowers very double and perfect in shape. *Viridis*, or *Rose verte*, is the far-famed green rose of France, which has several times been sent from that country as a great rarity : it is quite curious, its flowers being nearly green till fully expanded.

The varieties of this family form a beautiful group, not by any means gay and dazzling, but chaste and delicate, and contrast well with groups of the dark varieties of Rosa gallica and Hybrid China roses ; they also make good standards, often growing to a large size and uniting well with the stock; they always bloom abundantly and bear close pruning; in this respect they may be treated as recommended for the French roses.

HYBRID CHINA ROSES.

Rosa Indica hybridæ.

THE superior varieties of this fine division give a combination of all that is or can be beautiful in roses; for, not only are their flowers of the most elegant forms and colors, their foliage of extreme luxuriance, but their branches are so vigorous and graceful, that perhaps no plant presents such a mass of beauty as a finely grown hybrid China rose in full bloom. They owe their origin to the China, Tea-scented, Noisette, and Bourbon roses, fertilized with the French, Provence, and other summer roses, and also to the latter crossed with the former; the seeds of such impregnated flowers, producing Hybrid China roses. These have, in many cases resulted from accident, but latterly from the regular fertilizing process, as mules or hybrids have been raised from well known parents.

In England, but few varieties have been originated; as the common China rose does not in general ripen its seeds sufficiently for germination. The parents of Brown's Superb Blush, which is an English hybrid, was the old Tea-scented rose, Rosa indica odorata, impregnated with some hardy summer rose. Rivers's George the Fourth is also an English rose; but as this came by accident, its origin is not so well ascertained. Rosa Blairii is also English, and raised from the yellow China, impregnated with some variety of hardy rose. All these roses have the true charac-

ters of the family : leaves smooth, glossy, and sub-evergreen : branches long, luxuriant, and flexible. They
give a long continuance of bloom, but· they never put
forth secondary or autumnal flowers, except in a few insu-
lated cases. This is a most peculiarly distinguishing trait,
and an interesting fact. Impregnate a Bourbon, China, or
Noisette rose, all abundant autumnal bloomers, with the farina of a French or a Provence rose, and you entirely take
away the tendency to autumnal blooming in their offspring.
They will *grow* vigorously all the autumn, and give a *long*,
but not a *secondary* series of flowers. Some of these Hybrid China roses produce seed abundantly, which is rather
a remarkable feature, as so few hybrid plants are fertile.
It has been asserted that hybrids produced from the French
rose, impregnated with the China rose, are not of such robust and vigorous habits as when the China rose is the female parent ; but this is an assertion scarcely borne out by
facts, for the exceptions are numerous, and like many other
variations in roses and plants in general, they seem to bid
defiance to systematic rules. By scientific cultivators the
roses of this division have been divided into four classes,
Hybrid China, Hybrid Noisette, Hybrid Bourbon, and
Uncertain Hybrids.

Those that have been raised from Noisette roses have
a tendency to produce their flowers in clusters ; those from
Bourbon roses have their leaves thick, leathery, and round ;
those from the Tea-scented have a delicate and grateful
scent; but all have those distinguishing family traits as before given, and accordingly they group beautifully. It is
a difficult task to point out the best in each of these divisions as they are nearly all well deserving of cultivation.
However, by making a few remarks, such as cannot so
well be given in a descriptive catalogue, I may perhaps be
able in some measure, to direct the choice of amateurs to
those most worthy their notice.

I will commence with those classed in the English Catalogues and my own as Hybrid China, and in the French Catalogues as Hybrides de Bengale Roses.

Adolphe Cachet is a variety not much known ; it is well formed, very double and distinct. *A Fleurs blanches, Blanchefleur, White Climbing China,* or *White Climbing Unique* is full double, pure white, and blooms freely and profusely. *Anisette,* or *Odeur d'Anisette* is a beautiful roseate variety, fragrant and highly esteemed. *Assuerus* is carmine, full double, and beautiful. *Auzou* is large and of a crimson hue. *Belle Bouquet* assimilates to *A Fleurs blanches,* but the flower is of more compact form and the growth is more slow. *Belle Thérèse* is a dark shaded crimson, quite fragrant, and in clusters. *Beranger* is light red, full double, protuberant, and very beautiful.

Bonne Geneviève, or *Beauté ethérial.* This rose has, been sold extensively under the latter name, and described as " purple margined with crimson." It is a most beautiful and perfectly imbricated rose, of large size, full double, and of a violet crimson color. *Brennus,* the *Brutus* of some collections : and sometimes called *Queen Victoria* in South Carolina, is a very superb rose, and will form a finer object as a pillar rose* or standard than as a bush ; its luxuriant shoots must not be shortened too much in the winter pruning, as it is then apt to produce an abundance of wood, with but very few flowers. It often puts forth branches in one season from eight to ten feet in length ; if these are from a dwarf, and are fastened to a wooden or iron stake, and *not shortened,* the following season they will form a pillar of beauty but rarely equalled. *Blairii,*

---

* All the roses to which this term is applied make very long and flexible shoots, well adapted for training up columns, thus forming a pillar of roses.

is a very distinct and unique variety, so impatient of the
knife, that if pruned at all severely, it will scarcely put forth
a flower: it is perhaps better as a pillar rose, than grown in
any other mode, as it shoots ten or twelve feet in one season,
and its pendulous clusters of flowers which are produced
from these long shoots unshortened, have a beautiful effect
on a pillar. *Beauty of Billiard* is, of all roses, the most
glowing and beautiful : its color is described in the catalogues as scarlet ; but it is rather a fiery crimson, so vivid
that it may be distinguished at a great distance. This rose
also requires care in using the knife ; the extreme tips of
the branches may be cut off, and some of them thinned out ;
it will then bloom in great perfection, but care must always
be taken in winter pruning to leave its shoots nearly their
full length. *Becquet* is a pretty distinct dark crimson
flower, very double and well shaped. *Belle Marie* is a
first-rate rose, finely shaped, and a good show-rose. *Belle
Parabère* is a very remarkable variety of inconceivable
luxuriance ; its flowers are very large : it will grow in good
soils, as a standard, soon forming a large umbrageous tree.
Catel is one of our finest dark roses, very double, and finely
shaped, quite worth the notice of the amateur. *Camuzet
carnée* is a rich rose color, very magnificent and highly fragrant. *Celicel* is large, rosy blush, seeds freely, and is therefore suitable for hybridizing. *Cerisette* is small, bright red,
neat and pretty. *Cesonie* is large and bright crimson. The
three varieties last named have now been superseded by
newer varieties. *Charles Louis*, No. 1, is large, a bright deep
cherry color, exceedingly splendid. *Charles Louis*, No. 2, is
small, of ranunculus form, rich roseate blush. *Coccinea superba*, or "*Vingt neuf Juillet*," is a rose alike beautiful in its
flowers and foliage ; in early spring its leaves and shoots
are of a most vivid red, and this appearance they retain
the greater part of the summer ; its flowers are brilliant in

the extreme, crimson purple shaded with scarlet : the shoots of this rose must be left at nearly their full length. *Coupe d'Amour* richly deserves its name, for it is a beautiful neat rose, quite perfect in its form and color.

Coronation is one of those purple shaded roses, inclining to slate, imbricated, and very perfect in its shape. *Coutard* may be safely recommended as a most perfect and good rose, flowering with great freedom, and beautiful either as a dwarf or standard. *Daudigné* is one of the older varieties, violet shaded with purple, inclining to a bluish tint, well formed, full double, and distinct. *Delaage* is purplish crimson, full double, and beautiful. *Duke of Devonshire* is an imbricated rose, one of the great favorites of the day, and most deservedly so, for its rosy lilac petals are so delicately striped with white, and its shape is so perfect, that it will always be admired. *Egerie* belongs to the Hybrid Noisette family. *Emmeline*, although often placed under this head, belongs in reality to the class of Hybrid Sweet Briars. This and the preceding are described under their appropriate heads. *Fabvier*, or *Colonel Fabvier*, is large, imbricated, full double, fine rose color changing to red ; the growth is vigorous, and it is well suited for a pillar rose. *Dr. Guepin*, is a most perfect shaped, globular rose, quite distinct in its character : this, with a few others, which will be noticed in their turn, have beautiful spherical-shaped flowers, singular and pleasing. *Eugene Barbet* is also one of these finely formed roses, with dark ·purplish crimson flowers of first rate excellence. *Fimbriata*, or *A Petales frangés*, is purple, full double, with cut or fringed petals. *Fulgens*, or the *Malton* rose, is certainly one of the most brilliant and beautiful of roses ; the entire plant is also worthy of admiration, independent of its magnificent globular scarlet flowers, as its foliage is so abundant, and so finely tinted with red ; its branches so vigorous, and yet spreading so gracefully, that it forms one of the very finest of standard roses. *Fleurette* offers quite a contrast in its small delicately-colored, and finely shaped flowers ; it is a desirable and pretty variety, and belongs to the Hybrid Noisette family, although frequently placed in this. Flora Mac Ivor is a globular and beautiful rose, of very large size and of a rosy lilac hue. *General Lamarque,* or *Lamarque,* is a brownish purple, one of the darkest of roses, a most luxuriant grower, very peculiar and distinct. *General Kleber* is a deep, rich, rosy lilac. *Rivers's George the Fourth* is yet, perhaps, one of the best of this family : it was raised from seed by Mr. T. Rivers, twenty-three years ago, and contributed, as he says, probably more than any thing else to make him an enthusiastic rose cultivator.* It is now much esteemed in France, where it is comparatively a new variety. *Georgian* is one of the oldest varieties, rather tender, the flower bright rose colored. *Gloire de Couline* is brilliant carmine, shaded with crimson, superb. *Gloire des Hellenes* is a splendid new variety, double purple, striped and tessillated. *Grillony* is a new, large, and superb variety, of a purplish slate color, and first-rate form and character. *Hypocrate* is a most superb variety, one of the finest of its class, and well

---

* In his Rose Amateur's Guide he remarks : " Even now I have not forgotten the pleasure the discovery of this rose gave me. One morning in June I was looking over the first bed of roses I had ever raised from seed, and searching for something new among them with all the ardor of youth, when my attention was attracted to a rose in the centre of the bed, not in bloom, but growing with great vigor, its shoots offering a remarkable contrast to the plants by which it was surrounded, in their crimson purple tinge ; upon this plant I set my mark, and the following autumn removed it to a pet situation. It did not bloom in perfection the season after removal, but, when established, it completely eclipsed all the dark roses known, and the plant was so vigorous that it made shoots more than ten feet in length in one season. This plant is still living, and nearly as vigorous as ever."

adapted for a show-rose : this is not the Hypocrate of many catalogues, or of the French cultivators, which is a hybrid Bourbon, an inferior variety. *Helvetius* is large, rosy violet shaded, and full double. *L'Ingénue*, probably a misnomer, is full double, deep crimson, and fragrant. *La Naiade* is of a delicate roseate hue and fine form. *Lansczeur* is one of the older varieties, purplish crimson. *La Tourterelle, Parny*, or *Dove Rose*, is a large flower, of a crimson lilac hue, assimilating somewhat to dove color, whence its first and last titles : the growth is vigorous, and it soon attains a height of twelve to sixteen feet, and is well suited for a pillar rose, but it has been superseded, as well as the four preceding, by new varieties of greater beauty. *La Quintinine* is very large and superb, deep lilac rose color. *Lady Stuart*, like the Duke of Devonshire, is a gem of the first water, for no rose can surpass it in beauty ; the form of the flowers before expansion is perfectly spherical and exceedingly beautiful. This rose, for some years to come, must and will be a favorite. *La Grandeur* is, perhaps, nearly as much to be admired, but for qualities quite opposite, as this is when quite open an imbricated rose, exceedingly regular and pleasing in its form. *La Nubienne* is full double, of globular form, color lie de vin. *Le Troubadour* is a beautiful brilliant red rose. *Leopold de Bauffremont* is very robust, the flower delicate roseate, beautiful, perfect. *Lord Nelson* is a deep velvety crimson, of fine form, the habit vigorous. *Louis Phillippe* is one of the older varieties, light reddish crimson. *Marjolin* is very dark violet purple. *Miaulis* is a good dark rose ; but is certainly surpassed by *Miralba*, which has recently been named "*Chevrier :*" this is not a large rose, but decidedly one of the most brilliant and beautiful dark crimson roses we possess. *Montault*, or *Eveque d'Angers*, (erroneously called Manteau) is also an old variety, large, deep purplish velvety crimson, and has been superseded. *Moyenna*, a bright purplish rose, has flowers very double and finely shaped ; it proves a very good show-rose. *Pallagi*, *Ne plus ultra*, or *Gloire des Hybrides* is a favorite. Its flowers resemble in color the red stock, and are singularly brilliant. The growth is vigorous, but like many others of this division it is not at all adapted for a show-rose. *Malton*, which has been erroneously confused with it by an American writer, is an entirely different variety. *Princess* is roseate, tinged with blush, and blooms in large clusters. It attains less height than many other varieties. *Princess Augusta* is an English rose, a vigorous grower, and well adapted, either for a pillar rose or a standard. *Petit Pierre* is one of those rapid and diffuse growing roses, like Belle Parabere and the King of Roses in luxuriance and vigor of growth ; this is one of the largest and the most double of hybrids, and when grown as a standard, forms a magnificent tree. *Pompone bicolor* is rather a small, but well-shaped rose, its centre inclining to scarlet, with outer petals of fine crimson purple, a most distinct and desirable rose. *Pompon carmine* is brilliant red, and much admired. *Potart* is a light rich crimson, very showy and greatly admired. *Prolifère*, or *Prolific*, produces a profusion of fragrant flowers in clusters of a deep purple hue, but being one of the old varieties, is now surpassed by many others. *Reine de Belgique* rivals Lady Stuart in the fine and perfect shape of its flowers ; this rose has been sold for Reine des Belges, a hybrid Provence ; but, as that is of the finest white, and this is of a rosy lilac, the deception is soon detected. *Richlieu* (Verdier) is a very deep rich rosy lilac, cupped, very double, and superb. *Rosine Dupont* is a very pale flesh-colored rose, with remarkable glossy foliage and erect growth, very distinct and pretty. *Saphirine* is one of the largest globular roses, and most astonishingly robust and vigorous in its habit : in a very few years, in a strong soil, this rose would form a tree of the largest size that roses ever attain. *Saudeur, Saudeur panaché,* or *King of Hybrids* is a rarity among this class, being finely striped and tessillated, whereas it can as yet boast of but few variegated varieties. Like some few others its branches may be thinned, but scarcely at all shortened. It is very suitable for a pillar, or for a standard of the largest size, being of extraordinary vigor and luxuriance. *Souvenir d'une Mère* is a large rose, of that delicate but bright rose-color, always so much admired. Its flowers are not so double as some other varieties, but very large and magnificent. *Stadtholder* is an old variety, rosy pink, now cast aside. *Triomphe de Laffay* is a beautiful rose, not of a pure white, but rather what is called French white, the outer petals inclined to rose-color. *Triomphe de Guérin,* a very large pale rose, much resembles Lady Stuart, differing only in having the centre of its flowers of a warm rose-colored tint : this is a most beautiful and distinct variety. *Triomphe d'Angers* is perfectly unique, and no rose can be more deserving of admiration. Its perfume is much like ripe fruit, and its singularly brilliant crimson flowers are often striped with white : these two last-mentioned varieties are finer grown as standards than in any other mode, as their flowers are large and pendulous. *Titus* is a remarkably pretty purple rose, blooming in large clusters. Its flowers are not large, but finely shaped and very distinct. *Tuscany* is deep crimson, blooming in clusters, but has been superseded. *Vandaels* is large, splendid, of a brownish violet hue. *Velours Episcopal* is a new and beautiful variety, perfectly globular, of a fine crimson purple, inclining to the latter color. *Vibert* is purple, full double, and beautiful. *Violet de Belgique* is large, full double, of a violet hue. *Wellington* is now an old rose ; for some time thought to be the same as Bizarre de la Chine, but now found to be quite different in its habit and growth, though its flowers have an exact resemblance. *Yolande Fontaine* is deep violet, full double and protuberant. This and a large number of varieties which I have here described for the first time, are remarkably beautiful, and these new varieties greatly exceed in splendor and perfection those of older date.

As with the varieties of the French Rose, the new varieties of this family are too numerous for detailed descriptions, but *Saint Ursule, Comtesse de Lacepede,* and *Adalila,* ought not to be passed over; they are all of the most perfect shape and delicate tints. As rose-colored roses, *Fabvier and Richelieu* are quite perfection in the form of their flowers, and for vivid rose-colored varieties, *General Allard and Louis Fries* cannot be too much recommended; they are all truly beautiful. *Decandolle* and *Larochefoucault* are vivid red roses of great beauty.

To the family of Hybrid China Roses a great many varieties have been added during the last five years by French florists and others, from which I have selected only the most beautiful and perfect in forming the preceding descriptive list. A great many varieties that are enumerated in the different catalogues are not such as may be deemed really good roses, and of these the cultivation might better be discontinued, as they only occupy the place of choicer varieties. To one fine variety too much attention cannot be directed, and this is *Chenédolé,* so called from a member of the Chamber of Deputies for Calvados, a district in Normandy, where this fine rose was raised. It has often been asserted that no rose could compete with Brennus in size and beauty; but I feel no hesitation in saying, that in superior brilliancy of color, and size of flower, this variety is superior; the foliage and habit of the plant are also much more elegant and striking; in color its flowers are of a peculiar glowing vivid crimson, discernable at a great distance : it is indeed an admirable rose, and cannot be too much cultivated. *Le Météore* is from the same origin ; in color bright rosy red, very striking, and when blooming in large clusters on the plant, always much admired. *Julia* is a peculiarly elegant shaped rose ; in color brilliant rose, very distinct in habit and character, as is also *Jenny*, in color rather a deep rose, with flowers beautifully cupped.

Prince Albert is remarkable for its perfect and most elegantly-shaped flowers, very regularly cupped ; color delicate yet vivid pink. *Triomphe de la Queue* is another of these most elegantly-shaped cupped roses, blooming in large clusters ; of large size, color deep yet vivid rose, slightly tinged with lilac. Watts' Celestial, or Watts' Climbing China will be found under the head of Hybrid Climbing Roses ; Chatelin or Chatelaine, Duc de Cazes, and Victor Hugo being Hybrid Bourbon Roses, will be found under that head, Delice de Flandres will be found among the Hybrid Provence roses, and Hybride Parfaite will be found under its appropriate head of Hybrid Noisette.

With but few exceptions Hybrid China, Hybrid Bourbon, and Hybrid Noisette roses, may be cultivated as standards to advantage, as their growth is luxuriant and umbrageous, some of the most robust-growing varieties forming immense heads. To keep them in a healthy state, lay round their stems on the surface of the soil late in autumn a good proportion of manure ; and mind that before the blooming season commences this is added to, as they require the surface of the soil moist when in flower : they will also continue much longer in bloom if this is attended to.* The great objection to this summer surface-

---

* I have found night-soil, mixed with the drainings of the dunghill, or even with common ditch or pond water, so as to make a thick liquid, the best possible manure for roses, poured on the surface of the soil twice in winter, from one to two gallons to each tree. November and December

manuring, is its unsightly appearance, particularly around trees on well-dressed lawns and garden-borders; this may be obviated, by covering the manure with some green moss; and to keep the birds from disturbing it, which they will do after worms, place on the moss some pieces of rock or flints, thus forming an ornamental mound. In France, roses are cultivated with much and well-rewarded care; for even standards of thirty years' growth have, every spring, a large quantity of manure laid on the surface round their stems. This keeps the extreme heat of the sun from penetrating to their roots; and as they are abundantly watered in hot weather, it also prevents that rapid evaporation which would otherwise take place, so often rendering water useless. This practice is, after all, only imitating nature, for the Dog Rose, upon which all the fine varieties are ingrafted, grows naturally in woods and shady places; consequently, it is impatient of exposure in hot, dry soils and situations.

For rose beds on lawns the roses of this division are finely adapted, as they form such a mass of foliage and flowers. They may also be formed into a regular bank, rising gradually from the edge, by having dwarfs of different heights, and " petites tiges," or dwarf standards, in the back ground. They bloom remarkably fine on these little stems, and as the stem is protected from the sun by the branches of the plant, it increases in thickness much faster than when taller; tall stems, owing to exposure, are apt to become bark-bound and unhealthy, increasing but slowly in girth, and often requiring support. To have these hybrid varieties of roses in perfection as pillar roses, they re-

---

are the best months; the soil need not be stirred till spring, and then mere ly loosened two or three inches deep with the prongs of a fork; for poor soils, and on lawns, previously removing the turf, this will be found most efficacious, quire attention, and a superabundance of manure ; but they will amply repay it, for a column twelve to twenty feet high, covered with such roses as *Brennus, Blairii, Belle Parabère, Coccinea superba, Fulgens, Fimbriata, General Lamarque, George the Fourth, King of Roses, Petit Pierre,* or *Triomphe d'Angers, &c. &c.*, would be one of the finest garden ornaments it is possible to conceive. To make these varieties grow with the necessary luxuriance each plant should have a circle, three or four feet in diameter, to itself : and if the soil is poor, it should be dug out two feet in depth, and filled up with rotten mature and loam. This compost must be laid considerably (say one foot) above the surface of the surrounding soil, so as to allow for settling : in shallow or wet soils they will grow the better for being on a permanent mound. Place a single plant in the centre of this mound, or, if you wish for a variegated pillar, place two plants in the same hole, the one a pale-colored or white, the other a dark variety : cover the surface with manure, and replenish this as soon as it is drawn in by the worms or washed in by the rains. Water with liquid manure in dry weather, and probably you will have shoots eight to ten feet in length the first season. I scarcely know whether to recommend grafted roses on short stems for this purpose, or plants on their own roots ; this will in a great measure depend upon the soil, and perhaps it will be as well to try both. Most roses acquire additional vigor by being worked on the Dog Rose, but some of the robust varieties of this family grow with equal luxuriance when on their own roots ; finally, for dry and sandy soils, I am inclined to recommend the latter.

I shall now proceed to give a list of those roses from which, in combination with others, choice seedlings may be raised.

Aurora, a most beautiful purple rose, often striped with

white, may be made a seed-bearing rose of much interest ; if self-colored roses are desired, it should be planted with *Athelin*, which has abundance of pollen ; if striped and variegated roses, the *Village Maid* rose may be planted with it. The *Duke of Devonshire* will produce heps in tolerable abundance ; and as it is inclined to be striped, it would possibly form a beautiful combination with the French rose *Tricolor*, which should be planted with it.

Souvenir d'une Mère, a very large and most beautiful rose, will bear seed if fertilized ; the best union for this rose would perhaps be *Celine*, which is one of the most abundant seed-bearing roses we possess : very large and brilliant rose-colored varieties would probably be originated from these roses in combination.

Riego, which partakes of the sweet briar, might be made the parent of some beautiful briar-like roses by planting it with the *Splendid Sweet Briar*.

General Allard a hybrid Bourbon rose, from which Monsieur Laffay has raised his new perpetual rose, " *Madame Laffay*," is much inclined to give a second series of flowers ; this rose should be planted in a very warm border, or trained against a south wall with *Bourbon Gloire de Rosamène*, and if carefully fertilized with it, some beautiful crimson autumnal roses would probably be originated.

Henri Barbet, which is also a hybrid Bourbon rose of great beauty, should be planted with *Triomphe d'Angers*, with which it may be fertilized, but as the latter has but a small portion of pollen, and the former a great abundance, the process may be reversed ; if seed can be procured from *Triomphe d'Angers* it must produce fine flowers, as it is one of the most beautiful and fragrant of roses.

Petit Pierre, although very double, bears abundance of seed ; as this is a fine and large rose, deepness of color might be given by planting it with the French rose, *La Majestueuse*. *Legouvé* with the Tuscany would probably originate a fine class of rich dark crimson roses, of which at present we possess but few that are really perfect in form and color. Time will, no doubt, put us in possession of many other seed-bearing hybrid China roses that can be depended upon, in addition to those here recommended.

HYBRID BOURBON ROSES.

Rosa Bourboniana hybridæ.

THESE beautiful roses are remarkable for their distinct character ; their foliage is thick and glossy, and remains on very late in autumn ; their petals are also very thick and leathery, and endure sunshine or changeable weather better than most roses. For an avenue of standards, or for a group, they are admirably adapted. They are almost invariably of the most vigorous growth, and are suitable to grow on their own bottoms, or budded high as standards, or one foot from the ground as dwarf or half standards. In some catalogues they are erroneously confused with the preceding class.

A petales mucronés is full double, rose-colored, changeable. *Andrieux* is large, full double, and deep rose-colored. *Athelin*, or *Attelaine*, is not full double, but is well shaped, of that vivid rose color so peculiar to the Bourbons : very beautiful, and blooms in large erect clusters. As it produces seeds freely, it will no doubt be the parent of numerous fine varieties. *Belle de St. Cyr* is bright rose color, superb and perfect. *Brilliante* is large, brilliant rose color, spotted. *Chatelin*, or *Chatelaine*, is dove colored, finely shaped, and very good. *Celine* is a deep shaded blush, splendid. *Charles Duval* is a bright red, large, full double, superb and perfect. *Captain Sisolet* is a magnificent rich fulgent rosy lilac, and distinct. *Colonel Combes* is a brilliant red, occasionally spotted. *Countess Molé* is deep rose, large and superb. *Coupe d'Hébé,* or *Hebe's Cup,* is very robust, foliage glossy, sub-evergreen, and abundant : flowers large, of most perfect shape, petals thick and wax-like, of a delicate pink changing to blush, so beautiful that no description can do it justice. *Daphne* is one of the most beautiful varieties ; it has the usual brilliant reddish salmon color, and distinct; the flowers are much more double than the generality of the Bourbons, with fine foliage. *Dombrowski* is a beautiful flower, of a deep brilliant red hue, approaching to scarlet, well worthy of a place in the group. *Duc de Cazes* is of vigorous growth, the flower large full double, rosy lilac varying to purple, and fine. *Eliza Mercœur* is very large and superb, full double, rose-colored, perfect, and of very robust habit. *Ernest Ferray* is of the most vigorous habit, deep red, distinct and fine. *Esmerelda* is purple and full double. *Franklin* is red, beautifully tinged with lilac. *Great Western* is not a delicate but a *grand* rose, of the habit of Celine, but more robust, and makes shoots 6 to 8 feet in length, of the diameter of a moderate sized cane. The leaves are enormous, often nine inches from base to tip, leaflets three and a half by two inches ; its large clusters of flowers comprise ten to fifteen flowers in each, but as these are frequently too much crowded to expand properly, it is better to thin out each cluster by removing about half of the buds ; the color is a peculiar deep rich red, sometimes tinted with purple, variable according to the season. Budded on stout stocks of the Dog rose, this will form a large umbrageous tree.* It will form also a fine pillar rose, and as a bush

---

* In the Gardeners' Chronicle, " Rose Garden No. 5," Mr. Rivers has described this rose and its peculiar habit.

budded on a two feet stem, so that the whole plant is covered at once by the eye, it presents a magnificent display
at one view. *Henri Barbet* is large, brilliant reddish pink,
magnificent. *Hortense Leroy* is also a most elegant rose :
the foliage small, glossy, and distinct ; flowers very double
and perfect, of a pale roseate hue. *General Allard* is of
globular form, rosy red, fine and distinct. *Glorieux* is a
rich silvery blush, truly beautiful. *Las Casas* is of the
most robust habit, producing very large flowers of a deep
shaded rosy hue, nearly of the color and shape of the old
Cabbage Provence rose. *Le Gouvé* is large, full double,
and quite first rate in form, of a crimson color, and may be
grown as a prize or show rose. *La Dauphine* is a silvery blush, large, and splendid. *Lady Montgomery* is large,
fine blush, habit of Celine, very robust. *Le Vésuve* is of
globular form, purplish rose color, very distinct. *Lord
John Russell* is a fine light cherry color, most curiously
veined and marbled, and blooms in erect clusters. *Lussel-
dembourg* is a fine spherical-shaped rose, bright rosy lilac,
very beautiful and distinct. *Majestueux* is large, full double, of a bright deep rose color. *Miss Chauncey* is a rich
fulgent rose color, remarkably beautiful. *Olympia* is rosy
incarnate, tinged with lilac, very beautiful *Paul Perras*
is a shaded rose color, very large and splendid. *President
Molé* is of a brilliant purplish roseate hue, a superb flower.
Richlieu (Duval,) is perfectly beautiful, bright roseate, and
distinct, but its habit is meagre and unlike all others of this
generally robust family. *Striped Bourbon,* or *Striée,* is full
double, of a violet purple hue, and striped. *Sylvain* is a
superb brilliant crimson rose, of perfect form. *Victor Hugo* is one of the finest lilac colored roses, producing flowers
of large size, full double, globular, and finely formed ; it
is of erect and vigorous growth. *William Jesse* is very
large, deep rosy colored, of the form of La Reine, and
sometimes blooms a second time.

HYBRID CLIMBING ROSES.

INCLUDING HYBRID NOISETTE ROSES.

Rosa hybridæ scandens.

THE fine varieties of this interesting group partake of
the characteristics of the various families from which they
originated.   They are well adapted for training on pillars,
arbors, trellices, or sides of houses.   The varieties with
very weak and flexible branches may also be made to form
most beautiful ornaments, by cultivating them as standards
after the following method.   Select very strong Sweet
Briar, or other strong growing stocks, and bud these varieties upon them, at the height of eight to ten feet ; the flexible shoots will then drop quite to the ground, and when in
flower, will present a unique and splendid appearance.
This mode is adopted extensively in France and England.
There are several distinct classes of climbing roses, which
will be described under their appropriate heads.

Astrolabe is a very double, compact flower, of a brilliant
pink hue, distinct, very pretty, not so vigorous in growth
as some of the other varieties.   *Briseis* is a hybrid Noisette, of medium size, full double, and a delicate flesh color.
Bengale formidable is a cup-shaped flower, pale rose color,
and very double.   *Brookes' Climbing China* is a pale red
flower, of no great importance.   *Clair* is a small single
flower, bright crimson, cupped, pretty and attractive, said
to be a hybrid between the Sempervirens and Crimson
China, or Semperflorens.   It blooms all the autumn and
seeds freely, and will probably be the parent of many
beautiful climbers.   *Claire d'Olban*, is a hybrid Noisette,
of medium size, full double, and of a delicate roseate hue.
Drummond's Thornless, will be found under the head of
" Boursault Rose."   *Egerie* is a hybrid Noisette, of medium

size, deep purplish rosy color, and full double. *Elegans, Elegans Rosea*, or *Bengal Elegante* is of a cupped form, very distinct, nearly full double, and of a beautiful brilliant pink color, in large profuse clusters. The shoots are long and flexible, and it continues in bloom with a profusion of flowers for a much longer period than any other summer rose. *Fideline* is of medium size, full double, and beautiful rose color. *Fleurette* is of the same size as the preceding, of a very delicate roseate hue, and full double. *Hybride parfaite* is a full double rose of the usual size, and of same color as the preceding one. *Indica Major, Bengalensis scandens, Duchess of Dino, Walton Rose*, or *Rose Blanche*, is doubtless a hybrid between the China and Sempervirens : it is of the most vigorous and luxuriant growth, richly clad with large lucid foliage, nearly evergreen : it will make shoots of ten to fifteen feet in a season, and may be trained over a diameter of thirty feet or more, and to twenty feet or more in height ; the flower buds are edged with pink and peculiarly beautiful ; the flowers expand early, are very large, measuring about three and a half inches in diameter, full double, white, suffused with delicate touches of pale blush color. When a large and expanded plant is in full bloom, it is remarkably striking and attractive. It is well suited to cover unsightly buildings or walls. *Madame d' Arblay*, or *Wells' White*, is of rapid growth, attaining gigantic dimensions, surpassing almost any other climbing variety ; the foliage large and luxuriant ; the flowers creamy white, very double and pretty, and produced in large clusters. It is very hardy, and suitable for stocks to bud on. It will form a tree or pillar of the largest size. *Maheka* is a climbing Chinese hybrid, which grows vigorously and blooms early and profusely ; the flowers singly have but little beauty, as they are only semi-double, but being of a fine violet purple hue, the mass presented on large spreading plants is quite attractive. *Maria Stella*, is a hybrid Noisette, of medium size, full double, and deep rose color. *Miller's Climber* is a pretty pink rose, of small size, not quite double. *Madame Plantier* is a hybrid Noisette, of vigorous growth, producing pure white full double flowers of extreme beauty and in great profusion. *Pompon Carmin* is a hybrid Noisette, with small flowers, full double, of a beautiful carmine color. *Rivers' Queen* is a double cupped flower, dark purplish crimson. *Sir John Sebright* is semi-double, fragrant, bright vivid crimson scarlet, very showy, produced in great profusion in large clusters. *Sophie d' Houtetot* is a beautiful hybrid Noisette, of medium size, full double, deep rose color. *The Garland*, or *Wood's Garland*, has fragrant creamy white flowers, changing to pink after expansion; these are in corymbose clusters, often 70 to 100 united, fragrant, of compact form, and beautiful. The growth is very vigorous and rapid, making in a good soil, ten to twelve feet a year. *Triumph of Bolwiller*, or *Sempervirens Odorata*, is evidently a hybrid, and not a genuine variety of the Sempervirens, and therefore it should not be placed under the latter head. The flower is creamy white, large and beautiful, full double, globular, of agreeable fragrance, and produced in clusters at the extremities of the shoots in June, July and late in autumn. The foliage is handsome, luxuriant, and sub-evergreen. This variety is peculiarly suited to a southern climate, and to the south of the Potomac it attains a splendid development; but in this latitude it is somewhat tender, and liable to be partially injured in our severe winters. If planted against a wall or fence with a southern exposure, the difficulty is remedied, and it will then speedily spread 10 to 12 feet, or more, in each direction. *Watts' Celestial*, or *Watts' Climbing China*, is large, of a rich delicate rose color, the petals incurved, forming a fine cup-shaped flower.

As fine seedling climbers are very desirable, it is a happy circumstance that our glowing sun and climate cause those varieties which have the necessary parts for fructification, to produce seeds to a far greater extent than in England, and at least equally with France and Italy. We have also the advantage of already possessing a very considerable number of double and semi-double varieties of our native Prairie rose, or Rosa rubifolia, to aid us in the hybridizing process. A most desirable object is a dark crimson variety of Rosa ruga ; this may possibly be obtained by planting that favorite rose with the Ayrshire Queen, and fertilizing its flowers very carefully with those of that dark rose. It is remarkable that although these roses are both hybrids, from species apparently very remote in their affinities, yet both of them bear seed, even without being fertilized. The Blush Ayrshire, a most abundant seed-bearer, may be planted with the Ayrshire Queen, the Common Bourbon, Gloire de Rosamène, the Double Yellow Briar, Single Crimson Moss, Celine, Henri Barbet, the China Rose, Fabvier, Tea Princesse Helène (Luxembourg,) and its flowers fertilized with the pollen of these roses ; if any combination can be effected, pleasing results may reasonably be hoped for. To "make assurance doubly sure," the anthers of the Ayrshire Rose should be removed from some of the flowers with which the experiment is tried. The Red Boursault Rose, planted with Athelin, may perhaps become the parent of some brilliant red climbing roses. Rose Clair, if planted against a south wall, with Gloire de Rosamène, or fertilized with the flowers of Athelin, Sir John Sebright, or the Ayrshire Queen, would give some distinct and curious varieties. Sempervirens Scandens, of which the flowers are buff when they first expand, would be worth experimenting upon with the Old Double Yellow Briar, or with the Persian Yellow Rose, and as the Scandens is a most vigorous climber, its progeny, however much hybridized, would be sure to retain sufficient of that desirable quality.

THE SCOTCH, OR BURNET ROSE.

Rosa Spinosissima.

THIS dwarf species of the Rose derives its title from the profusion of small spines with which its shoots are clad. In France it is called Rosa pimprenellifolia, or Rosier pimprenelle, (Burnet-leaved Rose,) from the resemblance in its foliage to that plant. It approximates very much, in habit, to the Rosa lutea, or Yellow Austrian Briar. It is a native of several of the Alpine regions of Europe, but has, throughout Great Britain, obtained the exclusive name of Scotch Rose, from the circumstance of its being first brought into particular notice in a double state, by the Messrs. Brown, of Perth, Scotland. In the year 1793 they obtained seeds from some wild plants growing on an adjacent hill; the seedlings produced semi-double flowers, and by continuing the selection of seeds, and raising new plants annually, they obtained, by the year 1803, eight fine double varieties, comprising shades of white, blush, yellow, red and marbled; and from these the hundreds of seminal double varieties have been since produced, which are now disseminated throughout the world. In some of the European catalogues two or three hundred names are given, but in many cases these names are attached to flowers without sufficiently distinctive qualities. In my catalogue the names of a few of the best varieties are given.

The following varieties have generally proved good and

distinct. *Aimable Etrangère*, a French hybrid with very double pure white flowers. *Adelaide*, a large red rose, double, and good. *Athol* is much admired. *Blanche* is a fine double white variety. *Blanda* is one of the best of the numerous marbled Scotch roses, as these are generally much alike. *Countess of Glasgow*, *Cramoisie*, *Daphne*, *Erebus* and *Flora* are all good, vivid colored, dark roses, varying in their shades and very pretty. *Guy Mannering* is a very large and a very double blush rose, distinct and good. *La Cénomane* is a French hybrid, pearly white, with large and very double flowers; a beautiful rose, but not so robust as the pure Scotch varieties. *La Neige* is deserving of its name, being of the purest white, and very double and good. *Lady Baillie*, *Marchioness of Lansdowne*, and *Mrs. Hay*, are all pretty pale sulphur-colored roses, and from the seed of these, it is very probable that some good yellow varieties may be raised.

Painted Lady is a French hybrid, white, striped with red, but rather inconstant, as its flowers are often pure white : when it blooms in character, it is a charming little rose. *Princess Elizabeth* and the *Queen of May* are both bright pink varieties, very distinct and pretty. The *Single Yellow* is a neat and pretty variety, and blooms profusely. The *True Double Yellow* is a hybrid raised in France, and in most seasons is a pretty, sulphur colored rose, much admired; but in very hot weather it fades quite soon to white. *William the Fourth* is the largest white pure Scotch rose known ; a luxuriant grower, and a good variety. *Venus* is an excellent dark rose, with very double flowers and a distinct character.

To these may be added *Ianthe*, *Jugurtha*, *Rœser*, *Saturnia*, *Stephani*, and other choice varieties, where an extensive collection is desirable.

Scotch roses may be grown as standards, and the yellow,

and one or two of the more robust varieties, make good heads; but in general they form round and small dense heads, in ill accordance with good taste : when grown in beds or clumps, as dwarfs, they are beautiful, and in early seasons they will bloom nearly a fortnight before the other summer roses make their appearance, and this, of course, makes them desirable appendages to the flower garden. They bear seed profusely ; and raising new varieties from seed will be found a most interesting employment.   To do this, all that is required is to sow the seed as soon as ripe, in October, in pots or beds of fine earth, covering it with nearly one inch of mould; the succeeding spring they will come up, and bloom in perfection the season following.

With the exception of La Cénomane, Painted Lady, and the Double Yellow, all the Scotch roses bear seed most abundantly, and if this seed is sown indiscriminately, numerous varieties may be raised, many of which will prove very interesting.   The aim however should be to obtain varieties with large and very double crimson flowers, and this can only be done by slightly hybridizing; and to effect this it will be necessary to have a plant or two of the Tuscany, and one of the Superb Tuscany, or La Majestueuse, trained to a south wall, so that their flowers are expanded at the same time as the Scotch roses in the open borders, for unless thus forced they will be too late.   Any dark red varieties of the Scotch roses, such as Venus, Atro Rubra, or Flora, should be planted separately from others, and their flowers fertilized with the above French roses, and some very original, deep colored varieties will probably be obtained by this method.   Sulphurea and one or two other straw colored varieties may be planted with the Double Yellow Austrian Briar, and most likely some pretty sulphur-colored roses will be the result of this combination.

THE SWEET BRIAR AND CONGENERS.

Rosa Rubiginosa, &c.

WHO knows not the Sweet Briar ? the Eglantine, that flower of poesy and song, the rhyme of which jingles so prettily, that nearly all our poets, and even love-stricken rustics have taken advantage of its sweet sound.

"I will give to my love the Eglantine,"

has been full oft the beginning of the country swain's love ditty, and in sober truth, every one must love this simplest and sweetest of flowers, for what odor can surpass that emanating from a bush of Sweet Briar in the dewy evenings of June ? It pleases not the eye, for the single Sweet Briar produces flowers, in comparison with other roses, quite inconspicuous ; but it gratifies in a high degree by its delicious perfume, and gives to the mind most agreeable associations, for it is so often (at least in England,) the inhabitant of the pretty cottage garden—such a garden as one seldom sees elsewhere but in that country. The *Single Sweet Briar* is an European plant, growing in dry and chalky soils in some of the southern counties of England, and also abounding in various parts of France and other countries of Europe. It is likewise found in considerable numbers growing in the hedges and neglected grounds of our own country, more especially in the vicinity of long settled towns, near the Atlantic, it having been introduced among us by seeds and plants brought from Europe by some of the early settlers of our country. The *Montezuma Rose,* of Mexico, is identically the same species, but appears to be of more gigantic growth than the ordinary variety, and I have some in my grounds that are sixteen feet in height, with the stalks of proportionate diameter, and whose

branches assume a weeping position. The following varieties, with some others, have been originated, more or
less hybridized, and all but two have cupped flowers. The
American White is a beautifully shaped flower, creamy
white, and quite as interesting as any obtained from
Europe. *American Roseate* is of a bright rose color, and
estimable. The *Apple-bearing Briar*, or *Maliflora*, although a distinct species, particularly characterized by its
fruit, may nevertheless, from the similitude of its flowers
and general character, be comprised under this head ; the
flowers are semi-double, neat blush, early, and highly fragrant. The *Carmine* (Sweet Briar) is of a bright hue, in accordance with its name. The *Carnation* is a beautiful blush.
The *Celestial*, a beautiful little rose, with flowers very double
and fragrant, of the palest flesh color, approaching to white.
The *Chinese* is of a deep roseate hue. The *Cluster* has
semi-double rosy, lilac flowers. *Clementine* is rosy blush,
pretty and distinct. *Hessoise*, or *Petite Hessoise*, is a
pretty French hybrid, with bright, rose colored flowers,
and leaves not so fragrant as some others. The *Hip*, or
Dog Rose, (*Rosa canina*,) has, from its similarity for all
practical purposes, been incorporated with the Sweet Briar.
The best varieties are the old Double Red, the Single or
Semi-double Margined, or *Hebe's Lip*, creamy white, with
a pink border, and the *Double Margined*, which also
bears the names of *Emmeline*, and *Madeline*, full double,
white, shaded with pink, and a violet border. The *Iver
Cottage* (Sweet Briar,) is of a pale rose color. The *Monstrous* is a very old variety, with large and very double
flowers, distinct and good. *Maiden's Blush*, and *Manning's
Blush* are both double and pretty, with fragrant leaves like
the original. The *Mossy* has buds somewhat mossed, and
flowers of a light pink shade. *Riego* is a rose colored
hybrid, from the China Rose and the Sweet Briar, a re-

markable and most pleasing union, as it possesses a most delicious perfume. It has little or no similarity in appearance to the last named parent, and is ranked by some as a hybrid China rose. *Rose Angle* is a new variety, raised from seed by Mr. Martin, of Rose Angle, near Dundee: this produces large and very double flowers, of a bright rose color; its foliage is also very fragrant. The *Royal* is of a pale rose color. The *Splendid* is rightly named, a splendid rose, with large light crimson flowers, but its foliage is not very fragrant. The *Scarlet*, or *La Belle Distinguée*, *Lee's Dutchess*, or *La Petite Dutchesse*, for they are the same, is a pretty bright red, small, and compact rose, very distinct and good, but its leaves are entirely scentless. The *Superb* is of very robust growth, with rose colored flowers.

Sweet Briars form a pretty group, interesting from their origin and associations, and pleasing from their fragrance and peculiar neatness; they make also pretty trees, particularly on " petites tiges," as the French term them; they require the same culture as the other hardy roses.

Humble as are the claims of the Sweet Briar when contrasted with the gorgeous beauty of some of our new roses, yet, the raising of new varieties from seed will, I am sure, be found interesting.

The Scarlet may be planted with the Splendid Briar, which so abounds in pollen that fertilizing will be found very easy. The Carmine with the Scarlet semi-double will also give promising seed ; the beauty of their flowers might be increased by hybridizing with some of the French roses, but then their Sweet Briar-like character would be lost, and with that a great portion of their interest.

The Hybrid Riego, if planted with the Splendid Briar, would produce seed from which large and very fragrant double roses might be expected, and these would partake largely of the character of the Sweet Briar.

4

THE PERSIAN, OR AUSTRIAN BRIAR.

Rosa lutea, vel sulphurea.

THIS much admired, and very peculiar Briar is found
native, or naturalized, in the south of Europe, and particularly on the hills of the north of Italy, producing copper or
red, as well as yellow flowers; but, strange to say, though
the flowers are invariably single, they never produce
seed. In this country it is also with extreme difficulty,
and only by fertilizing its flowers, that seed can be perfected: if the flowers are examined they will all be found
deficient in pollen, which accounts for this universal bar-
renness. A splendid, perfectly double variety having been
obtained from Persia, and others being known to exist there,
it is extremely probable that it originated in that country.
All of this family have cupped, except where otherwise
designated.

The *Copper, or Red and Yellow Austrian*, the *Capucine*
of the French, is a most singular rose; the inside of each
petal is of a bright copper red, the outside inclining to sulphur. I have also in my collection a rose with single
flowers, imported from France under the name of *Capucine
de Semies*, which is totally distinct from the preceding; the
petals are yellow beneath, and the surface mottled with
dull red, and sometimes entirely of a dull red hue. The
foliage also differs from the preceding, being more delicate,
and the growth of the plant is much more vigorous. To
distinguish it I have called it *Capucine Ponctué*. A double,
copper colored variety is yet a desideratum. The *Double
Yellow*, or *Williams' Double Yellow Sweet Briar*, is a pretty
double rose, raised from the Single Yellow Austrian a few
years since; this blooms more freely than the original

species, and is a most desirable variety. *Rosa Harrisonii*, or *Harrison's Yellow*, was raised from seed by the late Geo. Harrison, Esq., of New-York, from whom I received the first plant he parted with, in exchange for a Camellia Aitoni, which I had just then imported at an expense of three guineas. It has proved not only brilliant and beautiful, but what was equally important, a most free and profuse bloomer; the flowers which are not quite full double are about two inches in diameter and globular before expansion, but a hot sun makes them expand and lose much of their beauty. It is a more robust grower than the Double Yellow Briar, often forming shoots of five to six feet in a season; its flowers are also a little larger, and do not fade so soon. Numerous seedlings have been raised from this variety, but all that have come under my notice have proved very similar, or inferior to it. To one produced in England the name has been given of *Harrisonii No. 1*. This I have imported, and find the flower to be pale yellow, tinged with copper. A plant obtained from Mr. Feast, and said to be grown from seed by him, has produced flowers undistinguishable from those of the parent. The *Single Yellow* is the most brilliant Yellow rose we yet possess; and it will probably be the parent of some double varieties, its equal in color.

To this peculiar family of roses a few new varieties have been added. *Cuivre Rouge*, a curious hybrid, partaking of the Boursault Rose, with smooth thornless branches and dull reddish single flowers, and the *Superb Double Yellow Briar*, a seedling raised by Mr. Williams, of Pitmaston, from the same rose, and, I believe, at the same time, as the Double Yellow Briar. This has larger and more double flowers, but they are perhaps not so bright in color. A third variety is the *Globe Yellow*, a very pretty pale yellow rose, of humble growth: this variety was raised in Italy.

A new yellow rose has been given to us from the land of flowers, Persia. This was introduced by the London Horticultural Society in 1838, and is now called the *Persian Yellow Rose*. In habit it is very like the Single Yellow Austrian Briar; it seems to grow readily budded on the Dog Rose, and plants so budded have made shoots three feet or more in length in one season. In color it is of a deeper yellow than the Harrison, quite double, cupped, and not so liable to become reflexed as that very pretty and brilliant rose. Like the Yellow Austrian Briar, it loves a pure air and rich soil, and will then grow and bloom most freely. The *Italian Yellow* has straw colored flowers with a yellow centre. The *Double Blush*, or *Victoria*, is of a salmon blush color, with a buff centre, large, but not fully double. *La bien Trouvé* is classed in some European publications under this head, but my own investigations have not yet enabled me to decide whether appropriately or not. The flowers are white, double, highly fragrant, and of globose form.

To bloom Austrian Briars in perfection, the soil should be moist, and the air dry as well as pure. But little manure is necessary, as they grow freely in any tolerably good and moist soil; neither do they require severe pruning, but merely the strong shoots shortened, most of the twigs being left on the plant, as they, generally, produce flowers in great abundance.

No family of roses offers such an interesting field for experiments in raising new varieties from seed as this. First, we have the Copper Austrian, from which, although it is one of the oldest roses in our gardens, a double flowering variety has never yet been obtained. This rose is always defective in pollen, and consequently it will not bear seed unless its flowers are fertilized: as it will be interesting to retain the traits of the species, it should be planted with and fertilized by the Double Yellow ; it will then in warm dry seasons produce seed not abundantly, but the amateur must rest satisfied if he can procure even one hep full of perfect seed. The French variety which I have called *Capucine Ponctué* seems to bear seed more freely, but as the color of its flowers is not so bright as the original, its seed, even from fertilized flowers, would not be so valuable.

The beautiful and brilliant Harrison and the Persian Yellow give us, however, the brightest hopes. They should be planted with the Double Yellow Briar ; and will then, as has been proved, bear seed abundantly : no rose will perhaps show the effects of fertilizing its flowers more plainly than this, and consequently to the amateur it is the pleasing triumph of art over nature. Mr. Rivers remarks that every flower on his experimental plants, not fertilized, proved abortive, while, on the contrary, all those that were so, produced large black spherical heps full of perfect seed.

The *Rosa Sulphurea*, or *Double Yellow Rose*, or *Yellow Provence*, is arranged as a distinct species in the botanical catalogues, but it is evidently of the same parentage as the varieties of the Rosa lutea. It has been traced to Turkey, being probably brought there from Persia ; and by some it is said to exist in China, the "Flowery Empire," that country which is not only the oldest in horticulture, but by far the most civilized and advanced in the development of those requirements that render human life most happy. In most European publications it is said to be a native of the Levant, whence it was introduced to the English gardens in 1629, but as it has never been found growing wild in its primitive character with single flowers, we may justly deem this hypothesis a mere fable. Nature has never yet presented us with *double* flowering species with which to commence the production of *single* flowering varieties, but directly the reverse. The process of producing new and

often double varieties by fertilization, has doubtless been
known to the Chinese for ages, else where would have
originated above two hundred varieties of the Pæonia Moutan, whose existence was announced by the first British
embassies ?   And whence the hundreds of double varieties
of the Chrysanthemum, Camellia, and other genera now
known to have flourished in China and Japan long before
the nations of Europe knew of the existence of a single
variety, or had imbibed the idea of producing double flowers ?
Recent developments are shedding a flood of light upon the
history of that country, and proving beyond all question
that the pretensions to original discovery of many of the
arts by Europeans, and their vaunted claims to civilization,
are as circumstances of yesterday, when contrasted with
the thousands of years that the same arts have flourished
in that ancient empire.

Be the origin of the *Rosa Sulphurea* what it may, it is
one of the most ancient and beautiful varieties known to
European gardens, introduced there in 1629.   The flower
is large, bright yellow, very double, and of globular form:
its foliage is particularly delicate, with a glaucous pubescence ; and its shoots have a greenish yellow tinge, very
unlike the single yellow, yet Mr. Rivers has ventured a
supposition that it was produced from that variety fertilized
by the Damask, which is also of oriental origin.   The *Pompone Yellow, Dwarf Double Yellow,* or *Pompone Jaune,* is
the variety deemed nearest allied to the preceding ; it is of
dwarf habit; the flower small, deep yellow and globular ; it
blooms more freely than the preceding one.   Both, however, are excessively shy of producing full blown flowers,
although they grow in any moderately good soil with great
luxuriance, especially if properly pruned, and show an
abundance of flower buds, but some " worm in the bud "
generally causes them to fall off prematurely.   To remedy

this, various situations have been recommended: some have said, plant it against a south wall ; others, give it a northern aspect, under the drip of some water trough, as it requires a wet situation. All this is quackery and nonsense. The *Double Yellow* Rose being a native of a warm climate, requires a warm situation, with a free and airy exposure, and rich soil.

At Burleigh, (England,) the effect of situation on this rose is forcibly shown. A very old plant is growing against a southern wall, in a confined situation, its roots cramped by a stone pavement; it is weakly and never shows a flower-bud. Another plant is growing in front of a low parapet wall, in a good loamy soil, and free airy exposure ; this is in a state of the greatest luxuriance, and blooms in perfection almost every season.

Mr. Rivers suggests that for the humid climate of England, it would be well to bud it on short stems of the Dog Rose, or Sweet Briar ; these to be potted in autumn, and forced late in the spring, giving the plants plenty of air, thus endeavoring to imitate the dry and warm climate of Italy, where it is said to bloom in perfection. With us such artificial means are unnecessary, as we have a sun quite as warm and glowing as that of Italy, and we doubt not that beneath the sunny skies of our own glorious country, a good soil and an open exposure will produce the desirable results.

CLIMBING ROSES.

UNDER this head we will describe six species or families of roses, the varieties of which bloom during the ordinary period. We have already described the class of Hybrid Climbing Roses, several of which bloom at different periods and we shall at a subsequent part of the work describe the Perpetual Flowering Climbers.

THE AYRSHIRE ROSE.

Rosa arvensis, et hybridæ.

IT is the opinion of some cultivators, that the varieties of the Ayrshire Rose have been originated from the Rosa arvensis, or creeping single White Rose of the woods and hedges of England. But this is contradicted by botanists, who assert, that the original Ayrshire Rose was raised in Scotland from foreign seed. This may have been ; but to judge from its habit, I feel no hesitation in asserting, that it is merely a hybrid seedling from the Rosa arvensis, having acquired much additional vigor, as hybrid roses almost invariably do, from some accidental impregnation. Perhaps no rose can be more luxuriant than this ; for the Single Ayrshire, and that semi-double variety, known as the Double White, will often make shoots in one season, twenty to thirty feet in length. Several of the prettiest varieties have been raised from seed by Mr. Martin, of Rose Angle, Dundee ; but the first in the catalogue, the *Ayrshire Queen*, the only dark Ayrshire Rose known, was originated by Mr. T. Rivers, in 1835, from the Blush Ayrshire, impregnated with the Tuscany Rose. But one seed germinated, and the plant has proved a complete hybrid. Its flowers are of the same shape, and not more double than those of the Blush Ayrshire, its female parent; but they have all the dark purplish crimson of the Tuscany Rose. It has lost a portion of the vigorous climbing habit of the Ayrshire, but yet makes an excellent pillar rose. Until we can get a dark Ayrshire Rose, double as a Ranunculus, this will be acceptable. The *Double Blush*, or *Double Red* of some catalogues, is a pretty early rose, a vigorous climber, and as a standard, forms a beautiful umbrella-shaped tree. *Bennet's Seedling*, or *Rosa Theresbyana*, of the Floricultural Cabinet, is a new variety, found growing among some briars by a gardener of the name of Bennet, in Nottinghamshire. It is a very pretty double, pure white variety. *Dundee Rambler* is the most double, and one of the best in this division; it blooms in very large clusters, much after the Noisette fashion, and is truly a desirable rose. *Elegans*, or the *Double White*, is one of our oldest varieties; its flowers are semi-double, and, individually, not pretty, as their petals in hot weather are very flaccid; but it blooms in such large clusters, and grows so vigorously, that it forms an admirable Wilderness Rose. *Jessica* is a pretty delicate pink variety, distinct and good. *Rose Angle Blush* is like Jessica in its color, but is much more luxuriant in its habit. I am sure that this rose in strong soils will make shoots in one season more than twenty feet in length.

Lovely Rambler, or the *Crimson Ayrshire*, is merely semi-double, and its petals too flaccid to be much esteemed; it is mentioned here to prevent its two imposing names from misleading the amateur. *Myrrh-scented:* this name has been applied to two or three roses having the same peculiar scent; this variety has semi-double flowers of a creamy blush. *Queen of the Belgians* is a fine rose, with very double flowers, of a pure white; this is a most vigorous climber, soon forming a pillar fifteen or twenty feet high. *Ruga* is now a well known variety, said to be a hybrid between the Tea-scented China Rose and the Common Ayrshire; it is a most beautiful and fragrant rose. *Splendens* is a new variety, with very large cupped flowers, of a creamy blush; this rose has also that peculiar "Myrrh-scented" fragrance.

Ayrshire Roses are, some of them, perhaps, surpassed in beauty by the varieties of Rosa sempervirens; still they have distinct and desirable qualities : they bloom nearly a fortnight earlier than the roses of that division ; they will grow where no other rose will exist; and to climb up the stems of timber trees in plantations near frequented walks, and to form undergrowth, they are admirably well adapted : they also make graceful and beautiful standards, for the ends of the branches descend and shade the stems, which in consequence, increase rapidly in bulk. It seems probable that Ayrshire Roses will grow to an enormous size as standards, and surpass in the beauty of their singular dome-shaped heads many other roses more prized for their rarity.

The following extract from the Dundee Courier, will give some idea how capable these roses are of making even a wilderness a scene of beauty :

"Some years ago, a sand pit at Ellangowan was filled up with rubbish found in digging a well. Over this a piece of rock work was formed for the growth of plants which prefer such situations, and amongst the rocks were planted some half dozen of the Double Ayrshire Rose, raised in this neighborhood about ten years ago. These roses now most completely cover the whole ground, a space of thirty feet by twenty. At present they are in full bloom, showing probably not less than ten thousand roses in this small space."

TIIF MULTIFLORA ROSE.

Rosa multiflora.

THE *Rosa multiflora*, or many-flowered rose, is a native of Japan, whence it was brought by Thunberg, and introduced to Europe in 1804. Several of the varieties in the catalogue have been raised in Italy, where these pretty roses flourish and bear seed abundantly. In the neighborhood of Florence the *Double Red* may be seen climbing to an enormous extent, and large plants, completely covered with thousands of its very double and perfect flowers, having a very fine appearance. The *Single White* is also grown in Italy ; from this Mr. Rivers has raised several hundreds of seedlings; all the varieties of this family are interesting, as they differ so much from other roses. *Alba*, or the *Double White*, is rather a misnomer, for it is not pure white, but rather a pale flesh color, pretty and distinct. *Crivellii* is a new variety, and one of the prettiest ; its flowers are of a brilliant and changeable red, very unique ; it is a free grower, and well deserves attention. *Elegans* is a most beautiful little rose, changing from blush to nearly pure white : it is a little hybridized, and consequently more hardy than the true Rosa multiflora. *Fragrans* is a most robust growing variety, but it has not yet bloomed in this country. *Scarlet Greville*, *Russelliana*, or the *Cottage Rose*, may be a hybrid of this family, but I much doubt it, as it differs in character from all the other varieties, and is in fact none else than the *Pallagi panaché*, a French variety of the Hybrid China, which I imported under the latter name from France, many years before it was introduced here from England under the former three titles. It evidently had been re-named in England, and there received the title of the *Russelliana Rose ;* it being a very common practice in that country, on the introduction of any very superior variety of the Rose, from France, (where new varieties are annually produced in great numbers,) to give to it an entire new title, which often prevents it being identified for years. Such was the case with the *Village Maid,* which is the *Panachée double* of the French ;

the *New Village Maid,* the *Panaché pleine* of the French;
the *Cloth of Gold,* the *Chromatella* of the French, and with
a multitude of others, and this practice of the English cultivators has been extended to a great number of varieties of
Fruits, which under new titles have absolutely been deemed
new varieties, and widely disseminated as such, before
these acts of chicanery were elucidated by the investigations of the London Horticultural Society, and by other
pomologists in Europe and America.   The *Grevillei alba* is
a genuine variety originated by Mr. Rivers, with pure white
flowers.   *Grevillei grandiflora* has very large deep roseate
flowers.   *Grevillei minor* is, as its name indicates, of more
dwarf habit with shaded roseate flowers.   *Floribunda* has
roseate colored flowers, tinged with buff.   *Coccinea* has
small flowers of a carmine roseate hue.   *De la Grifferaie*
is of vigorous growth, and produces the largest flowers of
this class, purplish carmine, and full double.   *Graulhie*
has double white flowers of a very small size, and particularly delicate and pretty.   *Greville,* or the *Seven Sisters'
Rose,* is a vigorous climber, blooming in large clusters,
which show a curious diversity of colors; for soon after
expansion, the flowers change from crimson to purplish
roseate, and then to pale rose, and some even to blush and
white, so that in the clusters may be seen many shades,
from white to rose and deep purplish crimson.   In wet
soils, it is often killed to the ground by the severe winter
frosts; and in the Middle States, it requires a warm and
dry position, and should also be bound in straw or mats
during the winter months.   If thus protected, it will form a
fine pillar rose, or covering for walls, or sides of buildings.
The winter covering should be removed at the opening of
spring, as this variety shoots very early.   This treatment
of the Greville Rose may be applied to all the varieties of
the Multiflora, except Russelliana, as they are impatient of

cold. *Hybrida*, or *Laure Davoust*, is a hybrid, and a most elegant and delicate rose, having all the peculiar neatness of the double red and white varieties, with larger flowers and more beautiful foliage. This is one of the prettiest climbing roses known, and also one of the hardiest of its class. A Genevese friend informs me that some pillars of this rose at Geneva are thirty feet high, and covered with flowers the greater part of summer. *Rubra*, or *Red*, or *Pink Multiflora*, is our oldest variety, but still interesting and pretty. Large plants of this rose may sometimes be seen, that seldom put forth flowers ; this is owing to close pruning, or to the winter killing the small spray-like shoots, by which they are produced, and it may be avoided by having recourse to the winter protection I have already recommended, and by pruning very sparingly. *Superba* is a variety approaching the Greville Rose in appearance, but much more dwarf and hardy, the flowers pencilled roseate.

These roses have but few adaptations. I have stated under Greville Rose their appropriateness for pillar roses, and for warm situations against walls, where they are very ornamental : they also bloom in the greatest perfection as standards, but they will then require additional protection in winter. Grafted on short stems and grown in large pots, they bloom freely, and form pretty objects, as they produce their myriads of elegant flowers during a great part of the summer.

THE EVERGREEN ROSE.

Rosa sempervirens.

The original of this beautiful family is the Rosa semper-virens, the climbing Wild Rose of Italy, with small single white flowers, and foliage nearly evergreen. Monsieur Jacques, the chief gardener at the Château de Neuilly, has had the pleasure of originating most of the varieties now in cultivation; two or three he has named after the daughters of his royal master, King Louis Philippe: *Adelaide d'Or-leans* is one of these, and a very pretty and excellent rose it is, with dark shining green foliage, and beautiful shaded pale rose colored flowers; in the Floricultural Cabinet, a figure of it is given, which is as much like a sunflower as this pretty and distinct rose. *Banksiæflora* is more fragrant than the generality of these roses; it seems hy-bridized in a trifling degree with the old Musk Rose, which has probably imparted a little of its delightful perfume; this has small and very double white flowers. *Brunonii* is not a true Sempervirens, but approaching so near its habit, that it cannot be placed in any other division with propriety. It has more color than usual in roses of this family, as they are all inclined to pale flesh color, or white. This is of a vivid rose color, and very pretty and distinct. *Carnea grandiflora*, this name conveys an accurate de-scription, as its flowers are large and flesh colored. *Donna Maria* is of the purest white, with fine dark green foliage, and very double flowers; a good and distinct rose. *Eximia*, imported as a new variety, proved on blooming to be the old Indica major. *Felicite perpetuelle* has been sold as " *Noisette floribunda*," "*Noisette compacta*," "*Mademoiselle Euphrasie*," "*Abéilard sempervirens :*" and probably under some other high sounding appellations, for it is a general favorite, and justly so, being one of the most beautiful of roses. No plant can be more lovely than a large specimen of this rose, covered with its double ranunculus-like cream-colored flowers. It will not bloom if pruned much; therefore its shoots must be tied in of their full length, and thinned out if too numerous, but not shortened.

Jaunâtre is a new variety, with yellowish white flowers. This is evidently hybridized with the Musk or Noisette Rose, as it is fragrant.

Mélanie de Montjoie has large flowers of the purest white, and foliage very abundant and beautiful, of a shining dark green, contrasting finely with its flowers. *Minor* is pale incarnate and blooms during the autumn.

Myrianthes, sometimes called *Ranunculacea*, is a charming plant: its flowers are so perfectly and elegantly shaped, and their color so delicate, that, if not the most beautiful of all, it is one among them. *Plena* is also known as *Sempervirens major*, and as the *Double White Noisette*. This is our oldest double variety, and a very good rose. *Princesse Louise* and *Princesse Marie*, as found in many collections, are identically the same rose, but the true Princesse Marie is a very neat and pretty bright rose colored variety, and entirely distinct. *Princesse Louise* is a fine and vigorous growing variety, with flowers of a creamy blush, very double and prettily cupped. *Rampant*, as its name implies, is a most vigorous and rampant grower and a very pretty pure white rose. This will cover a wall or building with nearly as much rapidity as the common Ayrshire. *Rose Foncée* has very dark shining green foliage, and varies in the color of its flowers; for in some seasons, they have not by any means been either a bright or deep rose color, though in others they were very distinct and in character. *Scandens* is a hybrid Sempervirens, having much of the Ayrshire habit, and making shoots of an immense length in one season. Its flowers are of a delicate buff when they first open, but they soon change to a pale flesh color. *Alice Grey* is the poetical name given to this rose by some cultivators. *Spectabile*, or *Rose Ayez* of some catalogues, is a fine and distinct climbing rose, with bright rosy lilac flowers, and curiously incised petals; a most vigorous growing and desirable variety. *Triomphe de Bolwiller*, or *Sempervirens Odorata*, is said to be a hybrid between the Rosa Sempervirens and the Tea-scented China Rose, and is decidedly the finest European climbing rose known: it will be found under the head of "Hybrid Climbing Roses."

The varieties of Rosa Sempervirens are of the easiest culture, as they seem to flourish in all soils and situations. In sheltered places and under trees they are nearly ever-green, retaining their leaves till spring. This makes them valuable for covering banks, trees, or walls. I know of no rose idea prettier than that of a wilderness of evergreen roses, the varieties planted promiscuously, and suffered to cover the surface of the ground with their entangled shoots. To effect this, the ground should be dug, manured, and thoroughly cleaned from perennial weeds, such as couch grass, &c., and the plants placed from three to five feet asunder. If the soil is rich, the latter distance will do; they must be hoed, and kept clean from weeds after plant-ing, until the branches meet; they will then soon form a beautiful mass of foliage and flowers, covering the soil too densely for weeds of minor growth to flourish. Those weeds that are more robust should be pulled out occasion-ally, and this is all the culture they will require. For temples, columns, and verandahs, the use of this rose is now becoming well known. One of the most complete temples of roses is that at the seat of Mr. Warner, Hertfordshire;

and the prettiest specimens of festooning these roses from one column to another, by means of small iron chains (strong iron wire will do,) may be seen near Hoddesdon, at the seat of Mr. Bosanquet. They also form elegant and graceful standards ; like the Ayrshire roses their shoots are pendu-lous, and soon hide the stem, in a few years forming a pretty dome of foliage and flowers ; for covering the naked stems of forest or ornamental trees they are also very use-ful, as their roots will not injure the tree which supports them ; and if strong copper wire is brought loosely round the trunk of the tree to support their branches, they will give scarcely any trouble in such situations. To make them grow vigorously, give them a supply of manure on the surface, annually in the autumn, to be carried to their roots by the rains of winter. In the autumn or winter pruning, their branches must be left at their full length, for, if shortened, they will make prodigious long shoots the fol-lowing season, but produce no flowers ; the shoots being very flexible, they can be laid in and twisted in any direc-tion, but the use of the knife must be avoided as much as possible.

THE BOURSAULT ROSE.

Rosa Alpina.

THIS is a most distinct group of roses, with long, reddish, flexible shoots ; they are not such decided climbers as the preceding three divisions, but they are exceedingly well adapted for pillar roses : they owe their origin to the Rosa Alpina, a single red rose, a native of the Alps, and also of the hills in the south of France. M. Boursault, formerly a great Parisian Rose amateur, gave his name to the group, by the first double, or rather semi-double variety, the Red, being named after him. *Blush,* or *Boursault Florida, Calypso, White Boursault, Bengale Florida, Rose de Lisle,* &c., for it is known by all these names, is a beautiful rose, and when trained up a pillar, its large and delicately-coloured flowers have a fine effect; they are very large, pale blush, with a deep pink centre, and protuberant; they are produced in great profusion, and expand among the earliest roses. It is one of the most vigorous of all the rose family, often throwing out shoots of ten to fifteen feet in length, and ascending to the height of thirty to forty feet, spreading latterally to an equal or greater extent. It serves well as a stock for budding other varieties, and the Tea-scented varieties, budded on it, bloom in great perfection. *Crimson,* or *Amadis,* is also a very fine pillar rose ; its clusters of large, deep purple and crimson flowers are inclined to be pendulous, consequently they have a fine effect when on a tall pillar. *Drummond's Thornless* is now an old variety, but it produces such a profusion of bright red flowers, that it ought to be in every collection of climbing roses. *Elegans* is a most beautiful vivid-colored rose ; its purple and crimson flowers are often striped with white : this has a long succession of bloom, as it is one of the earliest and latest of summer roses. *Gracilis* is a hybrid, of the most vigorous growth in good soils, often making shoots ten to twelve feet long in one season ; unlike the other varieties of this division, its shoots are covered with thorns. Nothing can be more graceful than the luxuriant foliage of this plant ; it has also finely-cupped flowers, of the most vivid rose-color, and must be reckoned a beautiful and desirable rose. *Inermis, Thornless,* or *Boursault Pleine,* is a pretty variety, with flowers of a bright red, and a fine and luxuriant grower. The *Red Boursault* is the oldest variety, and only semi-double ; the flower is however of large size, and brilliant color ; it may be deemed as superseded by the numerous climbers of a superior character.

THE BANKSIAN ROSE.

Rosa Banksiæ.
Rosa lævigata, Torrey & Gray.
Rosa sinica, Ait. Kew.

OF this splendid evergreen species, the original or single flowering variety has become widely disseminated throughout our more southern States, under the title of Cherokee, Nondescript, or Georgian Evergreen Rose, and this has at length been fully identified with the Rosa Sinica of China and Nepal, in the former of which countries the double varieties are known by the title of *Wongmoueheong.* This rose is so extensively diffused at the South and West, that many botanical writers have deemed it a native, and Mr. T. Rivers, the eminent writer on "The Rose," falls into the same error. So vigorous is the growth of this admirable climber that it ascends the loftiest trees of the forest to the height of 80 to 100 feet, and hedges of the most impervious description, clad with highly attractive glossy evergreen foliage, exist in some cases of more than a mile in extent. It appears to have been introduced at the same remote and unknown period, as the Melia Azederach, Prunus Caroliniensis ! ?, Sapindus Saponaria, Catalpa Syringæfolia ! ?, Stillingia Sebifera, and Sterculea Platanifolia, all of which have long been extensively naturalized in the southern section of our country, and two of which are still deemed to be natives by superficial botanists.

The *Large Single White Banksian,* or *Cherokee Rose,*

referred to, has flowers of cupped form, (which is common to all the varieties,) fragrant, and beautiful ; the foliage usually trifoliate, but occasionally pinnate, is very glossy, and peculiarly luxuriant and attractive.

The *Double White* was introduced to the European gardens in 1807, and shortly after to those of America. The flowers are very small, of a pleasant violet-like perfume, and are produced in wreaths on very long flexible shoots, the bark of which is green.

The *Double Yellow* was not brought to Europe until 1827. It is an unique and beautiful variety, with small pale buff scentless flowers, produced like the foregoing in wreaths, similar in form, but of a little larger size. The foliage of these two varieties, as well as of those which follow, is pinnate, dark green, glossy, and beautiful ; their flowers expand early in May, and large plants covered with clusters and wreaths of flowers, present a very pretty, but, as Mr. Rivers says, " a most unrose-like appearance."

The *Rose colored Banksian,* or *Rosea,* is a hybrid, with very bright roseate flowers, the whole plant partaking as much of the character of the Boursault Rose as of the Banksian : in fact, it is a most complete mule ; and though it has lost a little too much caste in the shape and size of its flowers—for they are a degree larger, and not quite so double as those of the true Banksian—it will prove a very pretty climber, and is also quite hardy.

The *Odoratissima,* lately introduced from France, was said to have rose-colored flowers, but proves to be a fragrant double white variety.

The *Blanc double superb* is also a fine double white variety. The *Jaunâtre pleine* is of a yellowish primrose hue. *Jaune vif,* or *Jaune serin,* is a superb bright yellow flowering variety. *Alba grandiflora* is, as its name denotes, a large single white flower. *Philadelphica* is an American variety, single, and of a creamy or pale yellow hue.

All the varieties are well adapted to the same purposes as other climbing roses, but the true Banksian varieties are too tender to be applied to these objects, north of Richmond, Va., unless planted against a wall, or in some other sheltered situation, and also well protected by straw or matting during the winter season. Their very early flowering also renders this course quite necessary, as the spring frosts, in exposed locations, would destroy their buds. They bloom more freely in dry soils, than in those retentive of wet ; in pruning, remove only the superfluous shoots, and do not clip any of the small twiggy branches unless absolutely required, as these produce the greatest profusion of flowers ; whereas, if these are shortened, the plant will put forth a great number of strong shoots, but will produce few or no flowers.

Often, towards the end of summer, large old plants will produce immensely thick and strong shoots ; these should be removed early in autumn, unless they are wanted to fill up a vacancy on the wall : the upper part of the plant, and its flowering twigs will not then be exhausted by them in the spring.

To see the varieties of this rose in perfection, it is necessary to witness their development in the States south of the 36° of latitude, where they may be justly pronounced the most luxuriant and graceful appendages of the Circle of Roses. They there spread their flexible branches, clothed with perpetual verdure, over extensive walls, the fronts, and often on all sides of dwellings, and have acquired the appellation of the " *Evergreen Multiflora*."

The variety first described under the title of Cherokee Rose, produces an abundance of seed, and in the south of France and Italy other varieties produce seed in tolerable quantity ; this is also the case in our southern states, where the rarer varieties are becoming considerably dis-

seminated ; and we may consequently expect ere long, to
be favored with crimson and other colored roses of this
charming and unique family.

THE PRAIRIE ROSE.

Rosa rubifolia, vel setigeria.

THE *Prairie Rose,* or *Western Multiflora,* has been heretofore most generally denominated, *Michigan Rose,* in consequence of its first introduction to our gardens from the
state of that name.   This splendid native of our western
prairies spreads its vigorous and luxuriant shoots over
thousands of miles of that mighty region, rearing its brilliant blossoms in immense corymbs, greeting the weary
emigrant as he locates his new home, amid those wilds
marked by the ruins of hundreds of ancient cities and forti-
fications, and whose plains have remained untilled for countless ages; but which are now destined to teem with myriads
of our enterprising citizens, and to yield a redundancy of
wealth to the millions of families which will hereafter comprise their population.

The character of this rose seems pre-eminently to distinguish it as an appropriate *National emblem,* for its ten-
drils have been found to extend to Oregon and California,
and its unrivalled properties as a climbing rose, admit no
limit to its aspiring propensities.

The hardy constitution of the Prairie Rose causes it to
flourish on the frigid banks of the St. Lawrence, and amid
the sunny regions of the tropics; and the genuine varieties
and numerous hybrids, which are being rapidly produced
from seeds, will be disseminated not only to every part of
our own country, but to every land where "The Rose"

has its votaries.   It is admirably suited for covering old buildings or walls, or any enclosures where perfect seclusion is desired, and for rock work, or to cover a glen, no climber can be more appropriate.   It flourishes exceedingly in a procumbent posture on its native plains, and may therefore be used to cover embankments, or any vacant spaces that it is either desirable to conceal, or to array in verdure and beauty in lieu of nakedness and sterility.

It is now about twenty-five years since the original single variety was introduced by my father to his gardens at Flushing.   Since that period several other single flowering, and three or four double flowering varieties have been introduced, found in a natural state in the prairies of the West, and there are doubtless very many other varieties, both double and single, that are yet doomed to blush unseen in their native locations.   A particular characteristic of this family of roses is the variableness of the flowers, which in some cases change so much that they would not be recognized as the same.   Of late years the amateur cultivator has lent a helping hand to produce new varieties. Numerous seedlings have been raised by Mr. Samuel Feast, Mr. J. Pierce, and by myself, and doubtless by others.   All these efforts have been eminently successful, and I have at the present moment 200 additional seedlings that will produce their first flowers in 1847.   The successful results up to the present period are comprised in the numerous admirable varieties which I shall hereafter describe.   The flowers of all this class begin to expand at the time when the general bloom of other varieties in June has nearly subsided ; they continue in flower until the middle of July, and scattering clusters spring forth even to a later date, thus prolonging the period of the rosy-bloom at the most desirable period, as a space is thus filled up between the first and second periods of bloom of the Chinese, Tea and other varieties. Only one variety has yet shown a disposition to produce flowers in autumn, but as we have not as yet been favored with any results from hybridized varieties, where the perpetual flowering classes are known to have been perfectly blended with the Prairie Rose, we have no reason for disappointment, but may look forward to the period of such developments with an absolute certainty of successful results.

I have already referred to the *Common Prairie*, or *Michigan Rose*, which has profuse clusters of bright, deep pink flowers, and produces an abundance of seeds. The *Kentucky Thornless* and the *Spotted* are both single, the latter with prominent petals. *Altonia* was found wild in Illinois, it is double but not full at the centre, brilliant pink and quite pretty: I received it direct from that State. *Anne Maria* is very double, pale blush, with a pink centre, and beautiful.

Baltimore Belle is a splendid variety, blooming in very large clusters, pale incarnate changing to white, full double, fragrant, and as large in diameter as the Queen of the Prairies. *Caradori Allan*, which we perceive has been confused by one writer with the Queen of the Prairies, has no similarity to that variety ; it is bright pink, tolerably double, and pretty. *Elegans*, or *Chilicothe Multiflora*, called also at that place *Kennickenick*, is bright pink, tolerably double, and very showy. *Eva Corinne* is a large flower, exceedingly double, light blush and beautiful. *Florinda* is very large, full double, of a very pale pink hue, and showy. *Gracilis* (Prince's) is one of our seedlings, of a roseate changeable hue, and very double. *Jane* is very double, of a deep rosy lilac color, and beautiful appearance.

Linnæan Hill Beauty was raised by Mr. Pierce, and is a fine pale blush flower changing to white, and very double.

Milledgeville is a peculiar variety, with beautiful glossy foliage ; the flowers brilliant carmine, and very splendid ; it was found in a natural state.

Mountjoy is also a natural variety, found by a lady of the name it bears, on an island in the Licking river, (Ohio) ; it is exceedingly beautiful when just fully expanded ; having a pale incarnate, or blush border, with a deep pink incurved centre, and being very double.

Mrs. Henry Clay is an admirable creamy white flower, extra beautiful, and produced in immense clusters. It is worthy in itself, as well as for its connection with this noble family of native roses, of being dedicated to the eminently worthy lady of that man, who stands apart, marked out in the minds of all candid Americans, and by the world at large, as the exalted combination of natural genius, of concentrated political knowledge, of energy of character, and of generous devotion to his country's prosperity ; thus presenting the concentrated amplitude of development, the veriest impersonification of Americanism.

Mrs. Hovey is a large and beautiful pure white variety, originated by Mr. J. Pierce, and kindly sent to Mr. Hovey and myself. There being several varieties which are nearly white, we may reasonably expect some pure white seedlings therefrom.

Pallida is a very fine full double flower, of incarnate hue changing to white ; so nearly resembling the *Superba* in color, and in the habit of the plant, that it cannot be distinguished, and although said to be of distinct parentage, may be deemed identical. It blooms perhaps a few days later than the Superba.

Pride of Washington is of a roseate hue changing to lilac, full double, and beautiful.

Priscilla is a new seedling, just introduced to notice, of a pale roseate hue, full double and very pretty.

5

Purpurea, or *Purple*, which is usually called, very inappropriately, *Perpetual Pink*, has no claim to be called Perpetual, as it but rarely produces any flowers after the usual period of flowering, and I have concluded to correct its erroneous title at once; the flowers are remarkably fine, full double, of a purplish violet hue, and as large as the Queen of the Prairies.

Queen of the Prairies, or *Beauty of the Prairies*, is a rose that any nation might be proud of; it was originated by Mr. Samuel Feast, and although among the first, is one of the very best we yet can boast of; the flowers are of the largest size of its class, being three inches in diameter, of exquisite cupped form, very double, deep pink, often striped with white through the centre of the petals ; these are produced in clusters, and retain their cupped form for several days unaffected by the excessive heat of that period; the growth of the plant is rapid, throwing up very strong shoots which often attain a length of ten to fifteen feet or more, in a season ; the leaves are large, dark green, and luxuriant, and the whole plant presents an imposing appearance.

Ranunculiflora is a flower of small or medium size, very pretty, of a light blush hue, with a pink centre, and greatly admired.

Sappho is a fine new seedling variety, full double, very pretty, and among the latest in the period of flowering ; the plants being small, have not yet afforded an opportunity for a more perfect description.

Seraphine is a very double flower, expanding among the later varieties, of a delicate pink hue, with a deeper pink centre.   It was named after one of my daughters.

Serena is a new and very pretty full double variety, of which, by inadvertence, no perfect description was made when in bloom.

Superba is of perfectly beautiful form, very double, of a pale blush or incarnate hue, varying to white ; it is an admirable rose, and one of the best of the incarnate varieties.

Triumphant is a magnificent variety, full double, of a deep roseate color, changing to pale violet, and greatly admired.

Worthington is a semi-double variety, found wild in Ohio, near the town whose name it bears. The friend who recently transmitted it to me omitted to describe it fully, and I am thereby prevented from doing so.

Having now described all the varieties that have, up to the present period, been brought to notice, and which are now under cultivation in my rose garden, I shall conclude by remarking that each succeeding year will, without doubt, increase the brilliant assemblage of varieties destined to become members of this unique family.

PERPETUAL FLOWERING ROSES.

The prolongation of the blooming season of the "Queen of Flowers," by the magnificent varieties belonging to several species, mostly of modern introduction, and some of which were scarcely known to exist fifteen years ago, has imparted to the amateur of the present day very great advantages over the cultivators of the last century, and has in fact produced a complete revolution in the selection of such primary varieties as should constitute an admirable rose garden. The Summer Roses, however splendid, soon fade from our view, but a sequence of flowers of the various classes of Perpetuals, will always be found to gladden us by their beauty and regale us with their perfume, until the chilling blasts of approaching winter shall arrest the expansion of their bloom.

DAMASK PERPETUAL ROSES.

This class has as much variety in its origin as in its appearance: it would indeed be a difficult task to trace the parentage of some of its justly esteemed varieties. The old Red and White Damask Monthly roses have, no doubt, contributed the greatest share of sweet assistance; for, in many of them, the powerful fragrance of these two very old Damask roses is apparent, and no perfume can be more grateful.

In preference to giving a slight history of the family at the commencement, I shall, as I describe the varieties, at the risk of being tedious, give the supposed origin of most of them: premising, that all those termed *true Perpetuals* have, generally, a terminal cluster of buds at the end of each shoot, whether produced in spring, summer, or autumn.

Amanda Patenotte, (by some ranked as a Hybrid Perpetual, and perhaps justly so,) is one of the very finest of this class; it is a most admirable flower, of a pale rose color, very double, protuberant, and of fine globular form; it is new, and in great request even in France at 15 to 20 francs each plant. I last year paid 22 francs, and was deemed favored.

Antinous is a new rose, evidently between the French Rose and the Crimson Perpetual, equalling that fine rose in form and fragrance, and surpassing it in beauty of coloring; but it partakes rather much of the French Rose, as it is not a true Perpetual. However, it often puts forth its fine crimson-purple flowers in September, and it will therefore be much esteemed, as we have hitherto been accustomed to roses of more sober hues in that pleasant month. *Beck*, one of Laffay's recent acquisitions, is a large and most superb flower, of a roseate hue, and very double. *Bifera venusta* is a new French variety, yet very rare; the flower is of a delicate rosy hue, and very double. *Billiard*, so named from a French rose amateur, is a pretty bright rose, very fragrant and double, and a true Perpetual. *Belle Italienne* approaches very near to the Crimson Perpetual, except that its flowers are larger, and not quite so double. This is also a true Perpetual. *Bernard* or *Perpetual Pompon*, is a most beautiful new rose, with rather small flowers, but they are very double and finely shaped, of a delicate carmine color : this is a true Perpetual, and a most desirable rose.

Claire du Chatelet is a very large flower, of a bright rose color, and fine form, distinct in habit, and of vigorous growth. The *Crimson Perpetual, Rose du Roi,* or *Lee's Crimson Perpetual,* is bright red, of perfect form, with the fragrance of the old Damask rose, and is a new constant and profuse bloomer. It deserves a few extra words of comment. This fine rose was raised from seed, in 1812, in the gardens of Saint Cloud, then under the direction of Le Comte Lelieur, and named by him Rose du Roi ; owing, I suppose, to Louis the Eighteenth being restored soon after that time, and thus presenting an opportunity for the Comte to show his loyalty : it is not recorded whether he changed its name during the hundred days to Rose de l'Empereur ! It is asserted that it was raised from the Rosa Portlandica, a semi-double bright-colored rose, much like the rose known in this country as the Red, or Scarlet Four-Seasons, or Rosa Pæstana ; which Eustace tells us, in his "Classical Tour," grows among the ruins of Pæstum, enlivening them with its brilliant autumnal flowers. This is treated as a traveller's tale by some English botanists, and the Rosa Pæstana is said to have been originated from seed in England : but was not that seed obtained from Italy ?

Every flower garden ought to have a large bed of Crimson Perpetual Roses, to furnish bouquets during August, September, and October ; their fragrance is so delightful, their color so rich, and their form so perfect.

Crispata, or the *Curled Perpetual*, is one of those whimsies of nature, more curious than pretty. Each leaf is curled, and forms a ring, giving an odd appearance to the plant. *De Rennes* is a true Perpetual, of first-rate excellence, with large and very double flowers. *Délice d'Hiver* is a splendid rose, with large and finely-shaped flowers, of that vivid rose-color so much admired ; also a true Perpetual. *Désespoir des Amateurs*, or *Perpétuatissima*, had its origin in Italy, whence it was ushered into France, with its high-sounding names, equally ridiculous; for, in reality, the rose, though pretty and fragrant, is much below many in this division. It is a hybrid of uncertain origin, and totally unlike other varieties in habit, being dwarf and rather delicate.

D'Angers, one of the older varieties, is a constant bloomer ; the flowers are in clusters, and of large size, exceedingly fragrant, of a delicate roseate hue, but not so finely formed as some of the other varieties. *De Trianon* is bright pink, blooming in large clusters; the plant is of dwarf habit. *Desdemona* is of a carmine red hue, delightfully fragrant, but sometimes fails to bloom well in autumn. *Duc D'Enghien* is a fine, full double, incarnate variety, distinct in color, as well as in growth and frequency of flowering. *Ebène* is the darkest of all the Perpetuals, being of a deep crimson purple hue, and superb. *Estelle* is a small neat Scotch Perpetual, of a roseate hue. *Feburier* is a large and beautiful light red rose, of perfect form, and very double ; it is of vigorous growth, but a rather inconstant Perpetual.

Flon, *Gloire des Perpetuelles*, or *La Mienne*, is a true

Perpetual, and abundant bloomer, with a peculiar and pretty habit; its foliage has a soft appearance, and when the plant is covered with its brilliant red flowers, no Perpetual Rose is more beautiful. *Ferox* is quite unique, and very magnificent, having larger flowers than any other in this division; but it is not a certain autumnal bloomer. The *Grand Perpetual*, or *Fabert*, is a true Perpetual rose of great excellence, requiring a rich soil and good culture to bloom in perfection. It has one great fault—the flowers produced in July are so large that they almost invariably burst; its autumnal flowers are much more symmetrical. *Grande et Belle*, or *Monstrueuse*, is a rose of immense size and beauty, and generally a good and true Perpetual. *Henriette Boulogne* is a good rose, but rather an inconstant autumnal bloomer. This, with some others, the French distinguish as varieties "*remontante rarement*," in contra-distinction to the true Perpetuals, which they style " *remontante franche-ment*." *Indigo* is a superb rose, of a dark rich violet hue, a new and very desirable French variety. *Isaure Lablée* is a full double flower of a delicate roseate hue and very fragrant. *Jeanne Hachette*, erroneously placed under this head by an American writer, is a Gallica or French variety. *Jenny Audio* is not remarkable for any peculiar beauty, but is fragrant, and a true Perpetual. *Josephine Antoinette* is now an old variety, but a true Perpetual of great excellence. *Lady Seymour* is of deep rose color, mottled with blush, of perfect form, and pleasantly fragrant. *La Gracieuse*, which has been by one writer placed under this head, belongs to the Bourbon family. *Laurence de Montmorency* is of expanded form, violet roseate hue and very superb. *Louis Philippe*, being introduced before Antinous, has had a large share of admiration : it is also a true Perpetual. *Lodoiska Marin* is a superb rose, very large and double, of a bright rosy hue, and blooming in clusters; but is rather an inconstant Perpetual. *Marie Denise* is a fine robust variety : its flowers resemble those of Lodoiska, but are more double, and the plant approaches nearer to a true Perpetual than that fine rose. *Minerva* is a fine new variety, of medium size, full double, and deep rosy hue. *Mogador*, or *Crimson Superb*, is a new and estimable variety, with splendid bright crimson flowers, shaded with purple, and of perfect form. *Noel* is a large pale red flower, very double ; the plant grows vigorously and blooms freely. *Pompon Four Seasons* is a very old rose, as its name may be found in many old catalogues ; still it is rare ; it blooms well in autumn, and forms a pretty little bush.

Pulchérie is a bright purple rose, that has been superseded. *Palmyre*, or *Blush Perpetual*, is of about the same standing as the Crimson : it is a true Perpetual and good. *Palotte Picotée*, is so like the Queen of Perpetuals, that it cannot be distinguished from that rose. *Pennsylvania Dwarf* is a small, very pretty blush rose, found full double in a wild state: the plant is very dwarf, attaining a height of only about eighteen inches. The *Perpetual White* and *Red Moss* varieties are described under the head of " The Moss Rose." *Portlandica carnea* is an exceedingly pretty, bright rose, somethimg like Rosa Pæstana in habit, with flowers of a paler color, and a true Perpetual. *Portlandica alba*, or *Portland Blanc*, is a new white rose of great beauty ; it rarely opens in the moist climate of England, but expands very well in ours ; a true Perpetual Rose like it would be invaluable. In rich soils it will frequently give a second series of flowers ; but it cannot be depended upon as a constant autumnal bloomer. *Preval* is a fine large flower, of a pale roseate hue, perfect compact form, and fragrant; a free bloomer. *Prud'homme* is a new and beautiful rose, bright rose-colored, fragrant, and a true Perpetual. *Red Damask Monthly, Red Four Seasons' Rose,* or *Quatre saisons rouge,* is a very ancient appendage of our gardens, and when well cultured in a rich soil, will yield a profusion of clusters of its delicate rose-colored flowers in succession at intervals throughout the season ; these possess so delightful a fragrance that they are favorites with every one, although many other varieties produce a far greater number of flowers. The *White Damask Monthly,* or *Quatre Saisons blanc,* is of a pearly white color at expansion, becoming perfectly white shortly after ; the flowers, like the preceding, are in clusters, and highly fragrant, and the genuine variety blooms quite as frequently. There are spurious varieties of both the red and the white flowering, which seldom bloom a second time. *Requien* is a large full double flower, of incarnate hue, expanded form, and beautiful : the plant is vigorous, with large foliage, and of very distinct character. The *Royal Perpetual,* or *Desquermes,* is a seedling from the Four Seasons rose ; its flowers are very double and perfect, of a fine vivid rose-color ; and the plant is a true Perpetual. *Scotch Perpetual* is a very pale blush rose, of twice the size of the ordinary Scotch varieties, fragrant and pretty ; the foliage and shoots are delicate, assimilating to its Scotch parent. The *Stanwell* Perpetual is in habit like the Scotch Perpetual, but it blooms more constantly and more profusely ; in short, it is a much better rose of the same family, and one of the prettiest and sweetest of autumnal roses. The *Sixth of June,* or *Six Juen,* so named by the French in commemoration of one of their "glorious days," is a miniature variety of the Flon, and a pretty vivid colored rose. The *Striped Crimson Perpetual,* or *Rose du Roi panaché,* which is qualified by the term "inconstant," it being a very fickle flower, is usually pale flesh color, striped with crimson, but some

5*

flowers lose the stripe entirely. *Triomphe de Montmorency*, is an inconstant Perpetual, with bright red flowers, highly fragrant, full double and of fine cupped form.

As the culture of this class of roses is at present but imperfectly understood, I shall give the result of my experience as to their cultivation, with suggestions to be acted upon according to circumstances. One peculiar feature they nearly all possess—a reluctance to root when layered ; consequently, Perpetual Roses, on their own roots, will always be scarce : when procurable, they will be found to succeed much better on dry poor soils than the budded plants, which require a rich soil. Perpetual Roses, as a general rule however, require a superabundant quantity of food: it is therefore perfectly ridiculous to plant them on arid lawns, and to suffer the grass to grow close up to their stems, without giving them a particle of manure for years. Under these circumstances, the best varieties, even the *Rose du Roi*, will scarcely ever give a second series of flowers. To remedy the inimical nature of arid soils to this class of roses, an annual application of manure on the surface of the earth is quite necessary. The ground must not be dug, but lightly pricked over with a fork in November ; after which, some manure must be laid on, about two or three inches in depth, which ought not to be disturbed, except to clean with the hoe and rake, until the following autumn. This, in some situations, in the spring months, will be unsightly : in such cases, cover it with some neat green moss, as directed in the culture of Hybrid China Roses. I have said that this treatment is applicable to dry poor soils ; but even in good rose soils it is almost indispensable ; as it imparts such increased vigor, and such a prolongation of the flowering season, as to amply repay the labor bestowed. If the soil is prepared as directed, the plants will twice in the year require pruning : in November, when the beds are dressed, and again a short time before the first flowering in June. At the November pruning, cut off from every shoot of the preceding summer's growth about two-thirds ; if the shoots are crowded, remove some of them entirely. If this autumnal pruning is attended to, there will be at the end of May, or early in June, the following summer, a vast number of luxuriant shoots, each crowned with a cluster of buds. Now, as June roses are always abundant a little sacrifice must be made to insure a fine autumnal bloom ; therefore, leave only half the number of shoots to bring forth their summer flowers, and shorten the remainder to about half their length. Each shortened branch will soon put forth buds ; and in August and September the plants will again be covered with flowers. In cultivating Perpetual Roses, the faded flowers ought immediately to be removed ; for in autumn the petals do not fall off readily, but lose their colour and remain on the plant, to the injury of the forthcoming buds. Though I have recommended Perpetual Roses to be grown on their own roots in dry soils, yet, on account of the autumnal rains dashing the dirt upon their flowers when close to the ground, grafted roses ought to be preferred, wherever it is possible to make them succeed, for on stems one and a half to two feet in height, the flowers will not be soiled ; they are also brought nearer to the eye, and the plant forms a neat and pretty object.

The Crimson, and, indeed, nearly all the Perpetuals, force admirably : for this purpose it is better to graft or bud them on the Dog-Rose, as it is so easily excited. It requires, also, but small pot-room ; as, previous to potting, its roots may be pruned to within two inches of the stem, and apparently with advantage ; for, if placed in gentle heat, an abundance of fibres are immediately put forth, and the whole plant will soon have an appearance of great vigor. Those who wish for the luxury of forced roses, at a trifling cost, may have them by pursuing the following simple method :—Take a common garden frame, large or small, according to the number of roses wanted ; raise it on some posts, so that the bottom edge will be about three feet from the ground at the back of the frame, and two feet in front, sloping to the south. If it is two feet deep, this will give a depth of five feet under the lights, at the back of the frame, which will admit roses on little stems as well as dwarfs. Grafted plants of any of the Perpetual Roses should be potted in October, in a rich compost of equal portions of rotten dung and loam, in pots about eight inches deep, and seven inches over, and plunged in the soil at bottom. The air in the frame may be heated by linings of hot dung ; but care must be taken that the dung is turned over two or three times before it is used, otherwise the rank and noxious steam will kill the young and tender shoots ; the hazard of this may be avoided by building a wall of turf, three inches thick, from the ground to the bottom edge of the frame. This will admit the heat through it, and exclude the steam. The Perpetual Roses, thus made to bloom early, are really beautiful. They may also be forced in any description of forcing-house with success, by plunging the pots in old tan, or any substance that will keep their roots cool. It will at once give an idea how desirable these roses are, when it is stated that, by retarding and forcing, they may be made to bloom for eight months in the year.

Perpetual Roses do not bear seed very freely, but Louis Philippe may be planted with the common Bourbon, as may the Rosa Pæstana, which both bear seed abundantly, and these would probably give some fine high-colored varieties. Grande et Belle, trained to a south wall, with Gloire de Rosamène, and Lodoiska with the Common Bourbon Rose, would possibly be the parents of some large flowering and splendid varieties. In endeavoring to obtain

Mossy Crimson Perpetuals, of which but one variety has yet been produced, it would be well to plant Louis Philippe with the Single Crimson Moss. To the culture of roses, and many other horticultural operations, the motto, although hacknied, may be appropriately applied, " Nil desperandum."

HYBRID PERPETUAL ROSES.

This class has now become so rich in beautiful roses, that a separate notice must be devoted to them. At page 55, is given the origin of Hybrid China Roses, which it is well known bloom but once in a season. Some of these hybrids or mules, unlike many plants of the same description, bear seed freely. These fertile varieties have been crossed with different varieties of Chinese and Bourbons. From seed thus produced we have gained a new race of autumnal roses, bearing abundance of flowers during the whole of the summer and autumn, and now called Hybrid Perpetuals. Certainly a more beautiful and interesting class of roses does not exist; their flowers are large, very double, most fragrant, and produced till the end of autumn. Their habit is robust and vigorous in a remarkable degree, and, above all, they are perfectly hardy, and will grow well in any climate however far north ; but caution will be required in selecting varieties for cold and damp localities, as those only that open freely should be planted. Some few are fine roses in a dry warm climate, and also when forced ; but in a moist climate, like that of England, will seldom or never open their flowers. I will mention such as may be chosen without the least fear of disappointment. And first, I must name the queen of this family, *Madame Laffay ;* this, like the Crimson Perpetual, in its

class, is at present unrivalled ; words cannot give the effect
of this rose, which with its fine large foliage and rosy crimson flowers, is perfectly beautiful, highly fragrant, and
ought to be in every garden. We have a fine contrast in
color in the *Dutchess of Sutherland,* which is a rose of
equally luxuriant habits and fine foliage, with flowers of
the most perfect shape, and of a delicate roseate hue. One
defect attaches to this rose, which ought not to be concealed—it will not give autumnal flowers constantly in a
moist climate, or during a wet period. *Aricie* is a large
globular rose, of a beautiful roseate hue, and much admired. *Arielle* is a splendid new variety, of small size,
full double, and of a rosy lilac hue. *Augustine Mouchelet*
is of very vigorous growth ; the flower large, very full,
and dark crimson. *Aubernon* is a beautiful brilliant crimson rose, opening freely, and blooming abundantly during
the summer and autumn. Of the same prolific habit is
Rivers, so named by Laffay, who frequently " dedicates"
roses to his friends. This is a rose of first rate quality ;
flowers red, something like Brennus, very large, and produced in clusters of great beauty, flowering profusely all
the autumn. *Baronne Prevost* is a rose colored flower,
full double, and of very large size. *Clementine Seringe* is
an exceedingly large flower, rosy blush, globular form,
with the peculiar odor of the Provence rose ; it is an invaluable rose for forcing. *Comte de Paris* is a globular flower,
of light crimson hue tinged with lilac, and blooms profusely. *Comtesse Tanneguy Duchatel* is a most splendid rose,
of large size, globular form, and of a brilliant rosy carmine hue ; it is yet very rare, and eagerly sought for at a
high price. *Coquette de Bellevue,* (of Laffay,) is a new
variety of vigorous growth, with small splendid flowers of
a brilliant rose color, spotted with white. *De Neuilly* is a
variety of great excellence, having all the peculiar beauty

of the Bourbon Rose, one of its parents, with the fragrance
of the Damask. It is a most abundant autumnal bloomer,
and ought to be extensively cultivated. *Docteur Marx* is
violet red shaded, large and very double. *Docteur Marjolin*
is a splendid flower of a brilliant cherry color. *Duchesse
de Montmorency* is an erect, free, and vigorous growing
plant, with very large, bright and delicate rosy flowers, full
double and distinct. *Mrs. Elliott* is a beautiful free-flowering
and free-opening rose, with flowers of light crimson, tinged
with lilac. Like some others in this class, barren shoots
are often produced in the autumn. *William Jesse* is a
large and superb rose, crimson, with lilac tinge, and of the
form of La Reine. This is certainly one of the most beautiful *very large* roses that exists; its flowers always open
freely : like the preceding, every shoot does not give flowers, but with good culture it will bloom well in the autumn.
Prudence Rœser is hybridized with the Noisette, blooming
in large clusters of exceeding beauty, and highly fragrant.
For a standard, or a pillar rose, this variety is peculiarly
adapted ; its flowers, not full-sized, are of a pale rose, with
a fawn colored centre, and elegantly shaped ; every shoot,
whether in summer or autumn, seems to give its terminal
cluster of flowers. Among the new varieties one of the
most beautiful is *Comte d'Eu ;* it is, strictly speaking, a
double dwarf Gloire de Rosamène, from which it was raised,
and is a brilliant-colored and fine variety. *Reine de Lyon*
is also a new and fine rose, with erect habit, and very double dark crimson flowers, of the same fragrance as the Provence Rose. *Duc d'Aumale* is a new and very erect-
growing variety, with brilliant crimson flowers of much
beauty. *Clémentine Duval* is a very pretty pale rose-colored variety, of quite neat compact growth, and giving
abundance of flowers. *General Merlin*, of the same origin,
also raised by Monsieur Duval, is quite a new variety,

with rose-colored flowers, rather bright, and elegantly shaped. *Reine Victoria*, or *Queen Victoria*, is of a very deep reddish rose, tinged with purple : it is of robust habit. *Duc d'Alencon* is a new and profuse flowering variety, of a lilac roseate hue, and very beautiful. *Duc d'Isly* is also a new and fine variety, of a brilliant red color, shaded with purple. *Earl Talbot* is a very large globular flower of a deep purplish rose color, and quite fragrant. *Edward Jesse* is of a fine lilac roseate hue, and highly fragrant. *Eliza Balcombe* is a small flower, with a slight incarnate tinge at opening, but changing to white; the foliage is peculiar. *Emma Dampierre* is of medium size, rose color, and very double. *Ernestine de Barante* is a small very double flower, of expanded form, bright rose color, very superb, and the plant blooms profusely ; it is quite new. *Fidouline* is of a delicate rosy lilac hue, large and full double. *Fulgorie* is a robust hybrid Perpetual, with flowers of a deep purplish crimson, very double and perfect, blooming freely all the autumn, and growing most luxuriantly. This is certainly one of the best roses of its class and color. *Iolande*, or *Yolande d'Aragon*, is of a rosy blush color, full double and beautiful. *Prince Albert* is a most beautiful rose, remarkably fragrant, being one of the sweetest of roses, of a deep velvety crimson hue, full double and finely formed ; as a forcing rose it is quite unrivalled. *Julie Dupont* is a fine very double crimson flower. *Lady Alice Peel*, is of perfect form, very double, and of a carmine roseate hue. *Lady Fordwich* is of vigorous growth, with highly fragrant flowers of a crimson roseate hue, which are produced in clusters. *La Reine* (of Laffay) is the largest and most magnificent of all the Perpetuals, often attaining the size of a double Pæony ; it is of a brilliant satin rose color, very slightly tinged with lilac, of most regular and perfect cupped form, and delightfully fragrant ; the growth of the plant is very strong and vigorous, and each new spring shoot is crowned with flowers. It is of so imposing an appearance, that amid hundreds of other varieties, it is sure to attract immediate attention, and it may with justice be deemed the most admirable acquisition that has yet been made to this brilliant class of roses. In the form of the flower, and the foliage and habit of the plant, it has a great affinity to William Jesse, and I risk the suggestion that such is its parentage. *Lindley* is a new variety, a large flower, full double, bright red and beautiful. *Louis Bonaparte* is a large globular flower, of a rosy crimson color, very double and perfect ; the plant grows vigorous, and attains a large size. *Madame Jobes Desgaches,* is of medium size, full double, very brilliant rose color, quite dazzling and magnificent ; this and the seven following are new improved varieties. *Madame Verdier* is a beautiful imbricate flower, full double, incarnate, of the same exquisite form, as Madame Laffay. *Marquis d'Ailsa* is a large flower, full double, of a shaded carmine hue. *Mérope* is of expanded form, full double, and satin lilac roseate hue. *Mrs. Cripps* is a large, full double expanded flower, of a delicate rosy hue with a carmine centre ; the plant is very vigorous, and blooms profusely. *Raynal* is a fine new variety, received from Mr. Laffay, but has not yet flowered with me. *Rose Cornet* is of a delicate roseate color, with imbricate petals. *Renufe d'Osmond* is a large, expanded, full double flower, of a velvety carmine hue, shaded with purple. *Marshal Soult* is a robust and free-growing rose, but rather dull in color when compared with Fulgorie. *Princesse Helène* is also a robust and free-growing variety, of a deep rose-color : in moist weather, and sometimes in autumn, its flowers do not open freely. *Reine de la Guillotière* is a superb brilliant crimson flower, with glossy foliage, distinct, and a constant autumnal bloomer. *Sisley* is hybridized with the Bourbon

Rose, and retains much of the fragrance of the Damask:
it is a large and beautiful autumnal rose, bright red, and of
perfect form; the plant of dwarf habit. *Thibault* is a
beautiful flower, of a brilliant carmine rose color. *Tri-*
omphante is a purplish crimson rose.

To the preceding might be added numerous other very
desirable varieties, many of which are of very recent origin, and have been introduced to our country from the Rose
gardens of France, Belgium and England, but all these the
amateur will find enumerated in recent Rose Catalogues.
Coquette de Montmorency, a bright red rose, is one of the
most delightful varieties yet introduced: its growth is so
compact, and its flowers are produced in such abundance,
always opening freely, and always elegantly shaped, that
it cannot be too much recommended. *Madame Laffay* is
perhaps a rose of equal merit, and if it had made its appearance before the Coquette, Monsieur Laffay would have
reaped more advantage from it; its habit is robust, and its
flowers a little larger than those of the latter: this was
raised from General Allard, a hybrid Bourbon rose, blooming generally but once in the season. Monsieur Laffay,
by persevering through two or three generations of seedlings, has at last obtained his object in getting a Perpetual
Rose of the same brilliant color. This information will,
I trust, be an incentive to amateurs in this country. Roses
of distant affinities cannot be brought together *at once:*
thus a Yellow Ayrshire Rose must not be expected from
the first trial, but probably a climbing rose, tinged with yellow or buff, may be the fruit of the first essay. This rose
must again be operated upon, and a second generation will,
perhaps, be nearer the end wished for: again the amateur
must bring perseverance and skill into action; and then if,
in the third generation, a bright yellow climbing rose is obtained, its possession will amply repay the labor bestowed.

But these light gardening operations are not labor, they are a delightful amusement to a refined mind, and lead it to reflect on the wonderful infinities of nature.

All the robust-growing varieties of this family form admirable standards, and are particularly well adapted for planting in rows by the sides of walks, giving them plenty of manure, and the necessary culture required by these roses—removing a portion of their bloom buds in June; thus, if there are twelve clusters of bloom making their appearance, cut off five to within about six buds of the base of each shoot; these will soon push forth, and give fine flowers in August. Constant care should be taken to remove in the same manner all the clusters of blooms as soon as they fade. Louis Bonaparte and a few others are very apt to make barren shoots without terminal flowers. As soon as this can be ascertained, cut all such shoots to within six or eight buds of their base; they will then, in most cases, give fertile branches: in short these roses require much summer pruning and attention to make them flower in great perfection in autumn. Madame Laffay, La Reine, Prudence Rœser, Fulgorie, Mrs. Elliott, and William Jesse, will, in rich soils, form very fine pillar roses, and be made to flower, with summer pruning, all the autumn.

THE BOURBON ROSE.

Rosa Bourboniana.

THIS family of Roses which has now become the most popular and desirable appendage of every rose garden, and which combines estimable properties long sought for, but until recently unknown, deserves at our hands some passing notice of its history. It is destined in connection with the Hybrid Perpetuals and other Perpetual classes, to take precedence over all the ancient families of Roses. The luxuriance of its growth, its large and beautiful foliage, and its magnificent flowers, with thick enduring petals of almost every hue, present a combination altogether unrivalled. Being perfectly hardy in this latitude, and requiring but slight protection even in more northern localities, it is destined to be widely disseminated at the north, while this and the Hybrid Perpetual Roses, attain a development so magnificent, that they astonish the most sanguine amateurs. It is now about fifteen years, since a beautiful semidouble rose, with brilliant rose colored flowers, prominent buds, and nearly evergreen foliage, made its appearance in England, under the name of the " L'Ile de Bourbon Rose," said to have been imported from the Mauritius to France, in 1822, by M. Noisette. It attracted attention by its peculiar habit, but more particularly by its abundant autumnal flowering; still such was the lukewarmness of English rose amateurs, that no attempts were made to improve this pretty imperfect rose, by raising seedlings from it, although it bore seed in large quantities. This pleasing task was left to their rose-loving neighbors the French, who have been exceedingly industrious, and, as a matter of course, have originated some very beautiful and striking varieties, and also, as usual in such cases, have given us rather too many distinct and fine-sounding names attached to flowers without distinctive characters. In a little time we shall be able to rectify this very common floricultural error. Many fables have been told by the French respecting the origin of this rose. The most generally received version of one of these is, that a French naval officer was requested by the widow of a Monsieur Edouard, residing in the island, to find, on his voyage to India, some rare rose, and that, on his return to L'Ile de

Bourbon, he brought with him this rose, which she planted on her husband's grave : it was then called Rose Edouard, and sent to France as " Rose de L'Ile de Bourbon." This is pretty enough, but entirely devoid of truth. Monsieur Bréon, a French botanist, and now a seedsman in Paris, gives the following account, for the truth of which he vouches :—" At the Isle of Bourbon, the inhabitants generally enclose their land with hedges made of two rows of roses, one row of the common China Rose, the other of the Red Four-Seasons. Monsieur Perichon, a proprietor at Saint Benoist, in the Isle, in planting one of these hedges, found among his young plants one very different from the others in its shoots and foliage. This induced him to plant it in his garden. It flowered the following year ; and, as he anticipated, proved to be of quite a new race, and differing much from the above two roses, *which, at the time, were the only sorts known in the island.*" Monsieur Bréon arrived at Bourbon in 1817, as botanical traveller for the government of France, and curator of the Botanical and Naturalization Garden there. He propagated this rose very largely ; and sent plants and seeds of it, in 1822, to Monsieur Jacques, gardiner at the Château de Neuilly, near Paris, who distributed them among the rose cultivators of France. Hence the name often given to the Common Bourbon Rose of " Bourbon Jacques." M. Bréon named it " Rose de L'Ile de Bourbon ;" and is convinced that it is a hybrid from one of the above roses, and a native of the island. Owing to the original being a hybrid, the roses of this family vary much in their characters ; those that retain the leading features I have termed true Bourbons. I shall now notice and describe some of the most striking and distinct varieties of this very charming group ; and begin with *Acidalie,* which is a large white, globular flower, slightly tinged at first with blush, very double and superb, and forces well. *Adela Plantier* is a new and brilliant red flower, changing to rose color. *Amourette* is a small pale incarnate rose with acute petals, very perfect and distinct. *Armosa*, or *Hermosa*, very double and perfect in the shape of its flowers, which are of a delicate rose color : the plant is of medium growth. *Asteroid* is of a delicate rose color, and very double. *Augustine Lelieur* is a well formed rosy crimson flower ; the plant vigorous, but it has been superseded by finer varieties. *Bizarine* is of a very brilliant deep rose color with a protuberant centre, very double and superb. *Bouquet de Flore* is of a deep carmine hue, very large, full double, with large stiff petals and superb. *Cardinal Fesch* is of a deep violet crimson hue, large, very double, with curiously formed petals. *Cendres de Napoleon* is a superb purplish roseate flower, pretty, shaded, and of globular form. *Ceres* is a dwarf variety, whose superb flowers are of a rich pink hue and perfect form, with imbricate petals. *Celimene* is of vigorous growth and very spiny, with flowers of a delicate rose color, but has been superseded. *Comte de Rambuteau* is of a deep reddish crimson shaded with violet, and very beautiful. *Comte de Nauteuil* is a new variety, red shaded with violet. *Coquette de Mélun* is a beautiful new variety of medium size and full double. *Crimson Globe*, or *Dr. Roques*, is a superb rose of perfect globular form, and purplish vermilion hue ; the plant of distinct habit. *Diaphane* is a small high-colored rose, almost scarlet. This is not a true Bourbon, but a very pretty rose of dwarf growth, adapted for the front of a border. *Duc de Grammont* is also a hybridized Bourbon, very dwarf in its habit, with flowers of fine shape and very double, inclining to purple. *Desgaches* is a superb flower of a bright rose color, and most perfect shape. *D'Yebles* is of a bright violet crimson hue, full double, somewhat resembling *Madame Desprez ;* the leaves are large and the growth vigorous. *Deuil Duc d'Orleans* is an expanded flower of blackish crimson hue, the darkest of this class, and very fine. *Duc de Chartres* is a splendid new variety, of a rosy incarnate hue, full double and protuberant. *Dumont de Courset* is a new and particularly splendid rose, of a rich very dark velvety crimson hue. *Dupetit Thouars* is a new vivid violet carmine variety, greatly admired, and yet very rare. *Earl Grey* is a genuine Bourbon Rose, with large and double flowers, of a fine rose color, and the plant of a compact though vigorous growth ; its flowers have a fault ; they do not open well in wet weather. *Emile Courtier* is a superb flower of a deep lilac hue, and of perfect form. *Faustine* is now an old variety ; but a very pretty little rose, very dwarf in its habit, with flowers of that silvery pale blush, so peculiar to some varieties in this group. *Fedora* is a very double crimson rose of vigorous habit. *General Dubourg* is a large pale rose colored flower, but has been superseded.

Gloire de Rosamène is a hybrid of most remarkable habits. Its large foliage, luxuriant growth, and showy semi-double crimson flowers, make it one of the most desirable of this division ; but not for grouping, as it outgrows all its congeners. As a pillar rose it will form a splendid object ; indeed, I cannot imagine any thing more imposing in floriculture than a pillar, from twelve to fifteen feet high, covered with the splendid flowers of this rose from June till October : it will also form a fine standard. *Gloire de Guerin*, like the last, departs from the characters of the group ; but, like all that I have retained, it has the pleasing feature of autumnal flowering. This is a dwarf rose, adapted for the front of the rose border. *Grande Capitaine* appears to be a seedling from Gloire de Rosamène, as it has a similar serrated foliage ; the flower is of globular form, very double, of a brilliant velvety scarlet hue, and very beautiful. *Hennequin, Splendens,* or *Crimson Madame Desprez* is of most robust habit, blooming constantly, and well adapted for a pillar rose ; the flowers are rosy crimson, very beautiful and fragrant. *Henri Plantier* is a very double rose, of a crimson roseate hue ; it is a profuse bloomer, and a fine pillar rose. *Ida* is also a beautiful rose, with smaller flowers, which are of a deep carmine hue. The plant is dwarf, yet possesses all the characters of the true Bourbon Roses in the prominency of its buds, and in its foliage. *La Tendresse* has flowers of a silvery pale rose color, very double and large. Its habit is robust, hardy, and luxuriant, fit for the centre of the rose bed. *Latifolia* is a fine bold rose, much like Augustine Lelieur in its color and habit : a good variety, but not required in a collection where that rose is grown, *La Bedèyere* is a distinct variety, bright red, and beautiful. *Lady Granville* is a new and beautiful light red variety, as yet scarce. *Madame Angelina* is a new and very superb rose, white, tinged with fawn color. *Madame Aude* is a superb rose of a bright deep roseate hue ; and is suitable for a pillar. *Madame Desprez :* this fine and robust rose blooms beautifully, its large clusters of very splendid lilac roseate flowers are indeed superb. It is, most probably, a little hybridized with the Noisette Rose, as it blooms in larger clusters than other Bourbon Roses. *Madame Margat,* or *Therèse Margat,* is of a bright rose color, perfect form, full double, and fragrant. *Madame Nerard* is of a delicate rose color and most perfect form ; a superb flower. *Madame Newmann, Dubrieul, Gloire de France, Le Brun,* and *Monthly Cabbage,* are the five titles by which this rose is announced in various catalogues ; it is of a bright roseate hue and very double, and although an old variety, continues to be much esteemed. *Mademoiselle*

Montesquieu is a very fine white variety, of recent origin, and in great request. *Marshal Villars* approaches to the China Rose in habit, which takes from it that compact growth peculiar to most of the Bourbon Roses : it has flowers of a bright purple tinge, very vivid and double. *Marianne* is a large flower, of a bright roseate shaded with lilac, very double and superb. *Marquis de Moyria* is a perfectly new variety, of a brilliant rose color shaded with vermilion, of large size and most beautiful form. *Marquis d'Ivry* is a delicate rose color, with a protuberant centre, and very beautiful. *Ninon de l'Enclos* is a beautiful violet purple rose ; its growth is vigorous, and it will not bloom profusely until it has attained a considerable size. *Phillipart* is a beautiful delicate rose colored flower of moderate size, produced in large clusters ; the plant in good soil is of rapid growth, and well suited for a pillar rose. *Premice des Charpennes* is a splendid variety originated at Lyons, and sold the last season by the grower at 25 francs each plant; it is of a satin roseate hue bordered with white, very double, with imbricate petals. *Pluto* is a dark crimson flower, of expanded form and much admired. *Phœnix* is a very fine rose of a bright rosy hue, fragrant and distinct. *Psyché* is a very remarkable rose, a hybrid of humble growth, with double pale pink flowers, of the most perfect shape.

Reine des Vierges is a pale delicate incarnate rose, superb, and of perfect form. *Rose Menoux* is a new and very magnificent flower, bright red, nearly scarlet, and very double. *Rivers*, so named by a French rose cultivator, who raised it from seed, is a pretty delicate rose, a true Bourbon ; and called by the originator an "extra fine rose :" it has not yet bloomed here well enough to support that character. *Theresita* is a bright rose-colored flower, but has been superseded by the recent improved varieties.

6

Thiaffait is of perfect form and brilliant rose color ; a fine new variety. *Thisbé* is a beautiful new variety, of expanded form and crimson rose color. *Phœnix* is a very fine rose of a bright rosy purple hue, fragrant and distinct. *Madame Nerard* is of a delicate rose color, and most perfect form ; a superb flower. *Madame Newmann, Dubrieul, Gloire de France, Le Brun,* and *Monthly Cabbage,* are the five titles by which this rose is announced in various catalogues ; it is of a bright roseate hue and very double, and although an old variety, continues to be much esteemed. *Mademoiselle Montesquieu* is a very fine white variety, of recent origin, and in great request. *Timocles* is a large and fine rose, very double, compact, and a genuine Bourbon, of luxuriant growth, and distinct character. *Souchet* is of a purplish crimson hue and perfect form, a superb flower. *Souvenir de Malmaison* is a large and splendid rose of pale incarnate hue, slightly tinged with fawn, very double, and of fine form ; it is deemed one of the richest acquisitions of this class of roses. *Souvenir Dumont d'Urville* is a beautiful rose of a violet cherry hue, and very double. *Triomphe de Plantier* is of the habit of Madame Desprez, the flowers of a rosy crimson hue, and perfect form ; the plant is of a robust climbing habit, suitable for pillars, &c. *Victoire Argentée* is one of those beautiful silvery blush roses, with very double flowers ; it is fragrant and blooms freely. The White Bourbon, called *Julie de Loynes,* was raised from seed by Monsieur Desprez, who annually raises immense numbers of Bourbon and other roses from seed, to procure new varieties. This rose is a little hybridized with the Noisette, which has given it a clustered character, and unfortunately, taken from its flowers that bold and peculiar shape, so beautiful in the Bourbon Roses. The French cultivators are at deadly strife respecting this rose ; some swearing, by all their saints, that it is a veritable

Bourbon, while others as stoutly maintain that it is a Noisette Rose. In listening to such warm disputants, (Frenchmen generally are so,) and to this "much ado about nothing," one is prone to smile at such violent altercation, and at their making a trifle "light as air," a matter of such grave importance. *Violet de Belgique*, erroneously placed under this head by some, is a Hybrid China Rose. *Vicomte de Cussy* is a very splendid new French variety recently imported, but which has not yet bloomed so as to be accurately described. *Victor Verangot* is a fine very double rose, of a pale blush color, a new and very desirable variety. *Walner* is a true Bourbon rose, dwarf, bright-colored, and very distinct and pretty. *Zulema* is a small delicate roseate flower, very double, and produced in profuse clusters, which indicates its proximity to the Noisette family, but its foliage is truly Bourbon.

A few very remarkable additions have been made to this family, which were it not for the endless variations in flowers in which we find pleasure, would seem to leave us nothing more to wish for in Bourbon roses. Dark crimson varieties, with double and finely-shaped flowers, *were* desiderata, but are so no longer. *Pucelle Genoise* is a fine large and double rose, apparently a hybrid of the China Rose, as its foliage approaches it in resemblance.

Among the novelties in Bourbon roses, one of the most remarkable is *Madame Lacharme*, a rose raised at Lyons, and named after the wife of a rose cultivator there ; this may with justice be called *White Madame Desprez ;* it produces its beautiful white flowers, the outer petals of which are slightly tinged with blush, in large clusters ; it is of robust habit, and will undoubtedly be a most popular variety. In fine contrast to the above are two new dark crimson Bourbons, *Proserpine* and *Paul Joseph*, which both produce their flowers on erect foot-stalks ; foliage large, thick, and of a deep glossy green, flowers of the most brilliant crimson, slightly shaded with purple ; the latter is possibly the darker of the two ; but it is really difficult to say which merits the preference. *Comice de Seine et Marne* is also a fine variety, with flowers of the most brilliant crimson, not quite so deep in color as the before-mentioned, and not tinted with purple ; this is a most splendid rose. *Enfant d'Ajaccio* and *Souvenir d'Anselme* are two new roses of precisely the habit of Gloire de Rosamène, with flowers of the same color, but quite double ; these are both beautiful and very fragrant roses. A race of delicately pale flesh-colored roses has sprung from Madame Nérard. Of these the most beautiful are *Manteau de Jeanne d'Arc*, almost white ; and *Reine du Congrés* and *Comtesse de Resseguier*, of the most delicate blush ; these are all elegant and beautiful roses. A profusion of other beauties have recently been presented to our notice, all of which will be found in the catalogue annexed.

In the preceding notices of sorts, I have purposely mentioned the habits of those that deviate a little from the characters of the generality ; in forming a clump, it will therefore be seen which to place in the front, and which in the centre ; several varieties in the catalogue not noticed here are equal in beauty to those that are ; but as their habits have nothing particularly distinctive, I have, to avoid being tedious, not described them.

Bourbon Roses most certainly show themselves to greater advantage on stems from one to three feet in height, than in any other mode of culture ; if on their own roots, they are too near the ground, and the autumnal rains spoil their delicate blossoms, by dashing the dirt upon them. They seem to grow well in all soils, but I should recommend, in spite of the above objection, those who have only a dry and poor sandy soil, to have plants on their own roots, as the

Dog-rose will not flourish in such soils; though cultivated roses in soils of the same description will grow most luxuriantly. Nature often seems to delight to puzzle the cultivator with anomalies that cannot be fathomed, however clever we may be in our generation.

These roses require but little pruning; towards the end of March or beginning of April their shoots may be thinned, any weak or useless ones removed, and long shoots shortened to within four or five buds.

I hope, in a few years, to see Bourbon roses in every garden, for the " Queen of flowers" boasts no members of her court more beautiful; their fragrance also is delicate and pleasing, more particularly in the autumn; they ought to occupy a distinguished place in the autumnal rose garden, in clumps or beds, as standards, and as pillars, in any, and in all situations, they must and will please. To insure a winter bloom, a collection of dwarf standards, *i. e.* stems one to two feet in height, should be planted in large pots, and during summer watered with manured water, and some manure kept on the surface; about the middle of November, they may be placed under glass, and they will bloom in fine perfection in a short period after. I consider the culture of these roses only in its infancy; and that we shall ultimately have the richest hues combined with perfection of form, and the complete plenitude of their flowers. During the excessive summer heat, their flowers are not as large and fully developed, as in the cooler spring and autumnal months, and the Bourbon varieties evidently flourish most when sheltered in some degree from the powerful rays of June, July and August.

It is difficult to point out roses of this family that bear seed freely, except the Common Bourbon; but *Acidalie* planted against a south wall, would probably give some seed. If any pollen can be found, it might be fertilized with the flowers of *Julie de Loynes.* A pure white and true Bourbon rose ought to be the object.; therefore it should not be hybridised with any other species. *Gloire de Rosamène* may be planted against a south wall, with the Common Bourbon, with which it should be carefully fertilized: some interesting varieties may be expected from seed thus produced. *Queen of the Bourbons,* planted with the Yellow China Rose, might possibly give some seeds, but these would not produce true Bourbon roses, as the former is a hybrid, partaking of the qualities of the Tea-scented roses. *Dubourg,* planted with *La Tendresse,* would give seed from which some very delicate Blush roses might be raised ; and *Phœnix,* fertilized with the Common Bourbon, would probably also produce seed worth attention.

THE CHINESE EVERBLOOMING, DAILY, OR BENGAL ROSE.

Rosa indica.

This species of Rose is said by botanists to be a native of China, whence it was introduced to our gardens in 1789. Its everblooming qualities have made it a favorite from the cottage to the palace ; and perhaps no plants have contributed so much to enliven the gardens of Europe and of our own country, as the common *Blush China Rose,* or *Rosa Indica,* and the *Crimson China Rose,* or *Rosa semperflorens.* These roses have been, and are, considered distinct species by botanists. Like all other cultivated roses, they sport much from seed ; but the descendants of each may generally be recognised by a close observer. The *Blush* and its varieties make strong green luxuriant shoots, with flowers varying in color from pure white to crimson. The *Crimson* also takes a wide range; for though its original color is crimson, yet I have reason to believe that the pure white, which was raised in England came from its seed. The varieties derived from both these species, which now comprise this family, are of a very hardy character, and will endure every variation of position and treatment, as well as an ordinary tree, sustaining the winters of this latitude; but when removed further north, they will require to be bound in straw, or protected by a box or frame, or they may be shortened to 6 or 12 inches, and covered with sand or common mould, or leaves. In describing the varieties, those that are decidedly of the Semperflorens family I shall mark with S. after the name. I should most certainly have placed them in a separate devision, were it not for the numerous intermediate varieties, on which it is impossible to decide to which species they lean.

Admiral Duperré, S., is a pretty, brilliant, crimson rose, distinct and worth cultivating. *Aglæ Loth*, and *Animated*, both old varieties, have been superseded by new and superior ones. *Alba elegans*, though not white, as its name implies, is a fine double rose of the palest flesh color, and a good distinct variety. *Archduke Charles* is a good rose and very beautiful. Soon after expansion, the tips of most of its petals change to crimson, giving it a pretty variegated appearance. *Arsinoe* is a fine rose of a delicate rosy hue, perfect form, quite distinct, and the plant blooms freely. *Assuerus* is a deep brownish crimson flower, but indifferent in form. *Baronne de Laage*, or *General de Laage*, is a new and beautiful rose, large, deep crimson shaded. *Bardon* is a pale colored fine rose, very double and good. *Beau Carmin*, S., is a rich dark crimson shaded rose, raised in the Luxembourg Gardens, and a fine and distinct variety. *Belle de Florence* is a very double and finely shaped pale crimson rose, very distinct and pretty. *Belle Isidore*, although pretty, and *Belle Clarissima* and *Bisson*, like some others, have been superseded by superior varieties.   *Belle de Monza*, S., an old variety, with full double roseate flowers, changing to crimson, of pleasant odor, still maintains its character as a hardy vigorous growing rose.   *Boisnard* is a splendid new variety, large clear yellow, with a deeper yellow centre, and greatly admired. *Buret* is a large deep crimson rose, partially fragrant.   *Camellia blanc* is an old variety, with large globular flowers of the purest white : this rose has a fine effect on a standard, as its flowers are generally pendulous.   *Camellia rouge* is also an old variety that has been rejected.   *Caméléon*, is a changeable rose, and very properly named : this has larger flowers than Isidore, though not quite so double, and a more robust habit, so that it forms a good standard. The two finest varieties of these mutable roses are *Archduke Charles* and *Virginie ;* during their change they are often variegated like a carnation, and are truly beautiful. *Carmin d' Yebles* is a deep carmine with white stripes, very perfect and beautiful.   *Cels multiflore*, or simply *Cels*, is a large and pretty incarnate rose, full double and perfect ; the plant grows vigorously, producing a profusion of bloom, and forces well.   *Citoyen des Deux Mondes* is a new full double rose, of a rich very deep velvety crimson, and greatly admired.   *Comble de Gloire* is also of vigorous growth, and a plentiful bloomer ; the flowers large, full double, violet red, and somewhat fragrant.   *Comtesse de Moloré* is said to be fine and distinct, but it has not yet bloomed here in perfection.   *Couronne des Pourpres* is a dark crimson changeable rose ; to this color the French give the name of " pourpre," or purple : this is apt to mislead, as our purple is, as I scarcely need say, so totally different. *Cramoisie éblouissante*, or *Eblouissante*, S., and *Cramoisie supérieure*, S., often called *Agrippina*, the last, the finest, and most double, are both brilliant and excellent varieties of Rosa semperflorens. *Countess of Albemarle* is now a rose tolerably well known ; this was a great favorite in France when first originated : it is a fine robust variety, very fragrant, and forms a good standard. *Don Carlos* is a fine new creamy yellow rose, but we see it stated by a Philadelphia writer, that "it closely resembles the common Sanguinea." He must have had in view some other variety, which possibly may have received the same title. *Duc de Bordeaux* is now an old, but still a pretty and distinct rose, with that bluish lilac tinge peculiar to a few varieties in this division. *Duchess of Kent*, S., has given way to new and superior varieties that have latterly appeared. *Eugene Beauharnais*, perhaps identical with *Roi des Cramoisies*, is a superb bright amaranth flower, large, full double, quite fragrant ; it is of vigorous habit, and blooms freely. *Etna* is a compact flower, of a changeable character, varying from rose to crimson, the petals sometimes tipped with scarlet. *Fabvier*, S., sometimes called *Noisette Agrippina*, approaches nearer to scarlet than any other China Rose ; its flowers are not quite double, but very brilliant and beautiful. *Gardenia* is a variety approaching to the Tea-scented roses in its habit ; its flowers have also a peculiar fragrance : this is a distinct rose. *Gigantea* is an old variety that has been superseded. *Grandiflora* is one of the most robust and finest of its class ; it a little resembles that well known rose, *Triomphante*, or *Pæony Noisette*, but has larger and more globular shaped flowers : it is a fine and distinct variety and forms a good standard. *Gros Charles* is a large imbricate roseate shaded flower, the plant is of vigorous habit. *Henry the Fifth*, S., is one of those vivid scarlet roses that in calm cloudy weather are so beautiful ; a hot sun very soon diminishes that excessive brilliancy of color : this is a fine rose, the flowers very double and perfect. *Hibbertia* is an American variety, originated 16 years ago, and has been widely diffused ; it is of feeble growth, the flowers large, full double, deep roseate, somewhat fragrant and quite pretty. *Indica* or *Old Blush China*, often called simply *Daily Rose*, from its frequent flowering, is, as has been already stated, one of the originals from which this entire family has been produced. It is of vigorous habit, and there are in some gardens strong bushy plants eight feet high ; the flower is a deep blush about three inches in diameter, not full double, but showy from their profusion, and appear well when in bud ; it is one of the best for forcing, and has been propagated in immense numbers until the present multitude of other varieties were brought forward. *Indica Alba*, or *White Daily Rose*, is a very good white variety, differing but slightly from the *White Tea ;* it is of freer growth, and a more abundant bloomer with thinner petals, and well adapted for forcing. *Icteros* is a new fragrant creamy white flower with a yellow centre, full double, and blooms profusely. *Jacksonia*, or *Hundred Leaved Daily*, is an American variety, produced from the same parcel of seed as Hibbertia ; it is bright red, full double, and a very good rose ; the shoots are vigorous and spiny. *Joseph Deschiens* has rather small but very double and perfect flowers of a reddish crimson ; this is a variety quite distinct and worthy of cultivation. *Le Camoens* is a rosy changeable flower, of the form of the White Camellia, very perfect and beautiful, and highly esteemed. *Louis Philippe d'Angers*, S., when planted in a rich soil, is of most vigorous growth, often throwing up shoots 4 to 6 feet in height ; the flower is of globular form, large, full double, deep crimson with a blush centre ; and very distinct. It has often been sent from France as " Louis Philippe," which has given rise to several mistakes, as there is a Tea-scented rose of this name, quite different in character, for which this has been substituted. It is also sometimes called *King of France*. *Madame Chauvent* is a new and large rosy lilac variety, as yet quite rare. *Madame Desprèz* is a very beautiful pure white variety, of delightful fragrance, and when blooming in full perfection, the flower resembles in form a Double White Camellia. *Madame Bureau* is a white globular formed rose, beautiful and distinct in habit; it is one of the prettiest white China Roses we possess. *Marjolin du Luxembourg* is a fine dark purplish crimson variety, likely to prove one of our most popular roses; but it is proper to mention that there are two Marjolins: this trick of giving the same name to two roses raised by opposition cultivators is very prevalent in France, and opens a door to deception; the Marjolin described here is a fine and distinct rose, robust and hardy, and will form a good standard. *Menes* is of recent introduction, the flowers of a purplish roseate tint, and quite beautiful. *Milliez* is a large expanded rose of a pale lemon color, and fragrant, the habit erect and vigorous. *Miss Sargeant* is an American variety, of a bright rose color; the plant very hardy, of vigorous growth, and a free bloomer. *Mrs. Bosanquet* is a very fine delicate waxy blush rose, full double; the habit vigorous assimilating to the Bourbons, and indeed it may by some be mistaken for the Queen of the Bourbons. *Napoleon* is a sterling good variety, with large bell shaped flowers of a fine bright pink. *Prince Eugene* is a full double purplish carmine rose, being intermediate in color with Eugène Beauharnais, and Cramoisie superieure. *Reine de Lombardie* is of a brilliant and beautiful cherry color, of globular form and full double; the plant is of rapid growth, very hardy and blooms profusely. *Rubens*, or *Ruban pourpre*, is a new and splendid rose from the Luxembourg Gardens:

this is one of the finest shaded dark roses known. *Romain Desprez* is a beautiful and very double large rose, finely shaped, of robust habit, distinct, and calculated to become a popular variety. *Reine de Pœstum* approaches the Tea Rose in habit and scent ; its petals are too thin and flaccid to bear exposure to our summer and autumnal showers. *Sanguinea*, S., this is not identical with the Semperflorens, as has been erroneously stated by a recent writer, but is a much improved variety of the latter, with flowers of larger size and more double ; the habit of the plant more vigorous and hardy, although not capable of sustaining as severe cold as most other varieties. The remarkably brilliant flowers are produced in such profuse clusters and with such constancy, that this old variety still finds a place in every garden. *Sulphurea superba* is a fine and very double variety of the yellow Chinese or Tea Rose : its flowers are large, rather flat, and quite unique. *Triomph de Grand* is a large flower, carmine and purple shaded ; the plant of robust habit, forming a fine standard. *Virginal* is a new and beautiful incarnate white variety, yet very scarce. *Triomphante, Pœony Noisette, Indica Superba, La Superbe*, or *Grande et Belle*, for like all very good and old roses, it has several names, is a fine and distinct variety, erect and robust in its growth, and forming a fine standard ; an entire clump of this rose, with its large, shaded crimson flowers, would have a fine effect.

Vanilla, S., is an old crimson variety, possessing the odor whence its name ; it is of erect growth, and blooms best in the hottest weather ; it makes but little display, and has been cast aside. *Washington* is a Philadelphia seedling of very indifferent character and has met the same fate as the last named.

New China Roses are raised with such facility in France the branches of standards will require thinning out, and that it is difficult to cultivate and describe all that are introduced. In our glowing summer climate, seedlings can be produced with equal facility, and this course is now being adopted to a considerable extent by myself and others, both with respect to this and other classes of roses.

Clara Sylvain, by some placed in this group, is a Tea Rose; it grows so freely, its flowers are so globular, and it produces them in such abundance that it must be a favorite. *Belle Emile,* and *Eugène Hardi,* are beautiful roses of their class; their colors are of the most delicate blush or flesh color. *Augustine Hersent,* or *Madame Hersent,* although not a new rose, is not enough known; it is one of the very finest bright rose-colored China Roses we possess, and of most hardy and luxuriant habit. *Fénélon* (Desprez) is a deep rose colored variety, with erect clusters of flowers, which are large and very double. *Prince Charles* is a Luxembourg rose of great excellence, raised by Mr. Hardi; the flowers are large and globular, of a fine rosy red.

In cultivating China Roses but little care is required, as most of them are quite hardy; all those marked S., as varieties of Rosa semperflorens, are adapted for the front edges of beds or clumps, as they are of more humble growth than the varieties of the Blush. It must also be recollected that the latter are those alone adapted for standards. The varieties of Rosa semperflorens, though they will exist for several years on the Dog Rose stock, yet do not form ornamental heads, but become stinted and diseased; on the contrary, the varieties of the China Rose, as standards, particularly on short stems two to three feet in height, form magnificent heads swelling and uniting with the stock, and giving a mass of bloom from June to November; on tall stems I have not found them flourish equally. About the end of March, not earlier, shortening to about half their length; in summer a constant removal of their faded flowers is necessary, and this is all the pruning they require.

Every well appointed flower garden ought to have a collection of China Roses worked on short stems in large pots; these, by surface manuring, and manured water, may be grown to a degree of perfection of which they have not yet been thought capable; and by forcing in spring, and retarding in autumn, and removing their bloom buds in August, they will flower early and late, so that we may be reminded of that pleasant season " rose-tide" the greater portion of the year.

To succeed in making these roses bear and ripen their seed in this country, a warm dry soil and southern exposure is necessary; or, if the plants are trained to a south wall, success would be more certain. If variegated China Roses could be originated they would repay the care bestowed. This is not too much to hope for, and, perhaps, by planting Camellia Panaché with Miellez, Cameleon with Camellia Blanc, and Etna with Napoleon, seeds will be procured from which shaded and striped flowers may reasonably be expected. Eugène Beauharnais with Fabvier would probably produce first rate brilliant colored flowers. Triomphante, by removing a few of the small central petals just before the flowers are expanded, and fertilizing them with pollen from Fabvier, or Henry the Fifth, would give seed; and, as the object ought to be in this family to have large flowers with brilliant colors and plants of hardy robust habits, no better union can be formed. China Roses, if blooming in an airy greenhouse, will often produce fine seed; by fertilizing their flowers it may probably be insured. In addition, therefore, to those planted as already suggested, some strong plants of the above varieties should be grown in pots in the greenhouse.

THE TEA SCENTED CHINA ROSE.

Rosa Indica odorata.

THE original *Rosa odorata*, or *Blush Tea Scented Rose*, has long been a favorite. This pretty variation of the China Rose was imported from China into England in 1810 ; whence it was sent to France, and there in combination with the Yellow China or Tea Rose, it has been the fruitful parent of all the splendid varieties we now possess. The yellow variety was obtained from China in 1824, and even now, after so many fine varieties have been raised, is surpassed but by few in the size and beauty of its flowers, although they are but semi-double. It has only a very slight tea-like odor, but its offspring have generally a delicious fragrance, which I impute to their being hybridized with Rosa odorata. Both the Chinese varieties referred to were introduced to our country by the late William Prince, the father of the author, many years before any other persons made similar importations, and the first considerable importation of varieties originated from these two Chinese parents, was made from Loddiges & Sons of London, by the author himself.

In France the *Yellow Tea Rose* is exceedingly popular, and in the summer and autumnal months hundreds of plants are sold in the flower markets of Paris, principally worked on little stems or " mi-tiges." They are brought to market in pots, with their heads partially enveloped in colored paper in such an elegant and effective mode, that it is scarcely possible to avoid being tempted to give two or three francs for such a pretty object. In the fine climate of Italy, and beneath our own radiant skies, Tea-Scented Roses bloom in great perfection during the autumn, and in the months of September and October hundreds of plants of yellow and other Tea-Roses may be seen covered with

ripe seeds and flowers. The French cultivators say that
the Yellow-Tea very rarely produces a variety worth notice. The culture of Tea-Scented Roses is quite in its infancy in this country, but surely no class more deserves
care and attention ; in early autumn, their large and fragrant flowers are quite unique, and add much to the variety and beauty of the autumnal rose garden.

Among the most distinct varieties known to be worth culture, are the following :—*Abricoté*, or *Fanny Dupuy*, is a
large rose of a bright rosy fawn color, with a deeper centre,
and superb. *Anteros*, or *Antherose*, is a blush white rose,
with a yellowish or fawn centre, and very double ; its
growth is vigorous, and it is well suited for forcing. *Arch-
duchesse Thérèse Isabelle* is a large and very splendid
variety, white with a yellow centre, of fine form, blooms
freely, and is greatly admired. *Arkinto* is an old variety,
of large size, incarnate, very double ; it grows freely and
blooms plentifully.

Aurore, or *Jaune panaché*, is an old but fine rose, a hybrid
of the Yellow Tea and Rosa odorata, and partaking of both,
for its flowers are, when first open, of a delicate straw color,
soon changing to blush. *Barbot* is a very large flower, of
rose color shaded with red, and a yellowish centre, very
fragrant ; the plant is vigorous, and an estimable acquisition. *Belle Allemande* is of Apricot or fawn
color shaded with blush, the colors prettily blended,
large and magnificent ; the plant is of vigorous growth
and very hardy. *Belle Hélène* is a pale variety of the
original Tea Rose, with flowers larger and more double ;
a distinct and good rose. *Belle Margueritte* is a large full
double rose, of a violet red hue ; the habit is vigorous and
erect, and it blooms freely. *Blush Tea*, *Odorata*, or *Old
Tea* is known to almost every one by its large rosy blush
flowers, of delightful fragrance, and although not as beautiful as many others, is nevertheless an estimable variety.

Bougère is a singular and splendid rose ; the buds and flowers are very large, full double, perfectly cup shaped, of a fine roseate hue, shaded with bronze ; the plant is of vigorous growth, blooms abundantly, and is one of the most hardy. *Boutrand* is a vigorous variety, with fine bright roseate flowers, of perfect form and much admired. *Boidron* is a new French variety, with very large flowers, of a rosy hue, beautiful, and as yet very rare. *Caroline* is a pretty rose, with flowers very double, of a bright rose color, and very perfect in their shape. *Clara Sylvain* is one of the most perfect shaped pure white Roses yet known, of globose form, fragrant, distinct, and superb. *Claudia Gourd* is a beautiful incarnate rose of globose form, very perfect, and greatly admired. *Comte d'Osmond* is a large and beautiful globular rose, of a cream color with a yellowish centre, very double, and perfect. *Duc d'Orleans* is of a bright deep cherry color, shaded. *Etienie,* a white variety, has been superseded. *Flon* is a new and beautiful rose, a sort of fawn-colored blush ; its flowers very large and fragrant, resembling those of the Triumph of Luxembourg. *Fragrans,* one of our oldest varieties, is but a very slight remove from the crimson China, but it has acquired by being hybridized, the pleasing perfume of this family. *Frederic Væber* is a new and rare variety, of medium size, full double, and shaded red color. *Gigantesque* is a Luxembourg variety, the flowers of the largest size, but not very perfect in form, of a pale incarnate hue, and very showy. *Goubault* is a most excellent rose, and remarkably robust and hardy, and will probably form a fine standard. *Hardy, or Gloire de Hardy,* is a vivid rose of large size, and most luxuriant growth, well calculated for a standard ; this will become a popular Tea Rose. *Hamon* is also a very fine rose ; but rather too delicate for the open border : this is a changeable variety ; sometimes its flowers are blush tinged with buff, and sometimes, when forced, they are of a deep crimson. *Hymenée* is an old variety, incarnate white with a fawn centre, full double, growing vigorously and one of the most hardy. *Hypolite* is a large rose of a salmon color, or sulphur and white blended, quite fragrant. *Jeune Arcole* is of medium size, full double, of a deep roseate hue, and much admired. *Julie Mansais* is a very large rose, pure white, very double and superb, sometimes with a lemon centre. *La Sylphide* is an admirable new French variety, of very large size, rosy incarnate hue changing to cream color; the habit of the plant is vigorous, blooming profusely, and it is one of the most hardy. *Le Pactole*, or *Pactolus* is also a new and distinct variety, with superb full double pale yellow flowers, approaching to bright yellow at the centre ; the plant is robust and hardy, blooms profusely, and is one of the most desirable yellow varieties known. *Lilacina* is an old lilac colored variety that has been cast aside. *Lyonnais* is a very large pale flesh colored rose, hardy, and worthy the attention of the amateur. *Madame Desprez* erroneously placed here by some, belongs to the previous class. *Madame Galet* is a fine new variety, of a yellowish hue; the plant is hardy and grows vigorously. *Mansais* must not be confused with Julie Mansais, being very distinct ; the flower resembles Noisette Jaune Desprez; it is large, buff with a rose centre, quite fragrant and superb : the plant is vigorous and hardy. *Marechal Bugeaud* is a large and superb new French variety, yet quite rare ; the flower is deep rosy, with a deeper rosette centre, and very double ; this is one of the most desirable of the whole family. *Melville* is a large and fine rose, buff and carmine shaded ; the habit remarkably vigorous, very hardy ; the foliage luxuriant and deeply serrated. *Mirabile* is a superb flower, fawn or sulphur color, tinged at the centre and edged with pink, and full double ; the plant grows and blooms quite freely. *Mondor* is another of the splendid varieties recently produced in France ; the flowers are very large, of a fawn color shaded with deep rose, and extra superb ; it is yet very rare. *Niphetos* is a large globular flower of a pale lemon color at opening changing to shining white, and like the Yellow Tea is most beautiful when in bud or partially expanded ; the growth is vigorous and it blooms freely. *Odoratissima* is a very free-growing and pretty lilac rose, more than ordinarily fragrant, and apparently very hardy. *Palavicini* has been much admired and also much depreciated, owing to the different appearances it has taken under cultivation. On its natural roots, and in a weak state, it is poor and insignificant, looking like a bad variety of the yellow China Rose ; but when budded on a strong branch of the Common China or the Blush Boursault, it will bloom in a splendid manner, so as to appear quite a different rose. I believe it is of Italian origin, as many fine Tea-scented and China Roses are raised from seed annually in Italy, but not distributed. *Pauline Plantier* is a beautiful creamy white rose, or rather pale yellow changing to white after full expansion, and well worthy of cultivation, although we have many others of the same color. *Pellonia* is a new and beautiful globular rose, of large size, straw color with a yellow centre, and as yet very rare. *Prince d'Esterhazy* is a very large flower of globular form, and rosy incarnate hue ; it is an admirable variety of vigorous habit. *Princesse Helene* (of Luxembourg) is a very large and fine straw colored rose, of globular form. *Princesse Helène*, (of Modeste) is a fine pure white rose. *Princesse Marie* is one of the finest roses in this group ; its flowers on strong plants are four to five inches in diameter. *Reine Victoria*, or *Queen Victoria*, is a splendid variety, yet rare, with large bright yellow shaded flowers, greatly admired. *Rêve du bonheur* is a singularly beautiful tinged rose, forming a fine large cup, but not very double. *Soliman* is a large full double flower, of a rosy buff hue, and the plant grows freely. *Silene,* or *Bon Silene* is a large and fragrant rose, very variable in color, and often described differently under different circumstances; the plant is robust and hardy, and will grow in any situation and make a fine standard. *Strombio* is now an old rose, but no variety can be more deserving of cultivation, being hardy and vigorous when growing on a standard, its large and pendulous cream-colored flowers are very beautiful. *Taglioni* is a full sized fine white rose, shaded with blush towards its centre, and a hardy and good variety. *Themistocles* is a fine white rose slightly incarnate at the centre, and of perfect form. *Thisbé* is a bright red rose that has been superseded. *Triomphe de Luxembourg :* this very large and imposing flower has probably attracted more attention and been more extensively disseminated during the ten years of its existence, than any other of the Perpetual flowering classes, and at first it was sold as high as thirty to forty francs at Paris ; the bud and flower are very large and distinct, the latter often five inches or more in diameter, of globular form, fragrant, usually of aurora hue shaded with pink, but varying somewhat according to the season and position ; the growth is remarkably vigorous and strong, plants in a rich soil form shoots of four to six feet in a season, and bloom most freely. *William Wallace* is a light blush rose, but has given place to superior varieties. The *Yellow Tea, Yellow China,* or *Flavescens* is placed here, as it has decidedly more of the habit and appearance of the Tea-scented Class than of the China ; its smooth glossy leaves and faint Tea-odor sufficiently show its affinity ; the flowers are very large, with broad petals of a straw color, not full double, but remarkably beautiful when in bud or half blown. In a congenial soil of rich sandy loam, it grows very vigorously, blooms profusely, and seeds freely, and if the flowers are judiciously fertilized it cannot fail to yield estimable varieties. *Valentine* is a large and beautiful new variety, full double, incarnate with a protuberant centre.

To these some varieties of extraordinary beauty have been added, among which *Eliza Sauvage*, a fine straw-colored rose, of rather a deeper tinge than the Yellow Tea, with flowers very large and double, richly deserves cultivation. *Duchesse de Mecklenberg* is of a more creamy yellow, and perfect in form, and really a most beautiful rose. *Lutescens Grandiflora* is one of the largest of these yellow Tea Roses; its flowers are cupped, very large, and deep yellow toward the centre.

Marechal Vallée is a rose-colored Tea rose, with flowers very large and double; this is a new and first rate variety.

Devoniensis takes a high rank; it is not yellow, as was at first supposed, but of a pale straw, changing to a fine creamy hue, and remarkably fragrant; when cultivated highly it produces flowers of a great size; in open culture it should have a rich soil and ample space, and it will then grow most vigorously; for forcing this is a most valuable rose. *Comte de Paris* is also a magnificent variety, with finely cupped flowers of pale rose color. This expands its flowers freely in any situation, and is very hardy and robust. *Josephine Malton*, equally hardy and robust, is a rose of the first class, having large and elegantly formed cupped flowers; color creamy white. *Adam* is one of the very largest roses in this family: its flowers are not so regularly shaped as the above; color rose, very fragrant, and showy. *Moiré*, a fawn colored variety, shaded with cream and rose, has petals of remarkable substance, so that it withstands heat much better than most of this class: it is a first rate and beautiful rose. *Safrano*, like the old yellow Tea Rose, is most beautiful in bud, or, half expanded, its flowers being of the brightest saffron; but, when fully opened and exposed to the sun, they soon fade; it blooms very freely and in clusters, and is a most desirable acquisition.

As these interesting roses require somewhat more care in their culture than most others, I will endeavor to give explicit directions, so as to insure success.

One most essential point for plants that are grown on their natural roots, is to select ground that is warm and rich, with a dry bottom, and in a somewhat sheltered position; as soils that are wet and cold are very uncongenial. The preparation of the soil need not differ in any wise from that of other roses further than is necessary to render it light and warm; and in this the plants may be placed about two and a half feet apart. In severe frosty weather which usually commences here in November, protect the plants by binding the tops in straw and raising the earth around them, or shorten their tops and cover them with leaves, sand or mould; another eligible mode is to protect the plants with branches of cedar, pine, or any of the spruces, or any other light spray that will keep off the severe frost. With this treatment they will seldom receive any injury from our severest winters, and will bloom in great perfection throughout the whole summer. If it is preferred to cultivate plants of this class that are budded on the Dog Rose or Blush Boursault, they will then flourish best in a more moist soil; and they can be arranged in beds of several rows each, placing those on the shortest stocks in front and allowing the rows to rise in succession, so as to form a bank of foliage and flowers. Grafted or budded plants when well established will in general brave our severest winters, but it is most prudent to bind their heads in straw, or to give to each an oiled paper cap; this

latter mode is practiced in the north of Italy and France
with great success to protect their tender roses and other
plants. In the more northern climates the budded roses
as well as those on their natural roots, can be planted in a
cellar or conservatory, or be buried in layers of sand or
light mould at a depth of four feet, where frost cannot
reach them, whence they can be removed at the first opening of spring, and planted in their appropriate positions in
the garden. This removal does them no injury, and they
appear to flourish and bloom quite as well as those not
subjected to removal. At the south of the Potomac there
is of course no winter protection required.

Some of the varieties are much more robust and vigorous
than others, and equally as beautiful as those of more delicate habits; it will therefore be scarcely worth while to grow
any but what are of known hardihood and vigor. I have
pointed out some of these in my notices, but time can only
make a knowledge of their habits more perfect. Budded
plants of Tea-scented roses force very well, and when
worked on neat stems about one foot in height, they form
beautiful plants; they do not require to be established one
year in pots, for if only potted in October or November,
and forced with a gentle heat in January and February,
they will bloom finely; in March and April the extreme
beauty of their foliage and flowers will amply repay the
attention given to them, as they have a peculiar softness
and delicacy of appearance when forced and growing luxuriantly.

With attention, some very beautiful roses of this family
may be originated from seed, but the plants must be trained
against a south wall, or in some other sheltered position,
and in a warm dry soil.

For yellow roses, Lutescens grandiflora and the Duchesse
de Mecklenberg may be planted with the Yellow Tea, which

abounds in pollen; some fine roses, almost to a certainty must be raised from seed produced by such fine unions: for the sake of curiosity a few flowers of the above might be fertilized with the Double Yellow or Rosa Harrisonii. The Yellow Tea bears seed abundantly, but it has been found from repeated experiments, that a good or even a mediocre rose is seldom or never produced from it; yet if fertilized with the Harrisonii, something original may be realized. Gigantesque and Hardy Tea planted with Prince Esterhazy, would produce seed of fine quality, from which large and bright rose-colored varieties might be expected. Archiduchesse Thérèse and Duchesse de Cazes, planted with Bride of Abydos, would give pure white Tea Roses; and Mansais with Dremont would probably originate first rate fawn-colored roses ; but the central petals of Mansais should be carefully removed with tweezers or plyers, as its flowers are too double for it to be a certain seed-bearer. Bélisaire, which is a hybrid, approaching very near to the China Rose, should be planted with William Wallace, as fine and large Crimson Tea roses are still wanting.

THE FAIRY OR MINIATURE ROSE.

Rosa Lawrenceana.

In the botanical publications, this curious little rose is said to have been introduced from China in 1810, and botanists have made it a species ; but Mr. Rivers considers it only a dwarf seminal variety of the Common China Rose, and holding the same relative position to that rose, that the Rose de Meaux and Pompone Roses do to the common Rosa centifolia. He may be correct, but I consider the point as not yet fully settled in the present case. Many plants that have been long under cultivation have a tendency to produce sometimes from seed, these pigmy likenesses of themselves : among these little " faerie queens," *Caprice des Dames* is a pretty morsel of beauty with vivid rose-colored shaded flowers. *Gloire des Lawrenceas* is one of the prettiest of the tribe ; its flowers are of a dark crimson. *Jenny* and *Lilliputienne* are both of them bright-colored and pretty roses. *Master Burke,* the most diminutive of all this class, was originated by Mr. J. Feast ; the whole plant when in bloom with full double flowers, not occupying a space of over two inches in diameter, and the same in height ; it is an object of curiosity only. *Nigra* has not black flowers, but they are of the darkest crimson, and very pretty. This was named by some florist with great exaggeration, and was not done wilfully to deceive, but is given as descriptive of what *he wishes the flower to be, rather than of what it really is.* Brugmansia sanguinea is a case in point ; and many other sanguineas and coccineas might be mentioned, in which the colors of the flowers which bear these imposing names approach to any thing rather than blood or scarlet. To return to Roses ; *Pallida* is the only variety in this division approaching to white. Its flowers, when they first open, are nearly of pure white, but they soon change to a pale flesh color : this is rather a delicate rose, seeming very impatient of cold and damp. *Petite Laponne,* or *La Laponne,* is a brilliant little rose, quite worthy a place in the group. *Pompone,* or *Indica minor,* is the oldest and largest flowering variety and more than double the size of the others ; it is blush and pretty, blooming in profusion. *Pompone Bijou* is of a bright roseate hue, very much resembling La Miniature, but of a deeper shade. *Pretty American* is a very diminutive variety, not exceeding six to eight inches in height. *Retour du Printemps* is different from all the others ; its pretty little flowers being surrounded by

7

a leafy calyx, and the whole plant tinged with a reddish coloring matter.

There are a few other varieties, but throughout this little family, the distinction between the different varieties is generally so very slight, that it requires a close observer to recognise them. They bloom throughout the entire year, the same as the China and Tea-scented classes.

These roses are all very impatient of moisture, and in all humid soils require a very dry warm raised border. They flourish best in the same soils and situation that I have recommended for the Tea-scented rose. In cold climates it will be advisable to grow them constantly in pots, protecting them in a cold pit or frame till January, and then if required to bloom early, remove them to a warm situation in the greenhouse, or force them with the Tea-scented Roses. A collection of these little rose-bushes, covered with their bright flowers in March and April, will be found one of the most eligible and unique ornaments for the drawing-room.

THE NOISETTE OR CHAMPNEY ROSE.

Rosa Champneyana.

PERHAPS no new roses ever excited more attention than the two varieties which were first produced of this interesting family. When first received in France, the Parisian amateurs were enraptured with it, its habits being so peculiar and distinct from every other class. The origin of the first varieties of this remarkable group, has been announced erroneously to the world by various writers, arising first, from the want of candor on the part of the late Philippe Noisette of Charleston, when he transmitted the plants to Paris; and, secondly, from the ignorance of those who have discussed the subject. The original variety is the *Champney Rose,* or *Champney's Pink Cluster,* a rose long well, known and very widely diffused. It was raised from seed by the late John Champney, Esq., of Charleston, S. C., an eminent and most liberal votary of Flora, from the seed of the White Musk Rose, or Rosa Moschata, fertilized by the old Blush China, and as he had been for a long period in constant correspondence with the late William Prince, he most kindly presented him with two tubs, each containing six plants, grown from cuttings of the original plant. From these an immense number were propagated and sent to England and France. The old *Blush Noisette* Rose was raised a few years after by Philippe Noisette, of Charleston, *from the seed of the Champney Rose,* and this he sent to his brother Louis Noisette of Paris, under the name of the Noisette Rose. It is more double than its parent, and of much more dwarf and compact growth; the flowers in very large dense panicles. The old *Champney's Pink Cluster,* although not full double, is still quite a favorite for its rapid growth, its appropriateness for pillars and other climbing positions, and for the profusion of its flowers which are in very large panicles much more diffuse than the preceding variety. The subsequent varieties have been produced from both the primitive ones I have named, but as the Champney rose produces seeds far more abundantly than the Blush Noisette, it has doubtless been the parent of much the greatest number.

To develope the beauties and admirable qualities of the Noisette Roses, proper attention must be paid to their culture; the soil must be warm, dry at the bottom, and well mellowed and enriched with old well-rotted manure, or black mould from the woods to the depth of two feet ; they will not flourish in a wet soil, and if the location is either a wet or heavy soil, a quantity of sand must be mixed with it sufficient to lighten it, and render it completely permeable so as to allow of the free passage of all rains through it.

The perfume of the Musk Rose is very apparent: its tendency to bloom in large clusters also shows its affinity to that old and very remarkable rose, but since its introduction to France so many seedlings have been raised from it, and so many of these are evidently hybrids of the Tea-scented and other roses, that some of the roses called "Noisettes" have almost lost the characters of the group ; for, in proportion as the size of the flowers have been increased by hybridizing, their clustering tendency and the number of them in one corymb has been diminished. Among the varieties most deserving of notice is *Aimeé Vibert*, or *Rosa nivea*, a seedling from the Rosa sempervirens plena, which it resembles, but it much surpasses its parent in the valuable quality of autumnal blooming. Nothing can be prettier than a large plant of Aimée Vibert Noisette, covered with its clusters of snow-white flowers, in September and October. These are small, of perfect form, and produced in profusion throughout the season ; it is perfectly hardy, and forms a fine standard rose. *Andreselle* is in color like that old variety, the *Noisette Bougainville*, but its culture has been discontinued. *Alba*, or *New White* is a small rose, pure white, blooming profusely in clusters ; it forms a dense and beautiful dwarf shrub of two and a half to three feet in height. *Alzand* is a pale blush variety, formerly much cultivated by amateurs, but has been superseded by superior new varieties. *Ariel* is a fine and vigorous-growing rose, blooming in immense corymbs; its flowers are of the most delicate blush tinged with buff : this is a distinct and pretty variety. *Belle d'Esquermes*, or *Camellia rouge*, is a flower of medium size, deep brilliant violet hue, not full double ; the plant grows vigorously, is suitable for a pillar, and blooms freely. *Belle Marseillaise* is of medium size, full double, of a rosy hue shaded with carmine. *Belle Violette* is a genuine Noisette, and a very neat and pretty little rose : its flowers are of a rosy lilac, and very distinct and good. *Belle Antonine* is a pillar Noisette, of very robust habit, with flowers delicately colored and well-shaped. In designating some of these as pillar Noisettes, those varieties that are very vigorous growers, making long and flexible shoots, are intended. *Boulogne* is one of the few dark-colored Noisettes, and when first its flowers open they are very beautiful, their color being a dark crimson-purple. *Beurre Frais* is singular, but scarcely double enough ; its delicate butter-color soon changes to white in the sun. *Bouquet tout fait,* a pillar Noisette, is a most vigorous grower, forming immense corymbs ; this may be taken for the original Noisette at first sight, but it is more fragrant, and its flowers buff towards their centre. *Belle Angevine* is a fragrant variety, with rose-colored flowers, tinged with buff. *Blanche d'Orleans* is a new and rare variety, with fine white expanded flowers. *Chloris* is a brilliant delicate red rose, shaded with carmine. *Comtesse de Tolosan* is white, with a pale roseate centre. *Charles X.* is a pretty rose in very dry weather, but in moist weather its buds will not open ; it has been superseded by superior varieties. *Castalie* is a variety, of a delicate flesh-color, very distinct and pretty. *Clara Wendel* is a beautiful and distinct rose of aurora hue, changing to pale straw color ; it is large, full double, and fragrant ; the plant blooms freely, and is a highly esteemed variety.

Clarisse Harlowe is a pillar rose of first-rate excellence ; its flowers are very large and double, and its growth excessively vigorous, so that it soon forms a large column. *Cleopatra* is a new and admirable variety, of a pale lemon color, recently introduced, and cannot therefore be fully described. *Comtesse d'Orloff* is a pillar rose, of vigorous growth,

producing abundance of very fine flowers of a rosy lilac color.
There is an old rose called *Orloff* by some, with rose colored flowers, very distinct from this, and now superseded.
Conque de Venus is an old rose, creamy white with a rosy
centre, quite double, very fragrant, and produced freely in
profuse clusters.   *Cora Barton* is a large and fine flower,
of a pink roseate hue, and fragrant ; the plant grows vigorously, blooms freely, and is suitable for pillars ; it is a seedling from Lamarque.   *Corymbosa* is a small white rose,
with rough dark green foliage, and unlike any other variety.   *Duc de Nemours* is a new rosy lilac variety, very
double, and of perfect form.   *Euphrosine* is a new and
admirable variety, a miniature likeness of Madame Desprez ; it is of medium size, with yellowish and rosy tints,
prettily blended, full double, of exquisite fragrance, and produced in clusters ; the habit is vigorous, and it is well
suited for a climber.   *Eugene Pirolle*, or *Admiral de Rig-
ny*, is of a carmine roseate hue, perfect form, and produced
in large clusters; the plant is of dwarf habit and forms a
beautiful dense border shrub.   *Eclair de Jupiter* is a pillar rose, with large vivid light crimson flowers, beautiful
and distinct.   *Eliza Le Maire* is a small rose, of incarnate
white hue, very neat and pretty.

Fellenberg has beautiful bright crimson flowers, which
it exhibits in the greatest perfection and in large clusters
during the autumnal months, those produced during the
summer being of less brilliancy ; the plant grows luxuriantly, is perfectly hardy, and blooms profusely.

Galaxie is a creamy white rose of dwarf habit.   *Grandiflora*, *Monstrosa*, *Blush Perpetual China*, *Lee*, *Triomphe
des Noisettes*, and *Celestis ;* all these names have been applied to one old variety, which is a pale blush colored rose,
produced in large diffuse clusters, but does not expand
well in wet weather, it is a very strong and rapid climber.

This must not be confused with the *Monstrueuse* or *Majestueuse* Noisette. *Hardy* is a pillar Noisette, quite worth cultivation ; its large pale flowers have a deep rose and buff centre ; its habit is so vigorous that it will shoot from six to eight feet in one season. *Isabelle d'Orleans* is a new and very beautiful pure white rose, of quite recent introduction, and calculated to excite general admiration. *Jaune Desprez Triomph d'Arcole*, or *French Yellow Noisette*, is a well-known and much-esteemed rose, of rapid growth and quite hardy ; as a pillar or standard it is equally beautiful ; its fragrance is also very remarkable. This was originated by M. Desprez about eighteen years since, and is still, and will be for some time to come, a very popular rose. It is, most probably, a hybrid between the Yellow Tea and a Noisette rose of some kind : it sold for a high price in France, when first sent forth to the rose world, its name being very tempting, for a yellow fragrant Noisette rose was deemed worth any price. Its rosy copper-colored flowers are very singular, and so powerfully fragrant that one plant will perfume a large garden in the cool weather of autumn. A pillar of this rose, twelve to twenty feet high, would be a grand object on a lawn. *Julia*, or *Julia Dante*, is a pale pink variety that has yielded precedence to the improved varieties. *Julie de Loynes* will be found under the head of Bourbon Roses. *Julienne le Sourd* is a small bright rose-colored flower, produced in very numerous clusters, often composed of fifty to one hundred flowers each ; the plant is of dwarf compact habit, forming a neat and beautiful shrub for the flower border. *Lactans* has very large full double flowers, of a delicate creamy hue, and very fine ; the plant is ranked with those of low growth. *Lamarque*, or *Le Marechal*, is another hybrid Noisette, approaching to the Tea-scented rose in the size and fragrance of its flowers. It is of most vigorous growth but not quite as hardy as Jaune Desprez. As a standard it is very superb, for its large pale sulphur-colored or nearly white flowers are pendant from their weight, and have a fine effect. It is rather impatient of cold, and requires a somewhat sheltered position until the plants attain age and strength. In a rich warm soil, it will grow fifteen to twenty feet in one season, and produce from May to December, a profusion of its drooping clusters, comprised of five to ten flowers each. In the Southern States it attains a magnificent development, extending its branches in some cases for fifty feet in length and above twenty feet in height. Even in this latitude there are plants twenty-five feet in length and ten in height. Like many others of this class, it is very much hybridized by the Rosa odorata, but the tendency to blooming in clusters has caused it to be placed here. It seems very evident, however, that a division of the Noisettes will be speedily required, by which those with small flowers may be placed in one section, and those with large flowers in another, the difference in the size of the clusters, and in the number of flowers comprised in them, being another important feature distinguishing the two sections; perhaps even a third section may be requisite in order to distinguish the climbing from the dwarf varieties, as the simple title of Noisette cannot at present convey a correct idea of the numerous discordant varieties, which are now embraced under this head.

Lamarque à cœur rose, or *Fleur de Jeune age,* is a large fragrant flower, creamy white with a rosy centre, and much admired; the plant has the vigorous habit of Jaune Desprez. *Landreth's Carmine,* or *Carmine Cluster,* does not expand its buds well, and has been cast aside to make place for superior varieties. *La Victorieuse,* or *Pictorium,* is yet rare; it is a large and fragrant incarnate white rose, very beautiful; it is strongly hybridized with the

Tea Rose, of dwarf habit, but blooms in clusters. *Le Pactole*, or *Pactolus*, is a Tea Rose and will be found under
that head, where it is placed by Laffay, Rivers, and others.
Lelieur is a pretty little dark purplish-crimson rose, and
deservedly a favorite, as its color is so vivid ; the point of
each petal is tipped with white. *La Biche* is a pillar Noisette, with very large pale flowers, inclining to fawn color
at the centre, and often changing nearly to white : a very
fragrant, beautiful, and distinct variety.

Luxembourg is a fine large, new, and distinct rose, very
double and fragrant, and of a bright purplish color; it is
of vigorous growth, blooms freely and will form a magnificent pillar ; it requires the shelter of a wall, in this
latitude, but is well suited for the Southern States. *Madame Byrne* is an American variety, large, full double,
cream-colored with a rosy centre ; the shoots are slender,
but of free growth, and it will answer for a climber. *Madame Guerin* is a fine new rose, white, and medium size,
yet rare. *Madame Laffay* was raised from seed by Monsieur Laffay, and sold at a high price; but its habit is so
delicate, and its flowers so small, that it has not pleased the
generality of amateurs. *Minette* is a pretty light crimson
rose, very double and compact ; it is a climber and well
suited for pillars. *Miss Glegg* is a small superb rose,
pure white with a delicate blush centre ; it is a new variety, yet scarce, and of medium growth. Mrs. Siddons is
a new and splendid variety, bright yellow changing to
straw color, but of irregular form. *Nankin*, or *Mutabilis*,
is a very distinct and pretty rose, very fragrant and of
rather dwarf growth. In the morning, before the sun has
much power, or in cloudy weather, its clusters of flowers
are of a bright nankin-color, changing to white a few hours
after expansion. *Narcisse* is a new and very rare variety,
with splendid flowers, large and expanded, of a sulphur

7*

color and fragrant. *Nemesis* is a new and desirable variety ; it is a small very double rose, of a deep brownish crimson hue, and inadvertently stated to be purple in my catalogue. *Ne plus Ultra* is a very fine creamy white rose, highly fragrant ; it forces admirably, but is as yet quite rare. *Philomèle* is a new French variety, with small full double flowers of an incarnate hue, very neat and pretty. *Pompone* is a fragrant full double rose of a light pink hue ; the habit vigorous with a profusion of foliage, well suited for covering walls and other places where concealment is desired. *Princesse d'Orange* is a French variety, with small and very pretty white flowers, full double and fragrant; they are sometimes very curiously and irregularly shaped. *Prudence Rœser*, erroneously placed here by some, will be found under its proper head of Hybrid Perpetual Roses. The *Red Noisette*, a very old variety, is a pretty bright semi-double rose, now eclipsed by new and finer varieties. *Rothanger* is a bright carmine flower, changing to a paler hue, of pleasant fragrance ; the habit is dwarf, and it blooms profusely. *Sir Walter Scott* is a fragrant and beautiful variety of a rosy purple hue with dark purple shades; the plant is of rapid growth and it makes a splendid appearance on a pillar. *Superba* is an old variety of pale rose color, and very vigorous, but not lofty growth, now superseded. *Smith's Yellow*, or *Lutea*, is certainly more nearly allied to the Tea-scented roses than to the Noisettes, for of this family it has not a feature : it is a fine rose for forcing, and remarkably beautiful when half blown, being of a very rich yellow hue, and when fully expanded the flowers are large and splendid.   In the Southern States, it grows vigorously, and expands its flowers in great perfection during dry weather, commanding universal admiration ; in this latitude it needs a wall or some other sheltered position for its full development. *Vitellina* is a rare variety, fragrant, white with a yellow centre, and very beautiful; it bears a strong affinity to Lamarque, and is much hybridized with the Tea Rose; it is of dwarf habit and when grafted two to four feet high, forms a splendid standard. *Zobeide* is a new and beautiful rose of medium size, full double, of a deep vivid roseate or cherry color : there are so many pale Noisettes, that such varieties as this are welcome additions.

Among the acquisitions to this class, that are worthy of especial notice, I will first describe two which have been raised at Angers from the Lamarque, and no roses have perhaps so well rewarded with their beauty the care of the cultivator. The first is the *Chromatella* of the French, which was quickly re-named *Cloth of Gold* on its reception by the English; it is a very large and splendid flower of a pale yellow color, and quite fragrant; the foliage is large, luxuriant and beautiful ; the plant unsurpassed in vigor and in the length of its shoots by any other of its class. It should be planted in a rich soil, and allowed ample space for development, when it will form a most magnificent plant; but it will not bloom well when small or if cramped in a pot. Another variety is the *Solfatare*, of the same parentage ; the flowers are not so globular as the preceding, but rather flat like those of Jaune Despres, very large, of a deeper saffron yellow than the preceding, and retaining its color more permanently. It is a splendid rose, universally esteemed, and the plant is of the same vigorous habit as the preceding variety. The *Ophirie* is of only medium size, full double, of a deep fawn or apricot color, very unique, a frequent bloomer, and greatly admired; the growth is vigorous and suited to any climbing position. *Poupre de Tyr*, one of the recent acquisitions, is not of the hue which we recognise as Tyrian purple, the French term " pourpre" not corresponding to *our* purple ; the flowers are of a brilliant violet crimson hue, of medium size, very double and greatly admired; the foliage large, dark green and abundant, and the habit of the plant exceedingly robust. Mr. Rivers pronounces this to be the finest crimson variety yet known, and he, with great kindness, presented me with five of the plants. *Similor* is a rare and admirable flower of medium size, full double, saffron color at expansion varying to an aurora hue, with a deeper centre, superb, and fragrant.

The individuals of this group are so varied in character that they may be employed as objects of ornament in a variety of ways. I will first give their culture as pillar roses, for which some of them are so finely adapted. Perhaps the most picturesque mode of growing pillar roses is to group them in clumps of three, five, seven, or nine, or to any extent in proportion to the space of ground required to be ornamented. A group of rose pillars, on an artificial mound, has a very imposing effect, and in wet situations this will be found the most advantageous mode of growing them. The posts should be made of yellow deal, or larch, or oak, and charred as far as inserted in the ground ; they should be from ten to fifteen feet in height, and stout, so that they can be firmly fixed in the ground; each post ought to be, at least, from nine to twelve inches in circumference. For roses of more humble growth, iron stakes, from six to seven feet in height, will be found more light and elegant in appearance than those of wood, and of course more durable. It must be borne in mind, that pillar roses cannot have too much manure; therefore, when they are planted, mix a plenty with the soil they are planted in, and give them an annual surface dressing.

As standards, Noisette Roses require but little culture ; the principal care is to be prompt in cutting off the decayed and decaying clusters of flowers, during the blooming sea-

son; and, in March, to thin out their superfluous branches.
All the pillar Noisettes form fine drooping standards : as
dwarfs for beds, many of the varieties are very eligible,
for they will grow and bloom luxuriantly in all soils and
situations. To insure their receiving no injury in very
cold and exposed situations, the plants of tall growth can
be well bound in straw in November, and the dwarfs can
be cut down to within a foot of the ground, and covered,
or rather thatched over, with a thick covering of straw, to
continue on till March. This will effectually protect them
from the frost. The covering, as elsewhere recommended,
must be removed at the opening of spring. For ornamenting wire fences these roses are also admirably adapted, as
they can be trained with great facility, and they will form,
in such situations, a blooming boundary for at least four
months in the year.

Many of the Noisette Roses bear seed freely, and the
following, if planted in a favorable position, and carefully
fertilized, would probably produce some. The object here
should be to obtain dark crimson varieties with large flowers, and for this purpose Fellenberg should be fertilized
with Cerise or Boulogne, and again Cerise with Fellenberg. Cerise may also be planted with the China Rose
Fabvier, and Boulogne with the same ; if seed can be produced, fine deep colored and nearly genuine Noisette roses
would be the result. It will be interesting also to try
Noisette Nankin fertilized with the Yellow China ; from
this union yellow or buff-colored Noisettes might possibly
be originated, and these of course would be unique and of
great interest. Beurre Frais with Duchesse de Mecklenberg would probably give straw-colored varieties, and these
would be large and fragrant, as in Lamarque and Jaune
Desprez. In these directions for procuring seed from roses
by fertilizing, I have confined myself to such varieties as

are almost sure to produce it ; but much must be left to
the amateur, as many roses may be made fertile by removing their central petals, and, consequently, very many
varieties that I have not noticed may be made productive.

THE MUSK ROSE.

Rosa moschata.

THE *White Musk* or *Musk Cluster* Rose with white flowers of a high musk odor, is one of the oldest inhabitants of
both the European and American gardens, and perhaps
more widely disseminated over the earth than any other
rose.   It is generally supposed that the attar or otto of roses
is prepared in India from this species, and that this is also
the rose of the Persian poets, in the fragrant groves of which
they love to describe their " bulbul," or nightingale, as enchanting them with its tuneful notes.   The probability that
this is the famed rose of Persia is strengthened by the fact,
that it is much more fragrant in the evening, or in the cool
weather of autumn, than at any other time or season, and
probably in the hot climate of Persia, *only so* in the cool-
ness of night, when nightingales delight to sing.   A recent traveller also remarks that the roses of Persia are remarkably small and fragrant.   There are doubtless many
seminal varieties of the species ; their flowers differing in
color, but possessing the leading features of the original.
Olivier, who travelled in the first six years of the French
republic, mentions a rose tree at Ispahan, called the " Chinese Rose Tree," fifteen feet high, formed by the union of
several stems, each four or five inches in diameter.   Seeds
from this tree were sent to Paris, and produced the common
Musk Rose.   It seems therefore possible and probable, that

this has been the parent of nearly all their garden roses; for, like most orientals, their habits are not, and have not been enterprising enough, to stimulate them to import roses from distant countries. Large and very old plants of the Musk Rose may sometimes be seen in the gardens of old English and American country houses.

A silly error is made by some writers who have supposed that the Musk Rose belonged to the Noisette family, but had been separated from it on account of its peculiar odor, whereas this is a distinct species of rose, and the first Noisette variety was a hybrid raised from this.

The *Blush Musk*, or *Fraser's pink Musk*, or *Rosa Fraserii*, is not a pure Musk Rose, but a hybrid of the Noisette class, which was raised at Charleston, S. C., about the same time as the Champney and Noisette Roses, and was carried thence to England by Mr. John Fraser; it is of a blush color, and quite fragrant; its flowers are semi-double, in large clusters, but it has now been cast aside. *Eliza Werry* is an expanded flower, quite fragrant, nankin color, changing to white, and suitable for climbing. *Eponine* is a pure white, fragrant and very double variety, one of the prettiest of the group. The *Fringed Musk* Rose has the end of each petal indented: this is a vigorous-growing and very fragrant little rose. *Herbemont's Cluster* originated by the late N. Herbemont, Esq., of Columbia, S. C., is blush color, of expanded form, and produced in large clusters. *Madame Plantier* is a very fine new variety, with pure white fragrant flowers. *Ophir* is a fragrant rose, yellowish white, and suitable for a pillar or wall. *Princess of Nassau* is a distinct and good variety, very fragrant, and blooming in large clusters; the flower-buds, before they open, are nearly yellow, changing to cream color as they expand. The *Ranunculus*, or *Superb New White Musk*, is merely an improved variety of the old or original Musk

Rose, with flowers more double. *Rivers' Musk* is a fine fragrant variety, originated by Mr. T. Rivers, of a pink color tinged with buff. *Tea-scented* is a hybrid, with large flowers of a pure white, and very pretty; this is apparently a seedling from the Musk Rose, fertilized with some variety of the Tea-scented Rose, as it has a most peculiar habit and perfume.

Moschata Nivea, or the " *Snow Bush,*" and one or two other roses from Nepaul, have the scent peculiar to this group; but as they bloom but once in the summer, and differ totally in some other respects from the true Rosa moschata, I have not included them. For the culture of the roses of this division, that recommended for Noisette roses, in beds and as standards, may be adopted, as their habits are very similar.

THE MACARTNEY ROSE.

Rosa bracteata.

THE single Macartney Rose was brought to Europe from China, in 1795, by Lord Macartney, on his return from his embassy to that country. It now forms the original of a pretty family; but as it has not produced seed freely, even in France, fine varieties, as yet, are not numerous; its strictly evergreen and shining foliage is a beautiful feature; and I hope ere long to see numerous varieties, with double flowers of the same brilliant hues as our other fine roses possess. It is perhaps not too much to anticipate, that, ultimately, we shall not be satisfied unless *all* our roses, even the Moss roses, have evergreen foliage, brilliant and fragrant flowers, and the habit of blooming from June till November. This seems to be an extravagant an-ticipation; but perseverance in gardening will yet achieve

wonders. The old *Double White* was the first double variety raised from seed. The growth is vigorous and the
foliage beautiful ; in this latitude the flowers are very apt
to drop off before expansion, but at the south, we believe,
such is not the case.

The *Double Blush*, or *Victoire Modeste*, is so much hybridized with the Tea-scented rose, that it has lost most of
the characteristics of the group, and has in consequence
been placed with the Tea Roses ; it is a most beautiful
rose. *Grandiflora* is a large single white flowering variety. *Lucida duplex*, or *Semi-double White*, is a fine free
bloomer, with beautiful white flowers, of globular form,
and semi-double. *Maria Leonida* is now an established
favorite ; its fine bell-shaped flowers of the purest white
sometimes slightly tinged with pink towards their centre,
and its bright red anthers peeping from among its central
petals, give to it an elegant and pleasing character. *Rosa
Hardii*, or *Rosa Berberifolia Hardii*, is a most interesting
rose, lately raised from seed, by Monsieur Hardy, of the
Luxembourg Gardens, from Rosa involucrata, a variety
of Rosa bracteata, fertilized with the unique Rosa berberifolia, or Single Yellow Persian rose. This curious
hybrid, like its Persian parent, has single yellow flowers
with a dark eye (much like Cistus formosus,) and evergreen foliage ; it seems quite hardy, and forms the very
prettiest little bush possible. It will probably be the parent of an entirely new group ; and what can be imagined
more interesting in roses than varieties with double yellow
flowers and evergreen foliage.

Scarlet Maria Leonida is a new variety originated by
Mr. Rivers, with bright red flowers. Macartney Roses
sometimes suffer when exposed to severe frost in the open
borders of the flower garden : they will therefore require
the same protection as recommended for the Noisette roses

in cold situations. *Maria Leonida* is a fine border rose, for, by pegging down its shoots as they are produced in summer, a few plants soon cover a bed, or clump, with a dense mass of foliage and flowers, ornamenting the flower-garden from three to four months in summer and autumn : it also forms a very fine standard.

It requires the burning sun of Italy, and of our own Country, to make these Roses produce seed, and we shall soon be able to boast of new American varieties.   To raise a double variety of Rosa Hardii is, at any rate, worth attempting.   A wall should be used to train the plants to ; and in small gardens, where there is not such a convenience, a hollow wall might be built, about six feet in height and ten or twelve feet long.   *Rosa Hardii* would bloom freely if trained to a south wall ; and, if fertilized with the Double Yellow Briar, seed may perhaps be obtained.   Lucida with the Yellow China Rose, will also be an experiment worth trying.   Maria Leonida, fertilized with the Tuscany Rose, might also give some curious hybrids.   This is all speculative ; but such speculations are, unlike many others, exceedingly innocent and interesting.

THE CHINESE SMALL LEAVED ROSE.

Rosa microphylla.

Rosa microphylla rubra, from which we have derived all our varieties of this pretty family, was introduced from the East in 1823.   It is somewhat allied to the Macartney, but apparently a distinct species.   The original imported plant bearing double flowers was undoubtedly an improved garden variety.   Mr. Rivers says he received seed from

Italy of this rose, and finds that plants from it, to use a florist's term, sport amazingly, no two appearing alike.

From Italian seed we have *Alba odorata,* a vigorous growing variety, partaking as much of the Macartney in its habit as of Rosa microphylla ; in fact, it is a complete hybrid, and a very good evergreen rose, producing an abundance of pale sulphur, or rather cream-colored flowers : these are sweet-scented, but do not in general open freely at the north. *Carnea,* or *Rosea Plena,* is a pretty and remarkable rose, forming a neat little blush, nearly evergreen; its flowers are double, and of a beautifully cupped shape. This and the old *Microphylla Rubra* bloom as frequently as any of the group. *Coccinea,* as in one or two instances which I have noticed, is named with the florist's license : it is *not* scarlet, but a very pretty double rose, of deep reddish rose-color, with the same neatly shaped flowers as the last.

Cramoisié, Violet Cramoisié, or *Violacea,* is a fine variety, with flowers of a violet crimson hue. *Grandiflora* was originated by Mr. Rivers, and is a very large rose colored variety. *Luxembourg Hybrid* is of rapid growth, and suitable for a pillar or wall, with flowers of a roseate hue. *Purpurea* is of vigorous habit, forming long shoots, suitable for a climber; the flowers are large and purplish crimson. *Rosea* is a single flowering variety, of a bright rose color, which will be useful for obtaining seeds. *Rouge Striée,* or *Rubra variegata,* is a large red flower, the centre partially striped with white. *Triomphe de Macheteaux* is a new French variety of a pale rose color and shaded.

A warm and dry border will suit these varieties admirably, protecting them in winter with some spray, &c., as directed for Noisette roses: but to see these very curious roses bloom in perfection, bud them on short stems of the Dog rose, and treat them exactly as recommended for the Tea-scented Roses; they will then bloom freely, either in pots or in the flower-borders, and form delightful little plants, quite unique in their characters and appearance.

A few of these may be planted against a wall, as recommended for the Macartney Roses; and, possibly Purpurea fertilized with a bright-colored China Rose, as Fabvier, would give some curious varieties. The Single Microphylla, with Athelin or Henri Barbet, would perhaps give some original and beautiful hybrids. Coccinea might also be fertilized with the Tuscany. If any of these roses can be made to produce seed, interesting and curious varieties must be the result.

There is no doubt that China, that ancient and noble empire, which had made the most consummate acquisitions in Floriculture, while Europe was yet laboring under abject barbarism, abounds in splendid varieties of this very unique rose, as well as of the other Chinese species; which the efforts now making to obtain from that country all desirable varieties of trees and plants, will without doubt speedily transfer to our shores. And as our further knowledge of that mighty country attains its development, it may serve to impart instruction to the world in the more refined arts of enlightened civilization; which will constitute a most singular return of favors to that nation, which in its spirit of *pure philanthropy and morality*, made use of *her civilized arts*, Paixham guns and gunpowder, to force the most *demoralizing* and deadly of all poisons down the throats of the inoffensive Chinese.

REARING ROSES FROM SEED.

This interesting mode of producing new varieties appears to have been adopted in China at a very remote period, and there can be little doubt, but they connected with it the artificial methods of impregnation, although these were, until recently, unknown to the less civilized nations of Europe. It is for Americans to improve upon the means adopted by them both, for to our view, the climax of European attainments should be deemed but the starting point for the attainments of American genius. The field is most ample, its path strewed by the Floral Goddess with the most exquisite tributes which her wreath can boast, and the object therefore, can be rendered pleasurable as well as profitable. The interesting art of impregnation can be so diversified as to amuse the fancy in an eminent degree, by planning and carrying into effect, through admixture of the pollen, the most singular combinations ; and the solicitude and attention which will be elicited in watching the progress of the young plants, and their ultimate development in foliage and flowers, are calculated to afford ample gratification to the mind. The many moments which often pass listlessly, might be filled up by the trivial initiatory arrangements, all resulting in the enchanting novelty of new Floral beauties.

It will have been noticed under the heads of the different families of Roses, that very many of those deemed the most desirable acquisitions, and which have served as the basis whence numerous similar varieties have been produced in Europe, were obtained from China, and that the most of them are double flowers. The difficult and dilatory process of producing double varieties of the Rose, as well as of the Camellia, Pæony, Chrysanthemum, &c., had already been applied by the Chinese, and it required only the simplest care to rear double flowering varieties from the seeds of plants which already produced double flowers, and consequently, the production of fine seedling varieties, was rendered one of comparative ease.

Many persons ignorantly suppose that new varieties are produced by proximity of the plants, and that the *existing* plant is effected and varied by such contiguity. Such is never the case under any circumstances, any more in the vegetable kingdom than in the animal one; and no person would be so weak as to allege that a red and a black cow or horses of those colors, by being placed in adjoining stalls, would affect and vary the color and qualities of each other.

New seminal varieties may be produced by planting any two or more distinct roses near to each other, when the pollen will admix in a greater or less degree, and the seeds of those flowers, where this admixture is perfected, will produce seedlings, a portion of which will be hybridized more or less, and will produce varieties intermediate between the parents, or sporting and approximating more fully to one or the other of the parents. The same results may however be effected with more certainty and precision by artificial means. To perfect this operation, the flowers of the plant intended to produce seed, should have the anthers removed the evening or morning before their full expansion with delicate pointed scissors, and in the course of the ensuing day, some pollen should be removed from the flowers of the other plant selected for crossing, with a camel's hair pencil, and applied to the pistils of the flowers whose anthers have been removed. This operation, though a delicate one, is attended with much less difficulty than would be supposed. It should be performed in dry weather, or if rainy, the flowers operated upon should be sheltered from its effects.

To ascertain precisely when the pollen is in a fit state for transmission, a few of the anthers should be gently pressed with the finger and thumb; if the yellow dust adheres to them the operation may be performed; it requires close examination and some practice to know when the flower to be operated upon is in a fit state to receive the pollen; as a general rule, the flowers ought to be in the same state of expansion, or, in other words, about the same age. It is only in cases where it is desirable for the qualities of a particular rose to predominate, that the removal of the anthers of the rose to be fertilized is necessary; thus, if a yellow climbing rose is desired by the union of the Yellow Briar with the Ayrshire, *every anther* should be removed from the latter, so that it may be fertilized solely with the pollen of the former. In some cases, where it is desirable to have the qualities of both parents in an equal degree, the removal of the anthers must not take place; and in an experiment made by Mr. Rivers, it was found that by removing them from the Luxembourg Moss, and fertilizing that rose with a dark variety of Rosa Gallica, the features of the Moss rose were totally lost in its offspring, and they became nearly pure varieties of the former; but if the anthers of the Moss Rose are left untouched, and it is fertilized with Rosa Gallica, interesting hybrids are the result, more or less mossy; this seems to make superfetation very probable; yet Dr. Lindley in " Theory of Horticulture," page 332, "thinks it is not very likely to occur."

By this artificial process of fertilization, the operator may form any combinations his fancy may suggest, and as it is said that pigeons may be bred to a feather, so may flowers, by assiduity and practice, be generated of a particular color, stripe, or formation of the petals.

To exemplify this, we will suppose that a climbing Moss Rose with red or crimson flowers is wished for: the flowers of the Blush Ayrshire, which bears seed abundantly, may be selected, and before expansion the anthers removed; the following morning, or as soon after the operation as these flowers open, they should be fertilized with those of the Luxembourg Moss; if the operation succeed, seed will be matured, from which the probability is, that a climbing rose will be produced with the habit and flowers of the Moss Rose, or at least an approximation to them; and as these hybrids often bear seed freely, by repeating the process with them, the present apparent remote chance of getting a climbing Moss Rose may be brought very near.

I mention the union of the Moss and Ayrshire Rose by way of illustration, and merely to point out to the amateur how extensive and how interesting a field of operations is open in this way. Mr. Rivers mentions the interesting fact, that about seven years since he discovered in a pan of seedling Moss Roses, one of a most peculiar habit, even when so young; this afterwards proved a hybrid rose, partaking much more of the Scotch Rose than of any other, and until the plant arrived at full growth he thought it a Scotch Rose, the seed of which had by accident been mixed with that of the Moss Rose, although he had taken extreme care: but to his surprise it has since proved a perfect hybrid, having the sepals and the fruit of the Provence Rose, with the spiny and dwarf habit of the Scotch Rose; it bears abundance of heps which are all abortive.* The difference in the fruit of the Moss and Provence Roses, and those of the Scotch, is very remarkable, and this it was which drew his particular attention to the plant in question; it was raised from the same seed, and in the same seed-pan, as the Single Crimson Moss Rose; and as this strange hybrid came from a Moss Rose accidentally fertilized, we may expect that art will do much more for us.

The following extract from the Botanical Register for January, 1840, will, I think, go to prove that these expectations are not without foundation :

---

* It is more than probable, that if the flowers of this rose were fertilized with those of the single Moss Rose, they would produce seed from which some curious hybrid moss roses might be expected.

" My principal reason for publishing a figure of this very remarkable plant, Fuchsia Standishii, is because it is a mule between Fuchsia fulgens and Fuchsia globosa, two plants as dissimilar as possible in the same genus. The former, indeed, figured in this work, (Botanical Register,) differs in so many respects from the common species of the genus, especially in having a herbaceous stem and tuberous roots, that it has been supposed impossible that it should be a Fuchsia at all. It now, however, appears, from the fact of its crossing freely with the common Fuchsias, that it produces hybrids, and really does belong to the genus. These hybrids are completely intermediate between the two parents ; in this case having the leaves, flowers, and habit of their mother, Fuchsia globosa, with the hairiness and tenderness of foliage of their father, some of his coloring, and much of his herbaceous character. It is by no means necessary to take Fuchsia globosa for the female parent, as Fuchsia fulgens is found to intermix readily with many other species. That which is now figured is the handsomest I have seen. It was raised by Mr. John Standish, nurseryman, Bagshot, who sent me specimens last July, together with flowers of several others of inferior appearance. He tells me that it is an exceedingly free bloomer, with a stiff erect habit; and I can state, from my personal knowledge, that the plant is very handsome."

Now this is from Dr. Lindley, who may be quoted as a weighty authority ; and this plant is a hybrid between two, one of which, I believe, it was seriously contemplated to place out of the genus Fuchsia, so dissimilar did it appear to any known species of that genus. After this we may hope for mossy roses of every class, combining all hues even yellow and yellow striped, and doubtless even Mossy Perpetual Climbers. We have a commencement, in Mossy Perpetuals and in Mossy Bourbon Roses. A Yellow Ayrshire now deemed so desirable, will not be long hoped for in vain. Who that has witnessed the acquisitions of art during the last twelve years, can doubt that the efforts now so general, for the production of new varieties, will be eminently successful?

In France and Belgium the practice of fertilization has been carried to a great extent, not only with roses, but with various other species of plants.

The heps of all the varieties of roses will in general be fully ripe by October or November, when they should be gathered and kept entire in a flower-pot filled with sand, carefully guarded from mice; in February, or by the first week in March, they must be broken and the seeds sown in flower-pots, such as are generally used for sowing seeds, called "seed-pans," but for rose seeds they should not be too shallow; nine inches in depth will be enough; these should be nearly filled with a rich compost of rotten manure and sandy loam or peat; the seeds may be covered, to the depth of about half an inch, with the same compost; a piece of kiln wire must then be placed over the pot, fitting closely at the rim, so as to prevent the ingress of mice, which are passionately fond of rose seeds; there must be space enough between the wire and the mould for the young plants to come up, an inch will suffice; the pots of seed must never be placed under glass, but kept constantly in the open air, in a full sunny exposure. Water should be given occasionally in dry weather; the young plants will perhaps make their appearance in April or May, but very often the seed does not vegetate till the second spring. When they have made their "rough leaves," that is, when they have three or four leaves exclusive of their seed leaves, they must be carefully raised with the point of a narrow pruning knife, potted into small pots, and placed in the shade: if the weather is very hot and dry, they may be covered with a handglass for a few days. They may remain in those pots a month, and then be planted into a rich border; by the end of August those that are robust growers will have made shoots long enough for budding. Such as have done so may be pruned, and one or two strong stocks budded from each; these will the ensuing summer make vigorous shoots, and the summer following, if left unpruned, they will, to a certainty, produce flowers.

This course serves to multiply a variety which might otherwise be lost, and also insures a vigorous specimen bloom. Seedling roses in our congenial climate and beneath our radiant sky, flourish quite as well, if not more so, than in Italy and the south of France, and they will very generally, especially the Chinese and Tea classes, produce flowers the second year, and all are sure to do so the third year.

PROPAGATION OF SUMMER OR JUNE ROSES.

THERE are four modes of propagation applicable to Summer Roses, viz. by layers, by cuttings, by budding, and by grafting. Layering may be performed in spring, summer, and autumn; the two latter seasons only can be recommended, but if any are forgotten or omitted by accident, the operation in spring will often give success; still, as summer layering is the most legitimate, I shall give directions for that my first notice.

About the middle of July in most seasons the shoots will be found about eighteen inches to two feet in length; from these, for two thirds of their length the leaves should be cut off close to the shoots, beginning at the base, with a very sharp knife; the shoot must then be brought to the ground, so as to be able to judge in what place the hole must be made to receive it; this may be made large enough to hold a quarter of a peck of compost : in heavy and retentive soils this should be rotten dung and pit sand in equal quantities, well mixed ; the shoot must then be "tongued," *i. e.* the knife introduced just below a bud and brought upwards, so as to cut about half way through ; this must be done at the side or back of the shoot, (not by any means at the front or in the bend,) so that the tongue does not close ; to make this certain a small piece of glass or thin earthenware may be introduced to keep it open. Much nicety is required to have the tongue at the upper part of the shoot, so it may not be in the part which forms the bow, as it is of consequence that it should be within two inches of the surface, in order to feel the effects of the atmospheric heat ; unless this is attended to, the roots will not be emitted quickly ; the tongued part must be placed in the centre of the compost, and a crotched peg be used to fasten the layer in its place. In October or November the layers may be taken from the parent plant, and either potted as required, or planted out where they are to remain. Those shoots not long enough in July and August may be layered in October, when the layers are taken from the plant, and, if any are forgotten, February and March will be the most favorable months for the operation, but as a general rule, July is the most proper season.

PROPAGATION BY CUTTINGS.

To procure early cuttings, so as to have plants ready for setting out in June, strong plants must be placed in the forcing-house in December ; these will make vigorous shoots, which, when thoroughly ripe in March, should be made into cuttings about six inches in length ; the leaves must be left on that part of the cutting above the surface.

Supposing the cutting to contain six buds, from three of these the leaves may be removed, or, if they are very large, even four, leaving two buds with the leaves attached. The cuttings may be planted singly in small pots, filled one third with small pieces of broken pots, (or several may be planted in larger pots;) and the remainder with light mound, or peat and sand in equal quantities; the cuttings must then be placed in a gentle hot bed and kept perfectly close, no air should be admitted, by raising the lights in the slightest degree, except for the operation of watering; they must be sprinkled with tepid water every morning and again in the afternoon, but the latter only in bright sunny weather: these operations should be performed as quickly as possible, to prevent their being exposed to the exhausting effects of the open air. They will have made roots in a fortnight or three weeks. When this is ascertained, which can be done by gently turning out a plant, they should be placed in a cold frame and still kept close. After being a week in this situation they may be potted into larger pots. This is a very interesting method of propagation, and the plants made in this manner, form very pretty bushes of compact growth; it is applicable to all roses; even Moss Roses will strike root if treated as above; they require more patience, as they are longer in forming their roots than many, as are also the Provence. Care must be taken that the shoots, before being formed into cuttings, are perfectly ripe: an invariable sign of their maturity is when the terminal bud is formed at the end of the shoot; this shows that they have made their first growth; to hasten this, the plants should be placed in the most sunny situation, so as to mature their shoots as early as possible.

Cuttings of Hybrid China Roses, Hybrid Bourbons, and of all the climbing roses, may be raised with facility by planting them in a shady border in September. They may be made about ten inches in length, two thirds of which should be planted in the soil : in fact, they can scarcely be planted too deep : one, or at the most two buds above the surface will be enough ; on these buds the leaves must be left untouched. These will be fit for planting out the following autumn.

PROPAGATION BY BUDDING.

This seems at present, owing to the strong wish manifested by the present generation to do every thing quickly, to be the favorite mode of propagation. A summer rose from a cutting, requires at least two seasons to form a large flourishing plant. A layer is occasionally very capricious, and very loth to make roots ; indeed, of some varieties, particularly of Rosa alba, they will not by any means be induced to form roots when layered, and are very difficult even to be propagated by cuttings from the forcing-house ; but these become perfectly docile and manageable when budded, and in one season only, form large and handsome plants. The operation of budding is difficult to describe. A longitudinal cut, not so deep as to cut into the wood, but merely cut through the bark, should be made in the clear part of the shoot; thus $\top$, making the diagonal cut at the top of the incision. I differ from most of those who have given directions for budding, as they make the incision thus, $\mathbf{T}$: my practice has arisen from the frequent inconvenience sustained by shoots from standard stocks being broken off by the wind, when the cut is made at right angles : with the diagonal incision such accident rarely happens; the bark on both sides this incision must be opened with the flat handle peculiar to the budding knife, and the bud inserted ; the slice of bark taken off the shoot with the bud in the centre should not be more than an inch in length ; but half an inch is enough, the incision being made of the same length ; this is the length used by experienced budders, who pride themselves upon performing the operation in the neatest manner possible. When the bud is inserted, cut off with your knife (which should be very sharp) a piece from the upper part of the plate, *i. e.* the piece of bark with the bud attached, so that it fits closely to the diagonal cut at the top ; then bind it up firmly with cotton twist, such as the tallow-chandlers use for the wicks of candles; the finest quality is best ; this is the most eligible binding known, and far preferable to matting or worsted. Many writers recommended the wood to be left in the plate ; in cases where the bud is unripe this may be very well ; but, as a general rule, always remove it. Take buds that are mature, and by placing the thumb nail at the top of the plate, peel cleanly the wood from the bark : if a remnant of wood is left on or near the eye of the bud, let it remain, it will do no harm ; but if attempted to be removed, the eye is liable to be bruised and injured. Budding may be commenced in June, and performed as late as the second week in September ; if done in June the only shoots fit to take buds from, are those that have shed their bloom : on these alone the buds are mature. I have occasionly known them to succeed in October. After August it is at the best uncertain, as the success of the operation entirely depends upon the state of the weather. In taking the wood from the bark, it will seem occasionally as if the eye or root of the bud is dragged out ; it will then appear hollow : this only appears so, and is not of the least consequence, at least with roses, as those apparently hollow buds take as readily as those with the eye prominent.

PROPAGATION BY GRAFTING.

THIS may be performed in the forcing-house in January, and in the open air in February and March. There are many modes of grafting; those most eligible for roses are the common " whip grafting," using clay as a covering, and " cleft grafting," using wax or pitch : the former is generally the most successful ; and if the stocks are potted a year before being used, strong blooming plants of the perpetual roses may be made in three months.

A neighboring amateur has been very fortunate in grafting roses, merely gathering his stocks from the hedges in January and February, and immediately grafting and potting them after the operation ; in doing so covering the union of the graft firmly with mould, using no clay, so as to leave only three or four buds above the surface, and placing them in a gentle hot-bed, in a common garden frame, keeping them very close. In this simple method of operating I have seen eighteen or twenty grafts grow, but owing to the stocks not being established in pots a year as they ought to have been, these plants have not made strong and luxuriant shoots the first season. Stocks many be potted in October if none can be had established in pots ; these may be used in January or February with much success.

In whip grafting of roses in pots it will be as well to omit the usual tongue by which in open air the graft is, as it were, hung on the stock ; this tonguing weakens rose-grafts too much ; as their shoots are generally pithy, a slice of bark with a *very small* portion of wood about 1½ inch in length, taken from one side of the stock where the bark is clear and free from knots, is all that is required ; then take part of a shoot about seven inches in length, and pare its lower end down quite thin till it fits accurately on the place in length and breadth, from which the slice of bark and wood from the stock was taken ; bind it firmly with strong bass, which has been soaked in water, and then place clay over it, so as to leave no crack for the admission of air : presuming this graft to be in a pot, it may be plunged in sawdust or old tan, leaving two buds of the graft above the surface in a gentle hot bed, and kept close till it has put forth its shoots : when these are three inches in length, air may be admitted gradually by propping up the light ; if perpetual roses, they may shortly be removed to the greenhouse, where they will bloom in great perfection in early spring. After this first bloom their shoots should be shortened, and if required they may be planted in the open borders, where they will flower again and again during the summer ; if summer roses they will flower but once, but they will make strong shoots and establish themselves for another season ; if a forcing-house is used instead of a hot-bed frame, they must be plunged in the same materials, as this keeps the clay moist, and generally insures success ; if convenient, grafting wax, made as follows, may be used in lieu of clay : 1 lb. Burgundy pitch, $\frac{1}{4}$ lb. common pitch, 2 oz. bees'wax, and $\frac{1}{2}$ oz . mutton fat, melted, and put on with a brush while warm : in cleft grafting, for a description of which I must refer to Loudon's Encyclopædia of Gardening, article " grafting." Grafting pitch must alone be used if the grafts are small ; this is a very nice mode, but difficult to describe, and the same result may be obtained by rind-grafting,* a very neat method : before this operation the stocks must be placed in the forcing-house for a few days till the bark will run, i. e.

---

* The best stocks for this kind of grafting, are the Blush Boursault and Rosa Menetti ; the latter was obtained a few years since from Italy.

part readily from the wood; the top of the stock must then
be cut off cleanly, and without the least slope; an incision,
as in budding, must then be made through the bark from
the crown of the stock downwards, about one inch in length,
which can be opened with the haft of a budding-knife;
directly opposite to this incision a bud should be left if one
can be found on the stem of the stock, the graft must then
be cut flat on one side, as for whip-grafting, and inserted
between the bark and wood, bound with bass, and covered
with grafting wax.   In March this may be done with young
shoots of the current season from the forcing-house; they
must be mature; as a rule, take only bloom shoots that
have just shed their flowers—these are always ripe.   To
those who love roses, I know no gardening operation of
more interest than that of grafting roses in pots in winter;
blooming plants of the perpetual roses are made so quickly, and they are so constantly under observation; but for
this a small forcing-house is of course necessary; a house
twelve feet by eight feet, with an eighteen inch Arnott's
stove, will do all that is necessary; and the expense of a
structure of these dimensions is very moderate.   What can
be done in the way of propagation in so small a house with
method is quite astonishing; a hot-bed frame will give the
same results, but the plants cannot be viewed in bad weather with equal facility; that interest attached to watching closely every shoot as it pushes forth to bud and bloom
in all its gay attire is lost.   To the mind happily constitu-
ted, this is a calm and untiring pleasure; the bud breaking
through its brown wintry covering into verdant leaves, replete with the delicate tints so peculiar to early spring, and
unchecked by cold and withering blasts, makes us feel ver-
nal pleasures, even in January; and then the peeping
flower-buds perhaps of some rare and as yet unseen variety, add to these still calm pleasures, felt only by those who

really love plants and flowers, and all the lovely creations
of nature.

PROPAGATION OF AUTUMNAL ROSES.

As with the Summer Roses, these may be propagated by
layers, budding, grafting, and by cuttings ; the latter mode
is the only one requiring especial notice, as the other
methods applied to Summer Roses are of equal use in
propagating these. All the families of this division are
propagated with great facility by cuttings ; in fact, with
China, Bourbon, and Tea Roses, it is the only eligible way
of getting plants on their own roots. There are three
seasons when this operation may be performed with success, in spring, summer and autumn.

For spring cuttings, it will be necessary to resort to the
forcing house in the month of March, when those roses that
were commenced to be forced in January, will be just
shedding their first crop of flowers ; these blooming shoots
will then be ripe, and as a general rule, fit for immediate
propagation, either for cuttings or buds. It must be borne
in mind, that no shoots are mature until their blooming is
past.

The cuttings may be made with three joints or buds,
from the lower end of which the leaf should be cut, leaving the others untouched ; the cutting must then be inserted about one inch into a very small pot of light mould, or
peat and sand, equal parts : with rare sorts two buds will
do, or even one ; in the latter case, the bud must have the
leaf attached, and a small portion of wood below the bud ;
it must be inserted in the pot so that the bud is slightly
covered with the mould. The pots should then be plunged

in sawdust or old tan, within a gentle hot-bed, and kept perfectly close, sprinkled with tepid water every morning, and
shaded from the sun.   In about a fortnight they will have
taken root, but they must not be removed from this close
frame till they have made a shoot from one to two inches
in length.   They are then safe, and may be removed into
another frame, still with gentle heat, and having air every
day to harden them.   In a week they will be fit to pot into
larger pots, and they may then be removed into the greenhouse or cold frame as convenient, till required for planting
out in the borders in April and May : the pots used for the
above purpose are *very small*, $2\frac{1}{2}$ inches deep and $1\frac{1}{2}$ inch
over at the top ; if more convenient, three or five cuttings
may be placed *round the side* of a larger sized pot, $3\frac{1}{2}$
inches deep by 3 inches over.   This method saves some
trouble, but the plants are apt to be checked when potted
off; pots of the latter size must be filled one third with
broken pieces of pots, on which the base of the cuttings
should rest; the small pots require no drainage.

For summer cuttings in June and July, ripe shoots may
be taken as above directed, planted in pots, and placed in
a cold frame, kept close, and sprinkled every morning.
These will root slowly, but surely ; for autumnal cuttings
any convenient and spare shoots may be made into cuttings,
and planted under a hand-glass in a warm exposure, about
the middle or end of September : these must have air in
mild humid weather during the winter, and be gradually
exposed to the air in April by tilting the light : by the end
of April they will be fit for potting.   All the autumnal
roses will grow readily if the above methods are followed.
The Damask Perpetuals only are slow in rooting, and are
propagated with more difficulty.

BUDDING ROSES IN POTS.

THE Blush Boursault and the Manetti, make the best stocks for budding on. My practice in budding on them is as follows :—The strongest shoots are selected early in July for layering ; flower pots of the two quart size are taken, and the aperture at the bottom is enlarged, so as to allow the end of the shoot to be passed through. After doing this the shoot is tongued ; the pot is drawn up till the tongue is about in the centre ; it is then filled with a mixture of rotton dung and sand in equal parts, and well pressed down. The shoot may be budded at the time of layering or afterwards, according as the buds are ready. *The shoots should be headed down at the time of budding* to within two eyes of where the bud is inserted.* The buds of all the Bourbon, Tea-scented, China, and Hybrid Autumnal Roses, will push immediately. These may be removed from the stools in August, potted in larger pots, and forced with great success the following spring.

DIRECTIONS FOR FORCING ROSES.

VERY few years ago forced roses were among the luxuries of gardening, and the matter was looked upon as a difficult operation in which accomplished gardeners only were successful ; but with modern varieties the difficulty has vanished, and every one may have roses, at least in February, with the most simple means.

---

* This heading down at the time of budding, although commonly practised, cannot be generally recommended. If applied to the Dog Rose when budded early in June, small heads will at once be formed, but the constitution of the plant will be much weakened.

A pit 10 or 12 feet long and 8 feet wide, just high enough to stand upright in, with a door at one end, and sunken path in the centre, a raised bed on each side of the path, and an 18-inch Arnott's stove at the further end, opposite to the door, with a pipe leading into a small brick chimney *outside*, (a chimney is indispensable,) will give great abundance of forced roses from February to the end of May. To insure this a supply must be kept ready ; so that, say twenty, may be placed in the forcing-pit about the middle of December, a like number in the middle of January, and the same about the middle of February ; they must not be pruned until taken into the house, when each shoot should be cut back to two or three buds or eyes, the latter for the strong shoots. The fire should be lighted at seven in the morning, and suffered to burn out about the same hour in the evening, unless in frosty weather, when it must be kept burning till late at night, so as to exclude the frost ; and for this purpose double mats should be placed on the lights. The thermometer should not, by *fire heat*, be higher in the day than 70° during December, January, and February ; at night it may sink to 35° without injury. The temporary rise in a sunny day is of no consequence, but *no air must be admitted at such times, or the plants will exhaust themselves, and immediately shed their leaves.* When the sun begins to have power, and in sunny weather in February, the plants may be syringed every morning about 9 o'clock with tepid water, and smoked with tobacco at night on the least appearance of the aphis or green-fly.

To insure a fine and full crop of flowers, the plants should be established one year in pots, and plunged in tan or sawdust in an open exposed place, so that their shoots are well ripened : the pots must be often removed, or what is better, place the pots on slates to prevent their roots striking into the ground ; but with the Hybrid and Damask Perpetuals, even if not potted in November previous, a very good crop of flowers may often be obtained, and a second crop better than the first; for the great advantage of forcing perpetual roses is, that after blooming in the greenhouse or drawing-room, their young shoots may be cut down to within two or three buds of their base, and the plants placed again in the forcing-house, and a second crop of flowers obtained. The same mode may be followed also with the Bourbon, China, and Tea-scented Roses; with the latter, indeed, a third crop may be often obtained.

Towards the end of March, when the second crop of flowers is coming on, the plants may be gradually inured to the air, by opening the sashes in mild weather. This will make them hardy and robust. Syringing should be practised every morning and evening; but when the flower buds are ready to open this must be confined to the stems of the plants and the pots, otherwise the flowers will be injured by the moisture; air must at first only be given about 12 in the day; care must be taken to remove the plants from the forcing-house to the green-house or drawing-room before their blossoms expand; they may then be kept in beauty many days. I have not found the check which the plants receive by this sudden change of temperature at all detrimental. During their second growth the plants should be watered once a week with manured water,* and the surface of the pot occasionally stirred. Those that are forced with the greatest facility are worked roses: these seldom or never fail to give an abundant crop of flowers; stems form 6 inches to $1\frac{1}{2}$ and 2 feet, are equally eligible; the latter form elegant plants, and I think generally grow with greater luxuriance than dwarfs. China and Tea-

---

* Two pounds of guano to ten gallons of water forms the very best species of liquid manure: this should be stirred before it is used.

scented Roses on their own roots are more delicate, and require more care; still one crop of flowers may always be depended upon, even from them. Instead of forcing them for a second crop, it will be better to place them in the greenhouse; they will then bloom again finely in May. I find, from experience, that all the autumnal roses may be forced every year without any disadvantage: to insure their well doing, they must be removed from the forcing-house early in June, the surface of the pots dressed with rotten manure, and plunged in the same, or leaves, or any light substance. Towards the end of September they should be carefully shifted, removing nearly all the earth from their roots, into a compost of light loam and rotten dung, equal quantities, (this is, on the whole, the very best compost for potted roses,) watered, and again plunged till required for forcing: this shifting would be better performed in June, but as the weather is then often hot and dry, roses worked on the Dog Rose are apt to suffer. Pots of the sizes called by the English 24's and 16's,* are the best sizes for strong plants of roses for forcing: when potted, the large and unyielding roots should be cut off close, so that the plants may stand in the centre of the pots, the fibrous and small roots merely tipped.

The treatment recommended for roses in a pit with Arnott's stove may be pursued with roses in a house with smoke-flues or hot-water pipes. Arnott's stove is recommended as an economical and eligible mode of heating, practised here to some extent with success for several years: on these stoves an iron pan, fitted to the top, should always

---

* The respective sizes of these pots are, 24's, 7¼ inches deep, and 8 inches over, measuring across the top of the pot; 16's, 8¼ inches deep, 9 inches in diameter.

be kept full of water. Roses may be forced slowly, but with perhaps greater certainty, by the uninitiated, by giving air freely and constantly in mild weather during the day, keeping the fire constantly burning during the same period as recommended when keeping them closely shut up.

CULTIVATION OF ROSES IN POTS FOR THE GREENHOUSE.

For this purpose a selection should be made of some of the finer varieties of China and Tea-scented Roses on their own roots ; it may also include such Bourbons as the Queen, Acidalie, Crimson Globe, Grand Capitaine, Madame Nerard, Madame Margat, Proserpine and Phœnix, and Noisette's Miss Glegg, Lelieur, Ne Plus Ultra, Victorieuse, and other choice and more rare varieties. Those I have named are all of dwarfish and compact habit, and free bloomers. Presuming these roses to be procured in the spring or summer, in the usual small pots they are generally grown in by the cultivators for sale, they should be immediately potted into pots called 32's, (these are generally 7 inches deep, by 6 over at the surface,) in a compost of turfy sandy loam and well-rotted manure, equal quantities, or leaf-mould ; if the latter is used, two-thirds to one-third of loam will be as well ; this compost must not be sifted, but merely chopped into pieces as large as a walnut : the fine mould, which will, as a matter of course, result from this chopping, must not be separated from the pieces of turf, but all must be well mixed with the manure or leaf-mould. The pots should then be filled about one-third with broken pieces of crockery or potsherds, the plants taken from the small pots, and the balls of earth gently pressed so as to loosen them ; place each plant in the centre of the large pot; press the earth well round them ; give a soaking of water, and plunge them in the sawdust or tan in some sunny exposed place where they may have all the sun our fine climate will give them.   They may remain here till early in October, when they should be removed into the greenhouse, but a fortnight before taking them into their winter quarters, lift every pot, and place it on the surface of the bed in which they have been plunged : their roots then become hardened, and bear the dry warm air of the greenhouse without injury : they should at this time also be pruned into any handsome desirable shape, (a compact bush is perhaps the prettiest,) or, if tall plants are required, the long shoots may be fastened to a neat painted stick. Roses thus treated will come into bloom in the greenhouse in April, and continue one of its brightest ornaments till the beginning of June; they should then be repotted into larger pots if large plants are wished for, and again plunged in the open air till the autumn : care must be taken to place the pots on slates, to prevent their roots getting through the bottoms of the pots.   If compact and pretty little plants are required the same pots may be used, merely reducing the roots, so that the pot will hold a small quantity of compost for the plant to feed upon.   A most excellent compost for potted roses may be made as follows :—Pare some turf from a loamy pasture ; the parings must not be more than one inch in thickness ; bake them in an oven about twelve hours when the temperature is equal to that just after it has been used for baking bread ; they must not be burned :* this, chopped as before directed, with equal

---

* Some persons have used, with much success, turf roasted on a sheet of iron (placed in temporary brickwork) under which a moderate fire has been kept: about one hour's roasting is sufficient. This chars the turfy side, and acts most beneficially.

parts of rotten manure, forms one of the very finest of composts. The plants must be looked to carefully in spring, and whenever infested by the aphis, or green-fly, tobacco-smoke must be applied : extraordinary luxuriance of growth may be given by watering them once a week with guano-water.

A season may be saved in the growth of these roses if plants in larger pots than those they are usually sold in are purchased : if these are procured in the autumn or winter, they may be placed in the greenhouse at once with a certainty of succeeding.

CULTURE OF HARDY ROSES IN POTS FOR EXHIBITION.

THE most elegant pot roses for exhibition may be selected from those families recommended for greenhouse culture ; but as it is now the fashion for Horticultural Societies to offer prizes for " roses in pots," it becomes my duty to offer a few observations on growing hardy varieties of roses in pots so as to form very large plants. I must here caution the reader, that occasional disappointment must be expected in growing them in pots for exhibition, as roses, like facts, are stubborn things, and will often, in summer, bloom just whenever it pleases them to do so, not being easily retarded or forced. Those roses recommended for green-house culture, from their producing a succession of bloom, must be most relied upon by the exhibitor; but if by a lucky chance a collection of moss roses, or some of the finer kinds of French and Hybrid Bourbon roses, could be enticed to show themselves in all their gay attire on *the* day, they would make the greenhouse roses " hide their diminished heads."

To form a collection of hardy roses in pots, the very best should be selected from the following families : Moss, Provence, Hybrid Provence, French, Damask, Rosa alba, Perpetual, and Hybrid Perpetual. Some good lists have been given in the *Gardener's Chronicle ;* but they contain too many varieties with flaccid petals, which will not bear removal when in bloom. As regards hardy pot roses, except Moss Roses, of which the choice is limited, only those with very double flowers, and stiff, waxy petals, should be selected.

To enable amateurs to make judicious selections, I have attached an S. to a considerable number of varieties of the different classes in my Catalogue, where they possess the requisite qualities in an eminent degree. Those so designated have flowers very double, with thick petals, and not liable to fade quickly. It is better to pot two, three, or four of any good variety, rather than to have a greater variety of second-rate flowers. Mr. T. Rivers gives the following directions, which are highly appropriate.

About the end of October worked plants should be selected on very straight stems, not more than from six to eight inches in height. *Care must be taken that their roots are so formed that each plant may be placed in the centre of the pot :* unless this is strictly attended to, they will make but a poor appearance. If any of the large roots interfere with the position of the plant in the pot, they may be much shortened, merely tipping the small roots and fibres.

Stems from six to eight inches may be taken generally as the most eligible height ; but, to form plants for the back row, varieties of the following families may be on stems one foot to eighteen inches ; they will increase the effect ; viz. Hybrid China, Hybrid Bourbon, and Hybrid

Perpetuals. Many of these will form, when in full bloom, fine pendulous heads. When plants of the above description have been selected, they may be potted in a compost of nice turfy loam and rotten dung, equal parts ; the loam should, if possible, be more rich and adhesive than that recommended for the plants under greenhouse culture ; the pots used should be sixteens, and, if some of the plants are very strong, even a size larger, called twelves, may be used ; these should then be plunged, in the open air on the surface of the soil, in sawdust, rotten leaves, or old tan, which should be four inches deep on the surface of the mould in the pots, care being taken to place the bottom of each pot on a slate, for reasons before given. I recommend the pots to be placed on the surface, rather than to be plunged in the soil, as they then receive the full influence of the sun to their roots. Towards the end of February each plant must be pruned to within six or eight buds of the base of the strong shoots, and to within two or three buds of those that are more weak : it will be as well, however, if the plants have very long shoots, to shorten these one third at the time of potting, as this prevents their being racked by the high winds of November, as before stated in this work. Autumnal pruning will tend to give an earlier bloom ; therefore, one half of the plants may be finally pruned when potted, if this is the object sought for ; the remainder in March, or even late as April ; indeed, this will give the exhibitor a chance of having *some* plants ready on the important day. In May, if the weather is hot and dry, the plants, although plunged and apparently moist, will require water daily ; and once a week a regular soaking with guano-water will insure a most vigorous growth, and defy all attacks of the aphis or any other little pest, the grub excepted, which must be carefully sought for in all those young leaves on the flower stems which appear glued together.

The plants will require shifting annually; in general, pots of the same size will do, shaking all the mould clean from their roots, and giving them a fresh and rich compost. The middle or end of October is the best period for this annual shifting. I have before said it is most difficult to retard or force into bloom roses grown in pots in the open air; however, a removal into the greenhouse for a week or ten days, to force them if required, may be tried; or to retard them, the method employed by the courtier, in the days of Elizabeth, to save his cherries for his queen, may be essayed, viz. stretch a piece of canvass on hoops over the plants, and keep it constantly wet, by sprinkling it with water.

PLANTING AND GENERAL CULTURE OF THE ROSE, IN THE OPEN GARDEN.

October, November and December are so well known to be favorable months for planting the Summer, or June, blooming Roses, that it is thought by many amateurs no others are or can be so eligible, and when applied to dry sandy soils this idea is quite correct; but on wet retentive soils, January and February, at the South, and March and April at the North, are quite preferable. In light soils a mixture of well rotted manure, and rich stiff loam from an old pasture, giving to each plant if a standard, a wheelbarrow full, or if a dwarf about half that quantity, will be found the best compost; if the soil is stiff, half a wheelbarrow full of manure mixed with the natural soil will be quite sufficient. The Damask and Hybrid Perpetuals should be treated in the same manner as the preceding roses, and the most hardy varieties of the Bourbons, of which there are now a very large number, and which are uninjured by the severest winters, require the same treatment. Among these are Madame Desprez, Madame Newmann, Crimson Globe, Bouquet de Flore, Triomph de Plantier, and numerous others.

The other Autumnal Roses which are more tender, comprising the Chinese Everblooming, Tea-scented, Noisette, Fairy, Musk, Microphylla, Macartney, and also the Multiflora should be planted in the spring at as early a period as the ground becomes free from frost and settled. If transplanted in autumn in a severe climate, they are very apt to be injured by the winter, as the roots have no hold upon the soil; but when planted in the spring their roots take a strong hold of the soil and they become well established during the growing season and are thereby enabled to sustain a far greater degree of cold. The Banksian Roses form the only class that can, in this latitude, be justly denominated *Tender Roses*, and they consequently require not only to be transplanted in the spring, but that they have additional protection by being placed against a wall, or in some other sheltered location, and bound in straw or matting during the winter. If equally convenient, and the plants not over large, they can be taken up and planted in a cellar or conservatory for the winter. Some varieties of the Macartney Rose are rather tender, but the usual covering of straw, leaves, or earth, will protect them amply. A nondescript variety of rose, raised by me from seed, which I presume must have been received from Asia, is the only other rose that has proved tender. It is a peculiar plant with small delicate foliage, and has not yet flowered. After sending it to several European correspondents, I received it back from Messrs. Loddiges & Sons, of London, under the name of *Microphylla striata*, but it does not belong to that family, and appears to be a perfectly distinct species. As so many inquiries are made as to the hardihood or tenderness of roses, I am thus particular on this point, and I have in every case, where any varieties are partially tender, stated the fact and recommended the requisite precautions.

In the planting of roses, the first point to be attended to, is, the proper preparation of the soil, and on this head I have already given specific directions, applicable to several classes, in the preceding part of the present work, and a few passing words here, will suffice as a general rule. Where the soil is not already rich, it will require to be deeply dug and mellowed, and a plentiful supply of well rotted manure, or wood soil from beneath the leaves of a forest, (half of each would be preferable,) must be incorporated and well mixed therewith. If the soil is wet or very heavy a proportionate addition of sand should be made, sufficient to render it light and porous. Particular care is requisite to have the holes made sufficiently large, so that the roots may not be at all cramped, and after the plant is placed in position, the earth first thrown in should be well pressed on the roots, but that near the surface should be left in a loose and porous state, so as to admit the rains, and the occasional waterings which should be given to them repeatedly for ten or fifteen days after planting. It is indispensable that the ground between the plants be kept free from weeds, and in a mellow state at its surface. In order, however, to intercept the sun's rays immediately around the naked stems of the Tree Roses, and to cause the earth to retain that moisture which their roots seem to require in a very considerable degree, I have found that the Parisians often cultivate strawberries among them, and I would suggest that little circles of Alpine Strawberries, or of neat annual or perennial flowers, be planted around each Rose Tree,

thus combining additional beauties with the benefits otherwise derived from them.

The autumnal dressings of the ground and requisite manuring have been already referred to, and I will only add
here, that whereever it is inconvenient to use ordinary manure, the liquid preparation of guano will answer every
purpose, and where this cannot be had, liquid manure can
be obtained from the barn-yard, or by filling a cask half
full of manure, and then pouring water thereon, and allowing it to remain a few days previous to drawing it off
for use. One other remark may not be without benefit,
and that is, that you can scarcely manure a rose too highly,
for no tree or plant will sustain advantageously a greater
degree of manuring than the rose.

In regard to pruning, the most requisite point will be to
cut from the body or roots of the budded roses all shoots
that may appear, and very many persons by neglect in
this particular, allow their standard roses to be destroyed.
The summer pruning of the Perpetual classes, for the purpose of strengthening the autumnal bloom has been already
discussed, and in regard to other prunings of the various
classes, they should consist in simply cutting away, from
time to time, such old or useless branches as an intelligent
observer may deem necessary to advance the general appearance or vigor of the plants : the autumn is the preferable season for such prunings, but they may be applied at
all periods without any injurious results.

It is with regret I have here to acknowledge that even
the Rose has its enemies, and as with others of the fairest
objects of creation, these enemies, although of the most con-
temptible description, are nevertheless extremely pernicious, until their efforts are thwarted. In my grounds,
happily I am not troubled with their depredations, but I
will tender some advice to those who are. The *Green Fly*

is the most common, but it is readily destroyed by syringing the plants at evening with tobacco water. Its depredations are most frequent in confined city gardens, or where the plants are shaded, or have not the benefit of free air and full sun, and also on plants in pots that are illy attended. In open locations the birds feed not only on these, but on almost every class of insects, and their presence should be encouraged in every garden, as the little innocents, in addition to gladdening us with their notes, render us most efficient aid in our garden labors. The *Slug* is much complained of in New-England, but I do not remember to have ever seen any here. Mr. D. Haggerston, a very intelligent gardener, has brought forward this remedy : take two pounds of whale oil soap and dissolve it in fifteen gallons of water, and apply it every evening with a syringe until the slugs are destroyed. In this case, as in every other of these syringings of insects, a purifying application of water must be made the ensuing morning by the same process. The *Rose bug* is another depredator, and often attacks the flowers as soon as they expand ; they are usually removed by hand, but no doubt proper syringing would extirpate them. The young vigorous shoots are sometimes injured in July and August by an insect that deposits its egg in them near the base, which becoming a grub, destroys the pith and causes the top of the shoot to fade and fall ; on seeing which, prune off the shoot some inches below the part injured, and destroy the worm. *Mildew* occasionally attacks plants under peculiar circumstances, but this is speedily eradicated by syringing them with sulphur water prepared in the ordinary way.

As regards position and distances at which roses are to be placed, that is so much a matter of taste, that every amateur prefers to decide the point for himself. They should not, however, be planted too close, as that will deprive them of sufficient space for their full development, and as a gene-ral rule, Tree Roses should not be planted nearer than four to five feet, and those on their own roots not nearer than three feet. Climbing Roses will of course form an excep-tion, and the greater space allowed them, the more ample will be their expansion, and the more brilliant the display of their beauteous flowers. In the study of position, too much formality should be carefully avoided.

In the formation of an admirable ROSARY the ground should be selected judiciously, and should comprise a suffi-cient space for a full display of the number of plants of which it is to be composed. Be this 50 or 500 feet in ex-tent, its effect will mainly depend upon the arrangement of the plants. Mere formal rows present few attractions, and the grouping process constitutes the only highly effec-tive arrangement. The ground plot having been selected, proceed to work out thereon in circles and other forms, the positions for the groups ; then prepare the ground, and plant the roses selected for the purpose. Wire pyramids for Climbing Roses should occupy conspicuous positions, as they serve as a variation and relief to groups of plants of the ordinary character.

The selection of the varieties will be the most important consideration, for on their beauty, and the diversity of their colors, will depend, in a great degree, the effect to be pro-duced. The groups should, in each instance, present the greatest contrast of colors, and each one should comprise such a combination as to be unique in itself, thus presenting throughout the whole area, an everchanging spectacle, re-lieving the eye at each variation of vision, and gratifying the fancy by an ever-varying spectacle of Floral enchant-ment. The taste of the fairer sex should not only be cal-led into requisition, but should preside over the whole ar-rangement ; for who will presume for a moment to dispute with them the prerogative of taste in all that is connected with selections of colors, with that refined discernment which discriminates most acutely between the slightest variations of tint, and with that acuteness of judgment which appears to possess by intuition, the most perfect knowledge of all those combinations, that are best calculated to arrest the fancy and enchant the mind.

Yield then, proud man, to the combined attributes of female supremacy, and her fairy wand will enforce your approval by adding to the mysterious enchantment of the ROSARY.

It is said that the Chinese display an exceeding degree of taste in the arrangement of their lawns and parterres, and when the multitude of plants already received, and of others known to exist in that Empire, are taken into consideration, we may well credit the accounts we have received of their Floral embellishments. When we count over the numerous varieties of splendid double flowering plants already received from China and Japan, it seems almost incredible to what an extent we are already indebted to those two countries, which have been hitherto so completely closed to us, that we have been kept in utter ignorance as to the extent of their Floral productions, except as regards those that have been obtained almost by stealth from their prolific shores. In this absence of knowledge which has so long prevailed, the title of the former country, "The Flowery Empire," was calculated to awaken our expectations, and it is most gladdening to the amateur, that these anticipations so long cherished, are now about to be realized by numerous importations.

The Horticultural riches of that mighty country have only commenced their developments; and while we are enriching our gardens with their choicest floral productions it is gratifying to know that not only the knowledge of other arts is being attained, but science, and most especially history, are both about to be enriched with stores of knowledge, which have been hidden from the world since the destruction of the famous library of Alexandria.

Baron Humboldt, in his elaborate work entitled " Researches in Central Asia," remarks, that it is to China we are hereafter to be indebted for our knowledge of the early history of Asia.

It forms a most singular anomaly in the history of nations, and a most astounding contradiction to the sage assertions of European wiseacres, that a country, shut apart as it were from the rest of the world, and which has hitherto pertinaciously *excluded the blessings* of European civilization, and which it has also been supposed was slumbering beneath a load of superstition and ignorance ; should now prove to be not only the most literary nation on the earth, but to have inculcated and absolutely carried into effect the fundamental principle of Christianity, as promulgated by Confucius 500 years before the Christian era ; and that " good will from man to man," and " to love thy neighbor as thyself," have formed for ages the universal basis of society, in an empire comprising more than one-third of the inhabitants of the globe.

It is probably to the general devotion of the Chinese nation to the refined enjoyments of the culture of Flowers, that is to be attributed the prevalence of that fraternal feeling and pure benevolence which exist so universally throughout that enlightened nation, a nation that seems animated by one general brotherhood, and where the raising the hand of man against his brother man is almost unknown.   Amid the myriads that swarm in the Canton river, in which boats almost innumerable are used as floating dwellings, and on which tens of thousands of human beings are born and end their days, such a circumstance as a quarrel is almost unknown ;

the principle of mutual aid seeming to pervade the entire congregated mass ; and the brutal disputes that disgrace human nature, are alone confined to the very enlightened and refined representatives of Christian civilization, and emanate from nations who most kindly and benevolently profess an ardent anxiety to civilize the Chinese.

AN ABRIDGED LIST OF ROSES,

Adapted for Amateurs possessing small Gardens, or for those beginning to form a Collection ; selected so as to give the leading variations of color, and comprising those only that are obtainable at moderate prices.

Provence.

Aspasie.
Duchesne.
Dutch.
Grand Agathe.
Unique.
Superb striped Unique.
Wellington.

Moss.

Blush.
Celina.
Crested.
Crimson.
Eclatante.
French Crimson.
Mrs. Wood.

Pompone.
Prolific.
Luxembourg Scarlet.
White Bath.

Hybrid Provence.

Blanche de Castille.
Emerance.
Garnier pages.
La Ville de Londres.
L'Ingénue.
Theodora.

Hybrid Chinese.

Blairii, No. 1.
Beauty of Billiard.
Brennus.

Chenedolé.
Comtesse Lacepède.
Coupe d'Amour.
Decandolle.
Duke of Devonshire.
Fulgens.
George the Fourth.
Lady Stuart.
Le Météore.
Ne plus ultra.
Saudeur panaché.
Triomphe d'Angers.
Triomphe de Laqueue.
Vandæls.

Hybrid Bourbon.

Charles Duval.
Colonel Combes.
Coupe d'Hébé.
Fulgens.
Great Western.
Paul Perras.
Sylvain.
William Jesse.

French, or Gallica.

Aglæ Adanson.
Agrémont.
Antonine d'Ormois.
Boula de Nanteuil.
Champion.
Cramoisie picotee.
Enchantress.
Fanny Parissot.

Grandissima.
Guerin's Gift.
Kean.
La tour d'Auvergne.
Ninon de l'Enclos.
Pourpre strié de blanc.
Renoncule ponctué.
Tricolor.
Village Maid.

White, or Alba.

Duc de Luxembourg.
La Séduisante.
Madame Campan.
Petite cuisse de nymphe.
Princesse de Lamballe.
Queen of Denmark.
Sophie de Marsilly.

Damask.

Calypso.
Déesse Flora.
La Cherie.
Lady Fitzgerald.
La Ville de Bruxelles.
Leda, or Painted.
Madame Hardy.
Pulcherie.
Semiramis.

Scotch.

Cramoisie.
Daphne.
Deep red.

Double yellow.
Erebus.
La Neige.
Marbled.
Venus.
William the Fourth.

Sweet Briars.
Celestial.
Margined Hip.
Rose Angle.
Scarlet.
Splendid.
White American.

Austrian Briars.
Capucine ponctué.
Double Yellow.
Harrison's Yellow.
Persian Yellow.

Hybrid Perpetual.
Aubernon.
Clementine Duval.
Comte de Paris.
Coquette de Montmorency.
Duc d'Aumale.
Fulgorie.
La Reine.
Madame Laffay.
Marquis Bocella.
Marshal Soult.
Prudence Rœser.
Prince Albert.
Rivers.

Ayrshire.
Ayrshire Queen.
Blush.
Dundee Rambler.
Jessica.
Queen of the Belgians.
Ruga.
Splendens.

Multiflora.
Crivellii.
Elegans.
Laura Davoust.

Evergreen.
Adelaide d'Orleans.
Banksiæ-flora.
Félicité perpétuelle.
Myrianthes.
Princesse Louise.
Spectabile.

Boursault.
Amadis.
Blush.
Gracilis.
Thornless.

Banksian.
White.
Yellow.

Hybrid Climbing.
Elegans rosea.
Indica Major.

Madame d'Arblay.
The Garland.
Triumph of Bolwiller.

Damask Perpetual.
Bernard.
D'Esquermes.
Du Roi, or Crimson.
Ebène.
Flon.
Jenny Audiot.
Josephine Antoinette.
Laurence de Montmorency.
Marie Denise.
Stanwell.

Bourbon.
Acidalie.
Armosa.
Augustine Margat.
Bouquet de Flore.
Comtesse de Resseguier.
Crimson Globe.
Emile Courtier.
Joan of Arc.
Julie de Loynes.
Madame Desprez.
Madame Margat.
Madame Nerard.
Marechal de Villars.
Mehemet Ali.
Phœnix.
Queen.

Chinese Everblooming.
Archduke Charles.
Boisnard.
Buret.
Carmin d'Yebles.
Comble de gloire.
Cramoisie supérieure.
Eugene Beauharnais.
Eugene Hardy.
Fabvier.
Henry the Fifth.
Madame Desprez.
Madame Bréon.
Marjolin du Luxembourg.
Mrs. Bosanquet.
Napoleon.

Tea-scented.
Abricoté.
Archiduchesse Therese Isa-
    belle.
Aurore.
Barbot.
Bougère.
Caroline.
Clara Sylvain.
Comte de Paris.
Devoniensis.
Eliza Sauvage.
Goubault.
Grandiflora.
Hardy.
Josephine Malton.
Le Pactole.

Princesse Marie.
Saffrano.
Silène.
Taglioni.
Triomphe de Luxembourg.
Yellow.

Fairy, or Miniature.
Caprice des Dames.
Gloire des Lawrenceas.
Multiflora.
Pompon bijou.
Retour du Printemps.

Noisette.
Aimée Vibert.
Boulogne.
Camellia Rouge.
Chauvineau.
Clarisse Harlowe.
Euphrosine.
Fellemberg.
Hardy.
Jaune Desprez.
Lamarque.

La Victorieuse.
Luxembourg.
Miss Glegg.
Nankin.
Ne plus Ultra.
Solfatarre.
Vitellina.

Musk.
Eponine.
Fringed.
Princesse of Nassau.
Rivers' Musk.

Macartney.
Lucida duplex.
Maria Leonida.
Scarlet Maria Leonida.

Microphylla.
Carnea.
Coccinea.
Purpurea.
Rouge striée.

CONTENTS.

CATALOGUE OF ROSES

IN THE NURSERIES OF

WILLIAM R. PRINCE & CO.

ROSES.

OF all the hardy shrubs that bedeck the Garden, none commands such universal admiration as the Rose, and there is none to which so much attention has been devoted in the production of new seminal varieties. Most appropriately, therefore, has this splendid appendage of the floral domain received the appellation of the "Queen of Flowers." To such an extent has the course of propagation referred to been carried, that above two thousand varieties are now enumerated in the European Catalogues. The most astonishing circumstance, however, is the *total change in the public taste* which has arisen since the production of hundreds of magnificent varieties of the Chinese Ever-Blooming, Tea-Scented, Noisette, and Bourbon, and other perpetual classes, all possessing the invaluable property of perpetual flowering, and thereby affording a long successive display of their floral beauties from the opening of spring until the autumnal suspension of vegetation. The result of this remarkable change in public opinion, has been the almost total abandonment of the Summer or June flowering Roses, usually denominated "Hardy Garden Roses," as they bloom but once, and then only for a very short period. Based as the taste of amateurs is in this case on the strongest reasons for their preference, its course must be progressive, and the period is not far distant when but few of the short-lived June varieties will be continued in gardens where the monthly varieties are obtainable. During a long course of culture, our object has been to select the most estimable varieties from the mass which have been presented to our observation, and in the formation of the present Catalogue, the whole have undergone a complete supervision and critical investigation; and the varieties now enumerated comprise a *Select List*, embracing only the most beautiful, and those most estimable for their form, size, fragrance, singularity, or delicacy. This assemblage, so extensive and so admirable, has been made at great expense, and many of the varieties have cost us from $3 to $6 for each original plant imported. Those which we have rejected, and discontinued the propagation of, are enumerated under a distinct head, and without descriptions. This *Select Collection* occupies four acres of ground, independent of an immense number in pots. During the period of their bloom they present an accumulation of varied beauties scarcely to be rivalled, and those who may desire it can make their selections during the flowering season. The different classes of Roses also present a great diversity in their style of growth, foliage, and in the form and size of their flowers. Some varieties are tall and erect, others procumbent or climbing, others have long flexible shoots adapted to training, and some are of a very dwarf habit. All the varieties will endure our winters, with the few exceptions which are noted in their place, and they are all double except the few which are designated as single.

The greater part of the Roses are on their own bottoms, but an assortment of about 400 varieties are also inoculated on strong stocks 3 to 4 feet from the ground, and thus form beautiful Rose Trees. These 400 varieties can therefore be furnished of either of the descriptions named. The prices, it will be perceived, are lower than they have ever before been offered to the public, and from these prices the following discounts are also made. Where a dozen plants are ordered, 15 per cent.; where 25 plants are ordered, 20 per cent.; where 50 to 100 plants, each different, are ordered, 25 per cent.; and to such Nurseries as purchase an assortment of a hundred or more to re-vend, consisting of two or more of a kind, 33 per cent.; and where a still larger quantity is desired, the terms will be arranged on the most liberal basis, it being our determination that our correspondents shall find *a great advantage in prices* in their dealings with us, as well as in other respects. We therefore particularly urge those who wish large supplies to communicate fully with us on the subject, as we will at all times furnish them lower than equally fine plants can be obtained elsewhere, to say nothing of the great number of estimable varieties we offer, which are no where else obtainable. In general, the plants we vend are much larger and stronger than are usually sold, and more may be saved in this respect than in the price. Mixed Roses, without names, will be supplied at $3 per dozen; $5 50 for 25; $10 for 50; or $18 per 100. The culture of Roses is of the simplest description, and the requisite information will be found under the proper head, and particularly in the Manual of Roses just published.

Particular care has been exercised in the arrangement, and all the varieties will be found under their appropriate heads. In some Catalogues gross blunders are made in this respect; and, for instance, the Solfatare and Similor are called Tea Roses by some, and in other cases, names are inserted as distinct, which are only synonymous, and many are also enumerated which are very inferior. These we do not cultivate, as there is an ample supply of estimable varieties, without wasting time on the worthless. In those classes of Roses which are not generally fragrant, the letter F is attached to such as are so. The Damask, Provence, French Roses, Moss, Hybrid Provence, Damask perpetual, Sweet Briars, Black, and Tea Roses, being all fragrant, need no such distinction, but an F has been added to some that are extraordinarily so. The letter P is attached to most of the varieties which have long flexible shoots adapted for rose pillars, arbors, or to train against the sides of buildings, &c. The following abbreviations are used in regard to form: glob. globular, or globose, the outer petals encircling the flower till fully blown; ex. expanded, the flowers rather flat, petals open; cup. cupped, the outer row of petals erect, rather incurved, enclosing the smaller petals; com. compact, petals stiff, close, and upright, resembling a double Ranunculus. The letter S has been annexed to a few Show roses, flowers full size, very double, perfect form, suitable for premium exhibitions.

A new distinct Catalogue of Roses is published annually, containing all the additional new varieties.

CLASS I.—CHINESE EVER-BLOOMING, DAILY, OR BENGAL ROSES.
Rosa indica.

This magnificent class of Roses comprises so many desirable qualities, that it is ranked by amateurs among the first in requisition. When cultivated in the open ground, as is now very generally practised, the varieties are particularly interesting, on account of their filling up the entire season with a continued profusion of bloom. They commence expanding their flowers in April, which present a constant succession of the most lovely and varied hues that can regale the fancy; and these are continued until their development is arrested by frost. All the varieties enumerated have cupped flowers, except the few that are noted as globular,

compact, or expanded. Where no remark is made as to the size of the
flower, it is of the ordinary or medium size. In the autumnal months
this and the seven succeeding classes present an accumulation of bloom,
which is the more grateful, as nature then seems the most to require
their cheering influence. In a mild climate they continue flowering
throughout the year. If potted and housed they will bloom during the
winter months, and form a most brilliant appendage to the parlor or
greenhouse. The new varieties obtained during the last few years are
more hardy than the older ones. Many of them are perfectly so, and
the most tender will withstand our winters with the simplest attention.
They can be bound in straw, and the earth raised around the base; or
a barrel or box can be placed over them ; or they can be cut off within
a few inches of the ground, and then be covered with ten or twelve
inches of common mould, sand, tan-bark, or leaves.

Name.	Color and Character.	$ cts.
1. Abbé Mioland,	Purple, large, globose, superb.	50
2. Adeline Come,	Large pure white.	1 00
3. Admiral Duperré,	Deep purplish roseate.	37
4. Aimé Plantier,	White, tinged with apricot.	75
5. Alcine, F,	Large deep ruby red.	1 00
6. Alexina,	Large creamy, centre yellow.	75
7. Alphonsine,	Roseate, beautiful.	1 00
8. Archduke Charles,	Rose changing to crimson.	37
9. Arsinoe,	Rosy, fine.	37
10. Assuerus,	Deep brownish purple.	37
11. Augustine Hersent, *Madame Hersent.*	Bright rosy, distinct.	37
12. Baronne Delaage,	Red, beautiful.	75
13. Beau Carmine,	Purple maroon, shaded, fine.	25
14. Belle de Monza,	Rose changing to crimson.	25
15. Belle Emelie,	Blush, pink centre.	75
16. —— Lawrence,	Roseate, marbled, beautiful.	1 00
17. —— Menes,	Incarnate, very double, fine,	1 00
18. —— Rosalie, or Petite, Rosalie,	Bright rosy, centre deeper hue.	37
19. —— de Florence,	Large, light carmine.	37
20. —— Isidore,	Rose and carmine, changeable.	37
21. Boisnard, F,	Large clear yellow, centre deep yellow, superb.	1 25
22. Buret,	Large deep purple.	50
23. Cameleon,	Rose, changing to purple.	37
24. Camellia blanc,	Pure white, globose.	50
25. panaché double	Red, shaded rose and white.	75
26. Carmine superb,	Deep carmine, beautiful.	75
27. Carmin d'Yebles,	Deep carmine.	50
28. Caroline de Berri, F,	Blush shaded fawn color, fine.	75
29. Cels multiflore,	Large incarnate, pretty.	50
30. Cæsar Cardet,	Very large pink, globose.	50
31. Citoyen des deux mondes,	Deepest velvety crimson, very d'ble.	1 50
32. Clarisse,	White incarnate, rosy centre.	75
33. Comble de gloire,	Large violet red.	50
34. Conquete heureuse,	Bright red, clear centre.	75
35. Confucius,	Roseate, beautiful.	75
36. Cramoisie supérieure, *Agrippina,*	Brilliant crimson.	25

Name.	Color and Character.	$ cts.
37. Dalinde,	Red, shaded with violet.	75
38. Darius, or Darieux,	Violet red, beautiful.	37
39. Desfontaines, F,	Pure white, perfect.	50
40. Don Carlos,	Creamy yellow.	50
41. Duchess of Parma,	Purplish crimson.	50
42. Eblouissant,	Deep purple, very double.	1 00
43. Ermite de Remistan	Red marbled.	75
44. Etna,	Red changing to purple, compact.	37
45. Eugene Beauharnais, or Roi des Cramoisies	Bright amaranth,	37
46. Hardy	Creamy blush, globose.	50
47. Fabvier,	Bright reddish purple.	37
48. Fenelon,	Deep rose, large.	50
49. General Lawœstine,	Deep purple.	75
50. Soyez,	Magnificent red.	37
51. Gold striped bark, or striata	Very singular, flowers blush.	50
52. Grandval, Hermite,	Fine purplish crimson.	37
53. Hamilton, Maximus,	Rosy purple.	37
54. Henneloup,	Bright rosy crimson, globose.	37
55. Henry V.,	Bright crimson, base white.	37
56. Hermine,	French white tinged with pink.	75
57. Hibbertia,	Deep rosy.	25
58. Hortensia,	Shaded deep blush.	25
59. Hospitalière,	Bright amaranth.	75
60. Icteros, F,	Cream, yellow centre, profuse.	50
61. Imperatrice Josephine,	Large brilliant crimson, superb.	1 00
62. Indica, or Old Blush China	Blush, vigorous habit.	25
63. alba, or White daily,	Fine White.	37
64. maxima,	Large red, fine.	25
65. Jacksonia,	Bright red.	25
66. Jeune Arcole,	Rosy lilac.	75
67. Joseph Deschiens,	Amaranth crimson.	75
68. Lady of the Lake,	Pure white, beautiful.	50
69. La regulière,	Bright purple, compact.	37
70. La superbe,	Large violet red.	50
71. Le Camoens,	Rose changeable.	37
72. Leonidas,	Velvety violet purple, globose.	75
73. Madame Breon,	Brilliant rose, erect.	75
74. Madame Bureau,	White superb, globose.	50
Infidelités de Lisette.		
75. Madame Desprès,	Pure white, beautiful.	50
76. Madame Chavent,	Rosy lilac, large.	75
77. de Crequy,	Bright red changing to crimson.	75
78. de Rohan,	Creamy white, globose.	1 00
79. Fries Morel,	Creamy, blush centre, compact.	50
80. Marie Therese,	Fine French variety.	50
81. Marjolin du Luxembourg,	Large deep purple.	37
82. Mars,	Red shaded.	50
83. Milliez,	Pale lemon, large, expanded.	50
84. Mrs. Bosanquet,	Pale incarnate, wax-like.	37
85. Napoleon,	Purplish pink.	37
86. Nemesis,	Shaded velvety brown.	1 00
87. Numa,	Bright red.	75
88. Olympic,	Lilac blush.	37

Name.	Color and Character.	$ cts.
89. Orpheline de Guillotiére,	Large rose-tinged yellow, profuse.	1 00
90. Pompone violet,	Fine full violet.	50
91. Prince Charles,	Brilliant carmine, superb.	50
92. Prince Eugene,	Carmine purple.	37
93. Queen of Naples,	Very fine full crimson.	50
94. Reine de Lombardie,	Beautiful cherry color.	37
95. des François,	Large blue shaded with rose.	1 50
96. Roi de Hollande,	Red.	50
97. Roi d'Angleterre,	Crimson.	75
98. Romain Després,	Purplish roseate shaded.	37
99. Romeo,	Deep red, very double.	37
100. Rubens,	Rose changing to deep crimson.	37
101. Sanguinea,	Bright deep crimson.	25
102. Stevens' new	Purplish crimson.	27
103. Sully, F,	Pale rose, shaded fawn.	1 00
104. Tancrede,	Hybrid Bourbon, rosy purple, very double, lucid foliage, distinct.	1 25
105. Triomphe de Gand,	Large shaded carmine and purple.	50
106. Victoire Daumy,	Purplish carmine shaded.	50
107. Virginal,	Incarnate white, beautiful.	1 00
108. Zephora,	Shaded violet crimson.	37
109. Zephyr,	Peach blossom, rosy centre.	50

CLASS II.—TEA SCENTED CHINA ROSES. *Rosa indica, var. odorata.*

The varieties of this class are particularly esteemed for possessing that peculiarly exquisite odor which is denominated tea-scented. They have the same qualities as the preceding class, in regard to perpetual blooming, and in the various beauties of color, size, and form. The same remarks will also apply as to the hardihood of the new varieties, and to their winter protection. In growth there are some varieties less vigorous than the preceding class, their shoots being more slender and delicate, while on the other hand there are many varieties which evince great vigor. The Bengal varieties are more vivid in their colors, while these excel in the delicacy of their tints, and combine among their varieties those most remarkable for their orange, yellow, and creamy shades. The same remarks are also applicable to the varieties of this class, in regard to the form and size of the flowers, as were made concerning the previous class.

Name.	Color and Character.	$ cts.
128. Abricoté,	Large bright rosy fawn color,	1 00
129. Adam,	Large delicate roseate,	75
130. Adeline Camille,	Pure white, very double,	1 00
131. Agathe,	Red with yellowish centre,	1 00
132. Anteros.	White with yellowish centre,	50
133. Antoinette Bouvage.	Pale incarnate, large, very double,	1 00
134. Archduchess Therese Isabelle,	White with yellow centre,	75
135. Arance de Navarro, F.	Bright red, projecting centre,	75
136. Arkinto,	Incarnate, large,	37

1*

Name.	Color and Character.	$ cts.
137. Aurore,	Fawn changing to rose,	50
138. Barbot,	Rose shaded red, yellow centre,	50
139. Bardon,	Delicate roseate,	1 00
140. Belle Allemande, F.	Apricot shaded, blush, large,	50
141. Belle Marguerite,	Large violet red,	37
142. Belle Melanie,	Incarnate, full double,	75
143. Belphegor,	Red, centre incarnate, globose,	50
144. Blush, or Odorata, F.	Old blush, fine, high fragrance,	37
145. Bocage,	Large, yellowish white,	1 00
146. Bon Silene, F.	Large changeable purple,	50
147. Bougère,	Large bronzed rose, superb,	37
148. Bourbon,	Fine white.	37
149. Boutrand,	Bright roseate,	1 00
150. Boidron,	Rose color, large,	1 00
151. Bride of Abydos,	White shaded with rose,	50
152. Calliope,	Yellowish white,	50
153. Carlin,	Large rose, changeable,	50
154. Caroline, F.	Bright rose, yellow base,	50
155. Charles Reybaud,	Deep incarnate, large globose,	1 00
156. Chrysocome,	Rose centre, yellow,	1 00
157. Clara Sylvain,	Pure white, superb, globose,	50
158. Chevalier d'amour,	Bright rose, yellow centre,	50
159. Claudia Gourd,	Incarnate, beautiful, globose,	50
160. Comte de Paris,	Rosy incarnate, fine,	50
161. " Osmond,	Cream, with yellow centre, globose,	1 00
162. Delice de Plantier,	Coppery roseate, globose,	1 00
163. Delphine Gaudot,	Rosy salmon, extra,	1 50
164. Desfontaines,	Pure white,	1 00
165. Devoniensis, F.	Straw, buff centre, superb,	50
166. Dremont, F.	White tinged aurora, expanded,	50
167. Duc d'Orleans,	Bright shaded, deep cherry,	37
168. Duchess of Mecklenberg,	Large pale yellow,	50
169. D'Yebles,	Incarnate, large, very double,	1 00
170. Duchesse d'Orleans,	Pale incarnate,	75
171. Eliza Sauvage,	Pale yellow orange centre, globose,	50
172. Elvira,	Deep blush, globose,	37
173. Eugene Desgaches,	Bright roseate, globose,	1 00
174. Eugenie Jouvain,	Incarnate white,	1 00
175. Favart,	Superb blush,	75
176. Flon,	Large fawn color, fine,	50
177. Fleur de Cypres,	Rosy incarnate, globose,	75
178. Fragoletta,	Bright rose, graceful form,	50
179. Floralie,	Incarnate, very double,	1 50
180. Frederick Væber,	Shaded red, very double,	1 00
181. Gama,	Large pale yellow, superb,	50
182. General Chassé,	Roseate, large, full double,	75
183. ———— Valèze,	Delicate incarnate, rosy centre,	75
184. Geraldine,	Light blush, veined, beautiful,	1 50
185. Gigantesque,	Large shaded rose, globose,	50
186. Golconda,	Creamy blush,	37
187. Goubault, F.	Bright shaded rose, superb,	50
188. Grandidier,	Shaded rose, large, very double,	50
189. Grandiflora,	Very large delicate rose,	75
190. Hamon,	Large deep red, aurora centre.	50
191. Hardy,	Very large brilliant rose,	37

Name.	Color and Character.	$ cts.
192. Heteroclite,	Fine straw color,	1 00
193. Hymenée,	White with fawn centre,	37
194. Hyppolite,	Large white and sulphur,	50
195. Irma,	Roseate large,	1 00
196. Jeune Arcole,	Deep roseate, very double,	1 00
197. Jaune panaché,	Pale yellow and white,	50
198. Jeannie Deans,	Delicate salmon color, beautiful,	62
199. Josephine Malton,	White yellow centre, large, globose,	50
200. Julie Mansais,	Very large, pure white, superb,	50
201. La renonmé,	White, yellow centre,	50
202. La Sylphide,	Rosy buff, large, beautiful,	75
203. Lady Warrender,	Large white, superb,	50
204. Leonie charmante,	White tinged with rose,	37
205. Le Pactole,	Deep saffron yellow, profuse flower'd,	1 00
206. Lutescens grandiflora,	Large lemon color, globose,	50
207. Lyonnais,	Large bright rosy,	50
208. Macarthy,	Deep pink, superb,	75
209. Madame Galet,	Yellowish white,	50
210. Madame Goubault,	Large,	1 00
211. " Jacqueminot,	New variety, from Laffay,	2 00
212. " de St. Joseph,	Salmon pink, very large,	75
213. " Villerin,	Creamy white, roseate centre,	75
214. " Depuis,	White, centre yellow and rosy,	1 00
215. " Guerin,	Pure white, deep centre,	1 00
216. " Roussel,	White, centre incarnate,	1 00
217. Malibran,	Large, flesh col'd, centre rose,	1 00
218. Mansais, F.	Large, buff and rose,	50
219. Marie de Medicis,	Large, bright rose, shaded with fawn,	1 00
220. Marechal Bougeaud,	Deep rosy, rosette centre, large, very double,	2 00
221. Ma tante aurore,	Yellow and rosy,	75
222. Miranda,	Cream, rose centre, beautiful,	50
223. Melville,	Large, buff and carmine,	50
224. Merlet de Loboullais,	Light yellow, rose,	1 00
225. Mirabile,	Sulphur, tinged and edged pink,	75
226. Miss Sargent,	Fine rose, pale margin,	50
227. Moiré,	Aurora yellow deep col'd. centre,	50
228. Mondor,	Fawn shaded with deep rose, very large, superb,	2 00
229. Narcisse,	Yellow, with deeper centre,	1 50
230. Nid d'amour,	Blush with rose centre,	37
231. Nina,	Large, blush,	37
232. Nisida,	Large, bright rose, yellowish centre, superb,	1 00
233. Nyphetos,	Large, shining white, globose,	50
234. Odoratissima, F.	Blush with deeper centre,	37
235. Pauline Plantier,	Creamy white, beautiful,	50
236. Perfection,	Pale blush, fine,	1 25
237. Pellonia,	Cream, aurora centre, large, glob.	1 50
238. Pharaon,	Deep rose, beautiful,	50
239. Philadelphia,	Fine pink, globose,	37
240. Prince d'Esterhazy,	Large incarnate, rosy tinge,	50
241. Princesse Marie,	Buff and rose shaded, globose,	50
242. " Helene, (Luxembourg,)	Large, yellowish white,	75
243. " Helene, (Modeste,)	Pure white,	50

Name	Color and Character.	$ cts.
244. Princess Adelaide,	Pale yellow, large, superb,	2 00
245. Reine des Belges,	Creamy white, large, very double,	1 50
246. " de Bassora,	Rose, centre buff, large,	75
247. " de Golconde, F.	Pale incarnate,	75
248. " Victoria,	Large, bright yellow shaded,	2 00
249. Rève du Bonheur,	Large, rose, centre aurora,	50
250. Rival de Pœstum,	Yellowish white, large, superb,	1 00
251. Roi de Siam,	White with yellow centre,	50
252. Rose du Luxembourg, F.	Brilliant rose color,	75
253. Robert Bruce,	White and cream color, globose,	1 00
254. Romain,	Aurora yellow, changeable,	1 00
255. Saffrano,	Bright yellow, cluster flowered,	1 00
256. Semelé,	Large, incarnate aurora,	75
257. Silene, F.	Rose shaded crimson, superb,	50
258. Soliman,	Rosy buff, large,	75
259. Souvenir 30th May,	Rosy salmon,	1 00
260. St. Cloud,	Rich creamy rose,	50
261. Strombio,	White pink, large,	50
262. Taglioni,	Creamy white, large, very double,	50
263. Thouin,	Shaded rose color,	75
264. Themistocles,	Fine white,	50
265. Theobaldine,	Bright rose, beautiful,	50
266. Triumph de Lille,	Rosy lilac, superb,	75
267. " de Luxembourg,	Large, aurora shaded pink, globose,	50
268. Vandael,	Rosy lilac, beautiful,	75
269. Virginie,	Incarnate, centre aurora,	1 00
270. Valentine,	Large, incarnate, protuberant,	75
371. Victoire modeste,	Blush pink,	37
272. Walter Scott,	Fine red,	50
	Pure white,	37
273. White, or Odorata alba,	White, very vigorous, has been	
274. American, P.	trained 20 feet in height,	50
275. Yellow, or Lutescens, F.	Fine, large, sulphur yellow,	50
276. Zebrina,	White shaded with yellow,	75

CLASS III.—BOURBON ROSES. *Rosa Bourboniana..*

The varieties of this class of Roses, although of but recent introduction among amateurs, are unrivalled in splendor, and their culture presents a new era in the combination of charms which comprise the Roseate wreath. Their habit is remarkable for its vigor in every respect. The shoots are very strong, the foliage broad and glossy, and the flowers are of large size, peculiarly beautiful and of regular form, and produced in profuse clusters. This charming family of Roses is now so perfect, and the splendid varieties recently added so numerous, that it is difficult to select from such a group of enticing beauties. The whole are suitable to cultivate on their own roots, their culture being as easy as the common garden rose, and their growth most rapid and luxuriant. Many of the varieties will throw up shoots three to four feet, crowned with most magnificent erect corymbs of flowers. The varieties marked P. form long flexible shoots, well adapted for training on the pillars or rafters of greenhouses, or on the sides of buildings and on trellices, arbors, &c. The letter F, designates those that are particularly fragrant.

They are perfectly hardy in this latitude, and even at Boston they withstand the winter with a slight protection of leaves or litter. Like the two preceding classes, they will, if housed, bloom freely in winter. All the flowers are cupped, except those noted otherwise.

Name.	Color and Character.	$ cts.
295. Abbé Plantier,	Deep rose color, large.	75
296. Acidalie, F,	Large white, very double, forces well.	50
297. Adela Plantier,	Bright red changing to rose.	1 00
298. Amarantine,	Cherry red, globose.	75
299. Amenaide,	Delicate rose, robust habit.	75
300. Amourette,	Small, flesh color, acute petals.	1 00
301. Anne Beluze,	Pale roseate, perfect, superb.	75
302. Ansegise,	Pale pink, beautiful.	50
303. Aristides,	Delicate rose color.	37
304. Armosa,	Globose, delicate rose, dotted white.	75
305. Asteroide,	Delicate roseate, very double.	50
306. Augustin Margat,	Deep rose color.	75
307. Aureny Zeb,	Rosy, shaded with white.	75
308. Beluze,	Rosy cherry color, large.	1 00
309. Bizarine,	Very brilliant deep rosy, projecting centre.	75
310. Bossuet,	Dark carmine, dwarf, beautiful.	1 00
311. Bouquet de flore, P. F.	Deep carmine, superb.	37
312. Bourbon, orig.; Jaques, P.	Bright rosy.	37
313. Cardinal Fesch,	Violet crimson, very double.	50
314. Cendres de Napoleon,	Superb purple shaded, globose.	75
315. Cent feuilles, or 100 leaved	Light rose color, fine.	75
316. Ceres,	Pink, imbricated, dwarf superb.	75
317. Charles Després,	Delicate roseate.	62
318. Charles Souchet,	Violet purple, very double.	75
319. Chatenay,	Blush white, cluster flowered.	75
320. Clementine,	Brilliant rosy,	75
321. Comice de Seine & Marne	Bright cherry color.	75
322. Comte d'Eu,	Bright carmine, large.	1 50
323. ——— de Nauteul,	Red shaded with violet.	1 25
324. ——— de Rambuteau,	Violet red,	1 00
325. Comtesse Resseguier,	Silvery blush, nearly white, large superb.	1 00
326. Comtesse de Colbert,	Rose shaded with lilac, large, form of Madame Després.	1 00
327. Coquette de Melun,	Beautiful,	1 25
328. Crimson Globe, or Dr. Roques,	Vermillion, dwarf, perfect, superb, globose.	50
329. Crimson Madame Després or Splendens, P. P.	Large, crimson, superb.	50
330. Cytherée,	Bright rose,	50
331. De Lamartine,	Violet red.	1 00
332. Deuil Duc d'Orleans,	Blackish purple, shaded, expanded,	1 50
333. Descrivieux,	Bright rosy lilac, distinct.	1 00
334. Desgaches, P,	Bright rose, superb, perfect.	
335. Don Alvar,	Large, crimson shaded,	1 00
336. Duc de Chartres,	Incarnate, pale border, protuberant.	1 50
337. Duchesne,	Crimson, fine.	1 00
338. Dumont de Courset,	Crimson carmine.	75

Name.	Color and Character.	$ cts.
339. Dupetit Thouars,	Dazzling violet carmine.	1 50
340. D'Yebles,	Violet purple.	75
341. Earl Gray,	Lilac roseate, large, splendid.	75
342. Edouard Desfosses,	Pale glittering rose, fine.	75
343. Emily Courtier,	Deep rose, perfect, superb.	50
344. Plantier, P,	Scarlet, very distinct.	75
345. Enfant d'Ajaccio, P,	Crimson scarlet, shaded.	1 00
346. Etoile de Berger,	Incarnate white, very double.	1 25
347. Faustine,	White, tinged incarnate, cluster flowered.	75
348. Fédora,	Purple, very double.	1 25
349. Gantin,	Incarnate, fine form, very double.	1 00
350. Gaston de Panck,	Incarnate.	1 00
351. George Cuvier,	Brilliant cherry, shaded blush.	75
352. Gloire d'Alger,	Bright crimson.	50
353. d'Rosamanes, P.	Large, deep brilliant scarlet.	37
354. Gloire de la Guillotière,	Light rose, large.	75
355. Gloire de Paris,	Bright crimson shaded, very double.	75
356. Grande Capitaine,	Brilliant velvety carmine, dwarf.	75
357. Hennequin, or Splendens,	Bright carmine, splendid, robust.	75
358. Henri Quatre,	Large, delicate roseate, very double.	50
359. Plantier,	Purplish roseate, very double.	50
360. Henry Le Coq,	Rosy carmine, full double.	1 50
361. Henry Clay,	Pale blush, beautiful.	50
362. Hermosa,	Pale rosy, beautiful, globose.	37
363. Hersilie,	Bright rose.	50
364. Ida,	Carmine, dwarf, pretty.	75
365. Ida Percot,	Bright rosy, superb.	75
366. Imperatrice Josephine, P.	Large, robust habit.	75
367. Jacquard,	Crimson purple, very double.	1 00
368. Jenny Cherie,	Beautiful French variety.	75
369. Joan of Arc,	Large, rose colored, superb.	1 00
370. Julie de Loynes,	(See Noisette Roses.)	75
371. Julie Sisley,	Large, rosy violet.	75
372. La Madeline,	Large, white, centre roseate.	1 00
373. La Bedoyere,	Bright red.	1 00
374. Lady Granville.	Light red, beautiful.	1 00
375. —— Canning,	Deep rose, globose.	75
376. Lavinie d'Ost, P.	Incarnate, very double.	1 00
377. La Gracieuse,	Reddish crimson, beautiful perfect.	1 00
378. Le Grenadier,	Brilliant deep crimson, purple tip'd.	1 00
379. Lelia,	Incarnate, shaded with rose.	75
380. Lilacea grandiflora,	Lilac rose, very large, perfect.	75
381. Louis XIV.	Bright rose.	1 25
382. Madame Aude, P,	Deep roseate, bright, superb.	75
383. Breon,	Bright carmine, white centre, large.	1 00
384. Despres, P,	Splendid lilac rose.	50
385. Nerard, F,	Delicate bright rose, perfect.	37
386. Lacharme, P,	White tinged blush, superb.	1 50
387. de Rohan,	Rosy pink, superb.	1 00
388. Margat,	Light roseate, beautiful.	1 00
389. Gros,	Pretty.	1 00
390. Souchet,	Light rose changing to deep.	1 00

Name.	Color and Character.	$ cts.
391. Madame Angelina,	White tinged with fawn, superb.	2 00
392. Newmann,	Brilliant roseate.	37
Dubrieul.		
Gloire de France.		
Monthly Cabbage.		
393. Mademoiselle Rachel,	French white, beautiful.	1 00
394. Madam'lle Montesquieu,	White, fine.	1 25
395. Manteau de Jeanne d'Arc,	White, rosy edge, ch'g to incarnate, beautiful.	1 00
396. Marechal de Villars,	Deep rose, shaded with violet,	37
397. Marianne,	Bright rose, large, very d'ble, superb.	2 00
398. Marquis de Moyria,	Bright rose, shaded vermillion, large perfect form.	2 00
399. Marquis d'Ivry,	Delicate rose, projecting centre.	1 00
400. Mehemit Ali,	Large, whitish rose colored.	75
401. Millesii,	Pale purplish pink.	50
402. Minima,	Small, deep roseate.	75
403. Miss Fanny,	Delicate incarnate, very double	1 25
404. Mrs. Bosanquet,	Flesh color, beautiful.	37
405. Nerine,	Deep purplish rose, brilliant.	1 00
406. Ninon'de l'Enclos,	Violet purple, beautiful.	50
407. Parquin,	Violet red, beautiful.	1 00
408. Paul Joseph,	Deep crimson purple, profuse flow'd	1 00
409. Phœnix, F,	Brilliant rosy purple, distinct, fine,	50
410. Phillipart,	Delicate roseate, beautiful.	50
411. Pierre de St. Cyr, P,	Pale rose, beautiful, robust.	75
412. Pluto,	Dark crimson, expanded.	1 25
413. Pourpre fafait,	Purple, very double, protuberant.	75
414. Premices des Charpennes,	Satin rose, white border, large, imbricated, very double.	3 00
415. Prince Albert,	Light rose, tinged buff, climbing, robust habit.	62
416. Prince de Salm,	Violet.	50
417. de Joinville,	Deep rose colored, beautiful.	50
418. Princess Clementine,	Violet carmine, very double, fine.	1 00
419. de Modena,	Delicate pink, pretty.	1 00
420. Princesse de Croi,	Large, bright red.	75
421. Proserpine,	Brilliant crimson, shaded purple, dwarf superb.	75
422. Pulchella,	Bright flesh color, dwarf habit.	50
423. Psyché,	Delicate pink, compact.	75
424. Queen, or Reine des Isles Bourbons, F.	Fawn colored rose, beautiful.	50
425. Reine des Vierges,	Pale incarnate.	2 00
426. de Fontenay,	Brilliant rose.	1 00
427. du Congrès.	Delicate incarnate, perfect, superb.	1 00
428. Rose Menoux,	Bright red, nearly scarlet, very double, superb.	3 00
429. Souchet,	Purplish carmine, very d'ble, fine.	1 50
430. Souvenir de Malmaison,	Incarnate, large, very double, fine form, splendid.	1 50
431. Dumont d'Urville,	Violet cherry color, very double	1 00
432. Therese Margat,	Bright rosy.	50
433. Thiaffait,	Brilliant rose, perfect.	1 00

Name.	Color and Character.	$ cts.
434. Thisbe,	Purplish rose, large expanded.	1 00
435. Timocles,	Large rose, very double, compact.	50
436. Triomphe de Plantier, P,	Rosy red, robust climbing habit, fine	50
437. Triomphe de la Guillotière,	Rosy red, superb.	1 00
438. Vicomte de Cussy,	Splendid new French variety.	2 00
439. Victoire argentée,	Delicate rosy, shaded with lilac.	50
440. Victor Varengot,	Pale blush, very double, fine.	1 50
441. Virgil, P,	Bright roseate, fine.	1 00
442. Zulema,	Delicate roseate, small, very d'ble.	50

CLASS IV.—NOISETTE ROSES. *Rosa Champneyana.*

This class of Roses owes its origin to the late John Champney, of Charleston, S. C., who raised the "Champney Rose" from the White Musk, impregnated by the old Blush China. The most remarkable characteristics of this class are the profusion of flowers produced, and the immense clusters or corymbs in which they are comprised. This applies to nearly all the varieties, many of which combine forty to sixty buds in a single cluster. The flowers vary exceedingly in magnitude, the greater number being of smaller or moderate size, and exceedingly delicate and beautiful, while others are so large that they may be ranked among the most splendid of the whole family of Roses. The large and magnificent yellow varieties recently produced, and enumerated in the following list, form a new era in this very desirable class of the Rose family. They possess the same property of blooming throughout the summer and autumn, as the three preceding classes, and the flowers of almost every variety are of cupped form. Most of the varieties are hardy, and others nearly so, requiring but slight protection. Those varieties marked P, form long flexible shoots, well adapted for training on the columns or rafters of greenhouses, or on the sides of buildings, and on trellises, arbors, &c.

Name.	Color and Character.	$ cts.
462. Aimée Vibert, or Unique,	Beautiful pure white in clusters.	50
463. Alba, or New white,	Pure white.	50
464. Antonine,	Yellowish, very double,	1 00
465. Belle Marseillaise,	Rose shaded with carmine,	50
466. Bicolor,	Flesh color shaded rose, beautiful.	37
467. Blanche d'Orleans,	White, medium size, expanded, full double,	50
468. Blush cluster, old variety,	Compact, fine blush in immense clusters,	37
469. Boulogne,	Brilliant rose color.	50
470. Belle d'Esquermes,	Brilliant deep violet.	50
471. Camellia rouge, P.	Rosy pink, full double, compact,	50
472. Champney's pink cluster, P.	Blush, blooms profusely, tall vigorous growth.	37
473. Chauvineau,	Blueish purple, cluster flow'd.	1 50
474. Chloris,	Bright delicate red, shaded with carmine,	75

Name.	Color and Character.	$ cts.
474. Chromatella, or Cloth of Gold, F. P.	Splendid large, pale yellow, vigorous growth,	1 00
Ditto, Extra large plants,		1 50
475. Clara Wendel, F.	Aurora, changing to straw color,	1 00
476. Clarisse Harlowe,	Creamy blush, large, very double,	1 00
477. Cleopatra,	Pale lemon,	1 50
478. Conque de Venus,	White with roseate centre,	37
479. Cora Barton,	Pink roseate, large,	50
481. Comtesse d'Orloff, P.	Rosy lilac, very fine,	37
482. Desiré Roussel,	Flesh color, shaded pink, very d'ble	1 00
483. Donna Maria,	Bright rose, very double,	62
484. Eclair de Jupiter, P.	Large vivid crimson, distinct,	75
485. Edmond Garrat,	Shaded rosy violet, very full,	75
Elegans rosea, P.	*See Class XIII.*	37
487. Eliza Le Maire,	White, incarnate, small,	1 00
488. Eugene Pirolle, *Admiral de Rigny.*	Carmined rose,	37
489. Euphrosyne, F. P.	Yellowish and rosy, clustered,	50
490. Fellemberg,	Bright crimson, beautiful,	37
491. Gabrielle,	Fine rosy violet,	37
492. Grandiflora, or Monstrosa, *Bengal Lee*, P.	Pale blush, large clusters, strong growth,	37
493. Hardy, P.	Large incarnate, rosy centre, robust,	50
494. Henry,	Bright incarnate, very double,	37
495. Isabelle d'Orleans,	Purest white,	1 00
496. Janne Després, F. P. *French Yellow Noisette.*	Large bright rosy fawn color,	50
497. Jeanne d'Arc, P.	Pure white, vigorous habit,	1 00
498. Julie de Loynes,	White, small, full double, in clusters,	75
499. Julienne le Sourd,	Small bright rose, dwarf, very pretty,	50
500. La Biche, P.	Deep blush, extra large,	50
501. La desirée,	White clustered flowered,	1 00
502. La victorieuse, F.	Large white, shaded incarnate,	50
503. Lactans,	Fine creamy yellow,	1 00
Le Pactole,	See Tea-scented Roses,	
505. Lamarque, P.	Large straw colored, lemon centre, superb,	37
506. Lamarque, à cœur rose, P. *Fleur de jeune age.*	Large white, rose centre, fragrant,	50
507. Lelieur,	Brilliant crimson, distinct,	50
508. Luxembourg, P.	Large bright purplish rose,	50
509. Madame Chalonge,	Yellowish incarnate,	1 00
510. Madame Guerin,	White, medium size, fine,	75
Madame Plantier,	*See Class XIII.*	
512. Magnanime,	Large white, rosy centre,	1 00
513. Minette, P.	Light crimson, very double, compact,	37
514. Miss Gregg,	Pure white, blush centre, superb,	75
515. Monstreuse, F. P.	Very large lemon, habit of Lamarque,	1 00
516. Mrs. Siddons,	Bright yellow, cha'g to straw color,	1 00
517. Nankin, F.	Nankin, changing to white,	50
518. Narcisse,	Sulphur yellow, expanded, large,	1 50
519. Nemesis,	Brownish purple, small, very d'ble,	1 00
520. Ne plus ultra, F.	Creamy white, very fragrant,	75
521. Nickmene,	White shaded, pink, singular,	50

2

Name.	Color and Character. $ cts.
522. Ophirie, **P.**	Bright salmon and fawn, distinct, beautiful, 1 00
523. Pauline Henry, ⸱	Rosy incarnate and chamois, 75
524. Philomèle.	Incarnate, small, very double, 1 00
525. Pourpre de Tyr, P.	Violet purple, medium size, full d'ble 1 00
526. Princesse d'Orange,	White, small, full double, 75
527. Prince's Pearl color, P. ⎱	Beautiful varieties, growing very vigorously, and can be trained
529. Superb White, P. ⎰	20 feet or more, 1 00
530. Coral,	Deep rosy cluster, 75
531. Rothanger,	Bright carmine, 37
532. Similor, F.	Saffron yellow, changing deeper yellow, superb, 1 00
533. Sir Walter Scott, P.	Dark purple, 37
534. Solfatare, F. P.	Splendid large saffron yellow, permanent, 75
Ditto, Extra large plants,	1 50
336. Suter's Pink,	Delicate incarnate, expanded, beautiful, 37
537. —— Susannah, P.	Yellowish white, 50
538. Smith's yellow, F.	Large splendid yellow, 50
539. Thélaire,	Pure white, 1 00
540. Theobaldine,	Light red, medium size, 75
Triomphe d'Arcole,	See 496.
542. Victoire Daumy,	Deep purple, small, 75
543. Vitellina, F.	White with yellow centre, 50
544. Zietrude,	Deep crimson, and purple, 1 00
545. Zobeide,	Cherry color, med'm size, very d'ble 1 00

CLASS V.—DAMASK PERPETUAL, OR AUTUMNAL ROSES.

These are hybrids obtained from the old Monthly Damask varieties, blended with the Ever-Blooming varieties, and they usually flower several times in a season, the autumnal blooming of some varieties continuing until arrested by frost. The flowers are beautiful, and in most cases highly fragrant, which, with their estimable property of flowering during autumn, renders them particularly desirable. They are readily distinguished from the Hybrid Perpetuals, by their flowers and fragrance, which have a great affinity to the old Monthly Damask. They require a very rich soil, rather moist, in order to force their growth, and thereby insure successive crops of flowers. They form admirable Tree Roses, when engrafted on strong stocks as standards. The flowers are all of cupped form, except such as are noted otherwise.

Name.	Color and Character. $ cts.
567. Amanda Patenotte,	Pale rose color, very double, protuberant fine globose form, large, splendid, 3 00
568. Antinous,	Deep purplish crimson, perfect form, 50
569. Arielle,	Rosy lilac, small, full double, 2 00
570. Beck, (Laffay,)	Roseate, large, extra superb, 1 00
571. Belle Faber,	Large, deep pink, full d'ble, convex, 50
572. Bernard, F.	Beautiful pink, small, full double, 50

Name.	Color and Character.	$ cts.
573. Bifera venusta,	Delicate roseate, full double,	1 50
574. Billiard,	Bright rose color, fine,	50
575. Celestine,	Brilliant rose color,	1 00
576. Claire du Chatelet,	Bright roseate,	50
577. Couronne de Beranger,	Crimson shaded, compact,	50
578. Damask monthly, Red, *Rose des quatres saisons.*	These are varieties long cultivated, and known as the Four Seasons	
579. ———, White,	Roses, or "*Rosiers des quatres saisons.*" They bloom but twice,	50
580. ———, Striped,	June and in autumn,	
581. D'Angers,	Large delicate rose, clustered,	50
582. D'Esquermes, or Royal,	Bright roseate.	50
583. De Montmorency,	Deep rose, very double,	1 00
584. Desdemona,	Carmine red,	75
585. Duc D'Enghien,	Incarnate, full double,	1 00
586. Du Roi, F. *Lee's Crimson Perpetual.*	Bright crimson, extra fragrant,	50
587. Du Roi strié, or panachè, *Striped Crimson Perpetual. Captain Renard.*	Flesh color striped with crimson, inconstant,	1 00
588. Du Roi moyenne,	Light purple, in long peduncles,	1 00
589. ——— pourpre,	Deep crimson purple,	75
590. Ebène,	Deep crimson purple, superb, the darkest rose known,	1 50
590½. Estelle, (Scotch,)	Rose, small size,	75
591. Fantesse,	Fine flesh colored,	1 00
592. Feburier,	Light red, full double, expanded,	1 00
593. Ferret,	Roseate, full double,	1 00
594. Ferox,	Light red, large, full double, protuberant.	1 00
595. Flon, or La Mienne, *Gloire des Perpetuelles.*	Bright red, compact,	50
596. Gentilhomme,		1 00
597. Indigo,	Dark velvety violet, superb,	2 00
598. Isaure Lablée,	Delicate roseate, full double,	50
599. Jenny Audiot,	Large, bright red, full double,	75
600. Josephine Antoinette, F.	Large rose, protuberant, ex. frag.	50
601. Lady Seymour,	Deep rose, spotted, full double,	1 25
602. Laurence de Montmorency	Lilac rosy, superb,	1 25
603. Lodoiska marin,	Large bright rose, full d'ble cluster'd,	50
604. Louis Philippe,	Violet purple, expanded,	50
605. Louise Puget,	Rose color, very double,	75
606. Marie Denise, F.	Bright rose, centre deeper hue,	75
607. Mauget,	Incarnate, full double, expanded,	1 50
608. Minerva,	Deep rose, full double,	1 25
609. Miroir,		1 00
610. Mogador, or Crimson Superb,	Purplish crimson shaded, superb,	2 00
611. Monstrueuse	Rose color, very large, fine,	75
612. Noel,	Light red, full double, large,	50
613. Olgerasie,	Incarnate, full double,	1 00
614. Palmyre,	Blush, cluster-flowered, compact,	50
615. Pennsylvania dwarf,	Small pompone, delicate blush, dwf.	30

Name.	Color and Character.	$ cts.
616. Philippe 1st.,	Violet purple,	1 00
617. Portland,	Large deep rose,	75
618. Portland blanc,	Large French white,	1 25
619. Portland rose,	Rose color, large, semi-double,	75
620. Portlandica carnea,	Dwarf pink, blooms freely,	1 00
621. Preval,	Pale rose, large, compact, fine,	50
622. Pourpre,	Deep bright crimson, semi-double,	75
623. Prudhomme,	Bright roseate, full double,	1 00
624. Reine des perpetuelles,	White and rose,	50
625. Renestine Audio,	Cherry color, large, full double,	1 00
626. Requien,	Incarnate, large, full double,	1 00
627. Rugueuse,	Roseate, full double variety of Palmyre,	1 00
628. Saint Barthelemy,	Rich pale pink,	75
629. Saint Fiacre,	Violet purple, beautiful,	50
630. Scotch perpetual,	Blush, blooms freely,	50
631. Six Juen,	Light rose, small, full double, protuberant,	50
632. Stanwell, (*Scotch*),	Pale incarnate, of the Scotch class,	50
633. Torrida,	Brilliant crimson, semi-double,	75
634. Triumph de Montmorency	Bright red, inconstant perpetual,	75
635. White perpetual moss,	For this, see class of Moss Roses,	

CLASS VI.—HYBRID PERPETUAL ROSES.

This class consists of Hybrid Roses, the most of which owe their origin to blending the old Perpetuals with the Chinese and Bourbon varieties. The growth is more robust, and their foliage more beautiful than the Damask Perpetuals, and they present a constant succession of bloom from June till November, and rank as the most beautiful of autumnal Roses, and with a few exceptions are among the most fragrant. The flowers are cupped, except where otherwise noted.

Name.	Color and Character.	$ cts.
656. Aubernon, F.	Brilliant crimson, sup. perf.,	75
657. Aricie,	Beautiful roseate, large, globose,	75
658. Augustine Mouchelet,	Purplish crimson, large, full double,	75
659. Baronne Prevost,	Rose color, very large, full double,	1 50
660. Calliope,	Bright carmine red, small,	75
661. Clementine Duval,	Beautiful brilliant rose,	75
662. Seringe, F. *Pauline Plantier.*	Roseate, odor of Provence, globose,	75
663. Compte de Paris, F.	Light crimson, lilac tinge, globose,	75
664. Comptesse Tanneguy Duchatel,	Brilliant rosy carmine, large, globose, superb,	3 00
665. Coquette de Montmorency,	Cherry color, distinct, superb,	75
666. Coquette de Bellevue,	Bright rose, spotted white, globose, vigorous,	1 50
667. De Neuilly, F.	Large, bright rose,	75
668. Deuil Dumont d'Urville,	Deep crimson maroon, mottled,	1 50

Name.	Color and Character.	$ cts.
669. Docteur Marjolin,	Bright cherry, superb,	1 25
670. ———Marx,	Violet red, full double,	1 25
671. Duc d'Aumale, F.	Brilliant purplish crimson, superb,	75
672. Duc de Chartres,	Lilac, centre carmine, very large, globose,	1 25
673. Duc d'Alencon,	Lilac, rose color, profuse flowered,	1 50
674. Duc d'Isly,	Bright red, shaded with deep purple, extra,	2 00
675. Duchesse de Montmorency,	Clear delicate roseate, large, full double,	2 00
676. ———Sutherland,	Incarnate, full double,	1 00
677. ———Nemours,	Delicate saffron rose color,	1 00
678. Earl Talbot,	Large, deep purplish rose color,	1 00
679. Edward Jesse,	Lilac rose, fine,	75
780. Eliza Balcombe,	White, somewhat incarnate at opening, small, full double, singular foliage,	2 00
681. Emma Dampierre,	Rose color, full double,	1 25
682. Ernestine de Barante,	Bright rose, small, very double, expanded, profusely flowered, superb,	1 50
683. Fidouline,	Delicate rosy lilac, full double.	1 50
684. Fulgorie,	Deep rose, purple tinge, globose.	75
685. General Merlin,	Rose color, shaded, full double, globose,	1 50
686. Gloire de Guerin,	Very brilliant carmine,	1 00
687. Iolande d'Aragon,	Rosy blush, fine,	7 50
688. Julie Dupont,	Purple, full double,	75
689. James Watt,	Large violet roseate,	1 00
690. La Bouquetière,	Deep rosy lilac,	1 00
691. La Reine,	Beautiful satin rose color, perfect form, delightful fragrance, exceedingly large, vigorous,	1 00
Ditto, Extra large plants,		1 50
692. Lady Alice Peel,	Carmine roseate, fine form, full double,	1 25
693. —— Elphinstone,	Delicate rose color, large,	1 00
694. —— Fordwich, F.	Deep rose, cluster flowered,	75
695. Lane,	Roseate, full double,	1 00
696. Lilacée,	Rose and lilac,	1 50
697. Lindley,	Bright red, large, full double,	2 00
698. Lord Peel,	Delicate roseate,	1 00
799. Louis Bonaparte, F.	Rosy crimson, distinct, globose,	62
700. Lucy Astaix,	Carmine roseate,	1 00
701. Madame Laffay, F.	Brilliant crimson rose, superb, perfect,	75
702. ——— Damême,	Bright rose color, fine foliage,	1 05
703. ———Jobes Desgaches,	Very bright dazzling roseate, sup'b.	1 50
704. ——— Verdïer,	Incarnate, full double, imbricate, exquisite form,	2 00
705. Marquis d'Ailsa,	Carmine, shaded, large, full double,	1 50
706. Marquise Bocella,	Rich rosy blush, distinct, perfect,	1 25
707. Marshal Soult, F.	Deep purplish rose,	62
708. Melanie Cornu,	Violet red, large, very double,	75
709. Mérope,	Satin rosy lilac, full double, expanded	2 00

2*

Name.	Color and Character.	$ cts.
710. Mrs. Cripps,	Beautiful delicate roseate, centre pink, large, full double,	1 50
711. Mrs. Elliott,	Rosy lilac, changeable, large, full double,	1 00
712. Pauline Levanneur,	Light roseate, very beautiful,	1 25
713. Ponctué, or Spotted (Laffay,)	Bright rose, spotted with white, imbricate petals, expanded,	2 00
714. Prince Albert, F.	Large, carmine, changing to dark velvet crimson, globose,	1 00
715. —— de Galles,	Light purplish pink, very fine,	1 25
716. Princesse Helène, F.	Deep purplish red, perfect,	75
717. Prudence Ræser,	Bright rose, very double,	50
718. Raynal (Laffay,)	New, beautiful,	1 50
719. Psyché,	Rosy pink, small, very pretty, dwarf,	1 00
720. Reine de la guillotière, F.	Superb brilliant crimson, glossy foliage, distinct,	75
721. —— Fontenay,	Light rose color, full double,	1 70
722. —— Victoria,	Light purple, full double,	75
723. Renufe d'Osmond,	Velvet carmine, shaded purple, large, full double, expanded,	2 00
724. Rivers (Laffay,) F.	Red tinged with lilac, very large,	1 00
725. Roch Plantier,	Brilliant carmine, white stamens,	1 00
726. Rose Cornet,	Delicate rose color, imbricate petals, extra,	2 00
727. Sisley,	Brilliant violet cherry, dw'f, sup'b.	75
728. Souvenir d'Anselme,	Carmine, beautiful,	1 00
729. Thibault,	Bright carmine rose color, fine,	1 00

CLASS VII.—HYBRID BOURBON ROSES.

These beautiful Roses are remarkable for their distinct character; their foliage is thick and glossy, sub-evergreen, and perfectly so in a mild climate, and remains on even here until very late in autumn; their petals are also very thick and leathery, and endure sunshine or changeable weather better than most roses. For an avenue of standards, or for a group, they are admirably adapted. In some catalogues they are erroneously confused with the preceding and following classes. All have cupped flowers except those otherwise noted.

Name.	Color and Character.	$ cts.
749. Adonis,	Lilac and red, globose,	1 00
750. Andrieux,	Large deep rose, fine,	1 00
751. A petales mucronés,	Rose color changeable, very double,	1 00
752. Athelin, or Attelaine,	Red, distinct, fine,	1 00
753. Belle de St. Cyr,	Bright rose, perfect, superb,	75
754. Brilliante,	Brilliant rose, spotted,	62
755. Capitaine Sisolet, S. P.	Rosy lilac, distinct, superb,	50
756. Celine, P.	Deep pinkish blush, splendid,	75
757. Charles Duval, S.	Bright rose, large, perfect, superb,	75
758. Chatelin,	Light lilac, large, full double,	1 00

Name.	Color and Character.	$ cts.
759. Claude Lorraine,	Brilliant rose, finely cupped,	1 50
760. Colonel Combes,	Brilliant red, sometimes spotted,	75
762. Comtesse Molé,	Pure flesh color, superb,	1 25
763. Coupe d'Hébé, S. *Hebe's Cup.*	Delicate bright rose, superb form,	1 00
764. Daphne,	Brilliant red, distinct,	75
765. Dombrowski,	Brilliant red, approaching to scarlet,	1 00
766. Duc de Cazes, S.	Lilac rose, very double, fine,	62
767. Edouard Delair,	Roseate, red centre, large, superb,	1 00
768. Elizabeth Plantier,	Superb rich crimson, shaded with velvety deep purple,	1 25
769. Elize Mercœur,	Lilac roseate, very large, full d'ble.	1 00
770. Ernest Ferray,	Deep rose color, fine,	1 00
771. Esmeralda,	Purple, full double,	1 00
772. Franklin,	Red, beautifully tinged lilac, glob.	1 00
773. General Allard, P. F.	Very brilliant rose, perfectly splendid, globose,	1 00
774. Glorieux, S.	Rich silvery blush, truly beautiful, globose,	50
775. Great Western, S. P.	Purplish carmine, very large, robust globose,	1 00
776. Henri Barbet, S.	Large brilliant pink, superb,	50
777. Hortense Leroy, S.	Bright rose, superb, distinct,	62
778. Hortensia, S.	Pink, tinged with fawn in clusters,	1 00
779. L'Admiration,	Delicate roseate, full double, graceful form, globular,	1 50
780. La Dauphine, S.P.	Large delicate flesh color,	50
781. La Superbe, S.	Bright roseate, large, imbricate, symmetrical,	1 50
782. Lady Montgomery, P.	Large pale blush, robust, habit of Celine,	1 00
783. Las Casas, S. P.	Very large deep rose, shaded,	62
784· Le Vésuve,	Purplish rose, very distinct, globose,	1 25
785. Legouvé,	Large violet, globose, fine,	50
786. Lord John Russel,	Light cherry, curiously veined and marbled,	75
787. Lusseldemberg,	Roseate, large, beautiful,	75
788. Madame Morel,	Carmine roseate, centre pale rose,	1 00
789. Majestueux, S. P.	Large bright deep rose,	50
790. Malton, or Fulgens, P.	*See Class VIII.*	
791. Marshall Soult, (Hooker,)	Bright rosy pink,	1 00
792. Miss Chauncey,	Rich fulgent rose color,	1 00
793. Olympia,	Rosy incarnate, tinged with lilac, superb,	1 00
794. Paul Perras, S.	Shaded rose, large, splendid,	75
795. President Molé,	Bright purplish rose, superb,	1 00
796. Richelieu, (Duval,)	Bright roseate, superb, globose,	75
797. Striped, or Striée,	Violet purple striped, full double,	1 25
798. Sylvain,	Bright crimson, superb, perfect,	75
799. Tippoo Saib,	Deep mottled pink, tinged salmon,	1 50
800. Victor Hugo, P. S.	Deep rosy violet, full double, fine,	75
801. William Jesse,	Deep roseate, monstrous, form of La Reine, sometimes blooms twice,	1 00

CLASS VIII.—HYBRID CHINESE ROSES.

This class of Roses owes its origin to the hybridizing of the French, Provence, and Damask Roses, with the Chinese Ever-blooming, Tea-scented, Noisette, and Bourbon Roses. The varieties produced from flowers thus blended, comprise the hybrids here enumerated. Their foliage is highly luxuriant, their branches very vigorous, long, and flexible; their flowers are of the richest hue and of the most elegant and diversified forms, and many of them are delightfully fragrant, thus presenting a combination of all that is grand and beautiful in this department of the Rose. They are peculiarly adapted for covering pillars and trellises, their shoots on strong plants frequently growing from 5 to 10 feet in one season. Although they bloom but once, yet that takes place at a much earlier period than the Summer Roses, and is of longer duration. If pruned after flowering, several of the varieties will throw out some autumnal blooms. They are propagated on their own bottoms, and also budded as standards, and are as hardy as the commonest Garden Rose.

The flowers of all the varieties are cupped except where otherwise denoted.

Name.	Color and Character.	$ cts.
802. A odeur, d'Anisette, F.	Deep rich pink, highly scented, globose,	75
803. A odeur d'Amande, F.	Bright red, almond scented,	62
804. A fleurs blanches, *Blanche fleur. White climbing Unique.'*	White, full double,	50
805. Amelie Guerin,	Pure white,	75
806. Auzou,	Dark purplish lilac, fine,	37
807. Assuerus,	Carmine, beautiful,	62
808. Aurora,	Crimson purple, white striped,	62
809. Beauty of Billiard,	Brilliant scarlet, in large clusters,	37
810. Beauty Bouquet,	Pure white,	50
810½. Becquet,	Very dark crimson,	37
811. Belle Ferronière,	Reddish violet, large extra,	1 00
812. Belle Marie, P. F.	Deep pinkish blush,	37
813. Beranger,	Light red, very d'ble, protuberant,	1 00
814. Blairii, No. 1, P. S.	Brilliant roseate, splendid, very fragrant,	50
815. Boullote, P. S.	Blackish purple, very double, extra superb, reflexed,	1 00
816. Brennus, S. P. *Queen Victoria.*	Very large, purplish crimson,	62
817. Bonne Genevieve,	Voilet crimson, large, full double,	50
818. Camuzet, carné, S.	Bright rose, magnificent,	50
819. Candeur,	Fine crimson,	50
820. Catel,	Deep crimson,	37
821. Charles Fouquier, P. S.	Deep purplish rose, very large, globose,	75
822. Charles Louis, No. 1, S.	Large, bright cherry, rosy border, globose,	50
823. Charles Louis, No. 2,	Rich lilac blush, beautiful, compact,	62
824. Chénedolé, P. S. F.	Vivid crimson, very large, beautiful,	1 00
825. Comtesse Plater,	Cream colored, beautiful,	1 50
826. ————, Lacepede,	Silvery blush, superb, perfect,	62

Name.	Color and character.	$ cts.
827. Coutard, S.	Large, flesh colored, perfect form,	37
828. Coupe d'amour,	Bright rose, superb,	50
829. De Laage,	Purplish crimson, marbled, fine,	50
830. Descartes,	Splendid new French variety,	1 50
831. Decandolle, P. F.	Scarlet crimson,	75
832. Docteur Guepin,	Large purple, violet shaded,	75
833. Duke of Sussex, S.	Deep roseate,	75
834. Duc de Richelieu,	Beautiful bright rose, large, full double,	1 00
835. Duke of Devonshire, P. S.	Large lilac rose, white striped,	75
836. Eliza Renou,	Delicate incarnate, large, full d'ble,	75
Emmeline, see Sweet Briar.		
837. Fabvier, F.	Large bright rose, changeable,	50
838. Fimbriata, or Frangée,	Cherry colored, fringed,	62
839. Flora Mc Ivor,	Rosy lilac, very large, globose,	75
840. Fulgens, or Malton, P.	Very brilliant carmine, globose,	50
841. General Kleber,	Bright purple,	50
842. George IV., P.	Violet purple, globose,	50
843. Georgia or Georgienne,	Rosy lilac,	50
844. Gloire des Hellenes,	Purplish rose, tessilated and striped,	75
845. Gloire de Couline, P.	Brilliant carmine, shaded with crimson,	1 50
846. Grillony,	Purplish slate color, very large,	50
847. Hypocrate.	Brilliant rose, perfect, superb,	37
848. La Grandeur, S.	Bright rose,	37
849. La Nubienne,	Violet purple, globose,	75
850. La Quintinine,	Lilac rose, in large clusters,	50
851. La Tourterelle, or Parny,	Delicate dove color, beautiful,	37
852. Lady Stuart, F. S.	Deep shaded crimson,	50
853. Le Meteore, P.	Brilliant red, beautiful,	75
854. Le Troubadour,	Rosy cherry color,	62
855. Leopold de Baufremont,P.	Delicate pink, large, splendid,	1 00
856. Lord Keith, P.	Purplish red, very large,	75
857. Lord Nelson,	Bright red, fine,	75
859. Madame de St. Hermine, P.	Deep cherry, rich, beautiful, globose,	50
860. Madame Lafayette,	Very dark purplish crimson,	50
861. Marjolin,	Black crimson, darkest of roses,	75
862. Ne plus ultra, or Pallagi,	Brilliant crimson, beautiful, globose,	37
863. Pallagi panaché,	Crimson and white, variegated,	50
864. Parigot, P.	Vivid crimson, beautiful,	75
865. Petite Pierre,	Bright rosy violet,	50
866. Pompone bicolor,	Violet, red centre, splendid,	50
867. elegante, F.	Pale flesh, bright rosy centre, pretty,	75
868. Potard P.	Large bright pink, very vigorous habit,	50
869. Quitterie,	Small rose, agathe foliage,	75
870. Reine de belgique, P.	Large lilac rose, fine,	37
871. Richelieu (Verdier,) P. S.	Bright rosy lilac, perfect, superb,	50
872. Saudeur panaché,	Red variegated with rose,	50
King of Hybrids.		
873. Triomphe d'Angers, F. P.	Fine purplish crimson,	37
874. ——— de la queue, F.	Purplish red shaded, large,full d'ble,	1 00
875. ——— de Laffay,	French white, outer petals tinged roseate,	50

Name.	Color and Character.	$ cts.
876. Vandaels, S.	Large violet purple shell,	50
877. Velours episcopal,	Deep purple, large,	37
878. Vibert,	Purple full double,	1 00
879. Violet de Belgique,	Large violet, splendid,	50
880. Vingt neuf Juillet,	Crimson purple, shaded scarlet,	
Coccinea superba.	brilliant,	50
881. William IV.,	Large pink,	37
881½. Yolande Fontaine, S.	Deep blueish violet, very double,	
	protuberant, superb,	1 00

CLASS IX.—FAIRY OR MINIATURE CHINA ROSES. *Rosa Lawrenciana.*

The varieties of this class are daily flowering, that is they produce a succession of flowers throughout the year in the same manner as Classes No. 1 and 2. They are remarkably dwarf or diminutive in the size of the plants as well as in respect to their foliage and flowers, many of the latter being no larger than a five or ten cent piece, and all of cupped form.

Name.	Color and Character.	$ cts.
882. Blush,	Blush,	37
883. Caprice des Dames,	Violet, shaded rose,	75
884. De Chartres,	Very small, roseate,	1 00
885. Dieu-donné,	Bright purple,	1 00
886. Gloire des Lawrencia,	Purplish crimson, very diminutive,	50
887. Jenny,	Brilliant rose,	1 00
888. La Miniature,	Crimson roseate, very small,	50
889. La Mouche,	Deep rose, very small,	1 00
890. La Laponne,	Very small, roseate,	50
891. Multiflora,	Deep roseate, very small,	50
892. Pompone bijou,	Delicate roseate,	50
893. Pompone, or Indica minor,	Blush, an old variety, larger than others,	37
894. Pourpre-brun,	Brownish purple, very small,	1 00
895. Retour du printemps,	Bright rose,	50
896. Rubra,	Deep crimson,	37
897. White or Blanc,	White with greenish centre,	50

CLIMBING ROSES.

The Classes X., XI. and XII., are Perpetual Climbing Roses, blooming more or less throughout the season, which is also the case with a very few of Class XIII. The other classes comprised under this section extend to No. XIX. *inclusive.*

CLASS X.—MUSK CLUSTER ROSES. *Rosa moschata.*

This class possesses a peculiar and delightful perfume. The flowers are produced in clusters, bloom from July to November, and are cupped, except where otherwise noted, and the plants require the same winter treatment as prescribed for the Chinese Ever-Blooming Roses.

Name.	Color and Character.	$ cts.
898. Double white, F.	White, old variety,	50
899. Eliza Werry, F. P.	Nankin, changing to white, expanded,	50
900. Eponine, F.	Pure white,	1 00
901. Fringed, F. P.	White, dentate petals,	1 00
902. Herbemont's cluster.	Blush, expanded, large clusters,	37
Madame Plantier, F.	Pure white, very fine,	1 00
903. New Double,	Creamy white,	75
904. Nivea,	White, shaded with rose,	50
905. Ophir, F. P.	Yellowish white,	75
906. Princess of Nassau, F. P.	Cream color, yellow centre, musk odor,	37
907. Ranunculus, or Superb, F.	Pure white, compact,	50
908. River's Musk, F.	Pink, tinged with buff,	75

CLASS XI.—ROSA MICROPHYLLA.

This class produces very large cupped flowers, of the most splendid description, from June to November. The foliage is remarkably delicate, peculiar, and beautiful, and the flower buds and entire plant are very distinct from every other class. The different varieties are hardy and well suited to train against fences or low buildings, or to form large dense shrubs.

Name.	Color and Character.	$ cts.
909. Alba odorata, P. F.	Creamy white, glossy foliage,	50
910. Carnea,	Pale roseate,	1 00
911. Coccinea,	Bright deep rose,	50
912. Cramoisie, *Violet cramoisie.*	Violet crimson,	50
913. Grandiflora, (River's,)	Roseate, very large,	1 00
914. Luxembourg Hybrid, P.	Rose color, vigorous,	50
915. Purpurea, P.	Purplish crimson, large,	50
916. Rosea,	Bright roseate, single,	75
917. Rubra, (old Microphylla,)	Rose, deep pink centre, large, hairy calyx,	50
918. Rouge Striée,	Large red, white striped or shaded,	1 00
919. Triomphe de Macheteaux,	Pale rose, shaded,	1 00

CLASS XII.—MACARTNEY ROSES. *Rosa bracteata.*

The varieties of this class have peculiar foliage and general appearance, and are very interesting, blooming more or less throughout the season. They have cupped flowers with the exception of one variety.

Name.	Color and Character.	$ cts.
920. Grandiflora,	Single white,	37
921. Lucida duplex, or double white,	White, semi-double, globose, beautiful,	50
922. Maria Leonida,	White, rosy centre, very fragrant,	50
923. Scarlet Maria Leonida,	Bright red,	50

CLASS XIII.—HYBRID CLIMBING ROSES. *Rosa hybridæ scandens.*

In this class are included the Hybrid Noisette varieties. All are fine hardy climbers, suitable for training on pillars, arbors, trellices, or sides of houses. The flowers are cupped except where otherwise designated.

Name.	Color and Character.	$ cts.
924. Astrolabe,	Bright pink, compact,	50
925. Bengale formidable,	Pale roseate, very double,	75
926. Briseis,	Delicate incarnate, full double,	1 00
Cherokee, or Sinica, *Georgia Evergreen.*	*See Bankeian Roses.*	
928. Clair,	Single, bright scarlet, showy, blooms all autumn,	62
929. Claire d'Olban, F.	Roseate, large, singular,	75
930. Egerie,	Deep purplish roseate, very double,	50
931. Elegans rosea,	Bright pink,	50
932. Fidéline,	Beautiful roseate, full double,	1 00
933. Fleurette, F.	Delicate roseate, very double,	50
934. Hybride parfaite,	Delicate roseate, full double,	1 00
935. Indica major, *Bengalensis scandens.* Ditto, per dozen $3,	Blush and white, robust, globose,	37
937. Madame d'Arblay, *Wells' white.*	White, monstrous clusters, a most rapid climber,	50
938. Madame Plantier,	Pure white, perfect, extra,	1 00
939. Maheka, Ditto, per dozen $3,	Semi-double, violet purple, profuse clusters, rapid growth,	37
941. Maria stella,	Deep rose color, full double,	1 00
942. Miller's climber,	Bright pink, small, pretty,	62
943. Pompon carmin,	Reddish carmine, small, very d'ble,	75
944. River's Queen,	Dark purplish crimson,	1 00
945. Sir John Sebright, F.	Vivid crimson, large clusters, semi-double, showy,	62
946. Sophie d'Houdetot, F.	Deep rose, very double, large clusters,	1 00
947. The Garland, F. · *Wood's Garland.*	Creamy, changing to pink and lilac, small, compact, immense clusters, elegant,	75
948. Triumph of Bolwiller,	White, globose, beautiful, in clusters, blooms in June, July and autumn,	50
949. Watts' Celestial, *Watts' climbing China.*	Large, rich roseate, blooms profusely,	50

CLASS XIV.—MULTIFLORA ROSES. *Rosa Multiflora.*

The varieties of this Class are vigorous and rapid climbers, and their flowers are remarkably neat, pretty and interesting, and are produced in large profuse clusters. The 1st Division comprises those with the smallest flowers and diminutive foliage; the 2d Division those with the largest flowers and foliage—the latter are the most hardy and appear to be nearly all varieties from the Greville. None of either division require protection in this latitude, unless in very exposed locations, and then binding them well with straw will suffice.

1st Division.

Name.	Color and Character.	$ cts.
950. Achilles,	Purplish roseate, fine,	75
951. Alba, or White,	Blush white, very neat,	37
952. Elegans,	Rose, very pretty,	50
953. Floribunda,	Rose, tinged with buff,	50
954. Fragrans,	Bright rose, superb,	75
955. Graulhié,	Pure white, pretty,	1 00
956. Laura Davoust,	Rose and white, very pretty,	50
957. Pink Garland, or Rubra, *Common pink Multiflora. Flora's Wreath.*	Deep roseate, compact, pretty,	37
958. Purpurea,	Light purplish pink,	75

2d Division.

Name.	Color and Character.	$ cts.
959. Carmin velouté,	Large deep roseate,	50
960. Crivellii,	Bright red, superb,	75
961. De la Grifferaie,	Carmine, vigorous, large of this class,	1 00
962. Grevillei, or Seven sisters,	Many colors, white to purple,	37
963. ——— alba, (Rivers,)	Pure white,	50
964. ——— grandiflora,	Deep rose, very large,	50
965. ——— minor,	Shaded rose,	75
966. Russelliana, or Cottage Rose, same as 863, *Scarlet Greville.*	Vivid purplish crimson and white variegated, changeable, beautiful,	50
967. Superba,	Pencilled roseate,	50

CLASS XV.—BOURSAULT ROSES. *Rosa Alpina.*

This class of Roses is distinguished by the young shoots being usually of a reddish purple hue. The varieties are also of remarkably vigorous growth, forming shoots of 12 feet or more in a season, and producing a great profusion of elegant flowers. They are perfectly hardy, as their

3

Alpine origin would indicate. The flowers are cupped where not otherwise noted.

Name.	Color and Character.	$ cts.
968. Amadis, or New Crimson,	Large brilliant purplish crimson,	50

969. Blush, or White,
   Bengal Florida?
   Belle de Lisle.
	Large pale flesh color, pink centre,
	  protuberant, globose, splendid,
	  vigorous growth, very early
		50

970. Drummond's Thornless,	Vivid roseate,	37
971. Elegans, *Purple Boursault.*	Purplish crimson, white stripes, expanded, profuse clusters,	50
972. Gracilis,	Bright pink, very pretty,	50
973. Thornless, or Inermis,	Large bright violet red, very early,	50

CLASS XVI.—AYRSHIRE ROSES. *Rosa arvensis.*

This class has very long, small, flexile shoots, which grow 12 to 15 feet or more in a season. The flowers are small, peculiarly delicate and beautiful. All are cup-shaped but No. 979 and No. 989. All the varieties are of the most hardy character, having originated from the common hedge rose of England.

Name.	Color and character.	$ cts.
974. Alice Grey,	Large beautiful blush,	50
975. Ayrshire Queen,	Dark purplish crimson,	50
976. Bennet's seedling,	Pure white, large clusters,	1 00
977. Blush, or Pearly,	Blush, pretty,	37
978. Countess of Lieven,	Shaded white,	62
979. Crimson,	Purplish red, expanded,	50
980. Dundee Rambler,	White, often edged with pink,	62
981. Feast's new white, F.	Creamy white, fragrant, beautiful, buds equal to Yellow Tea,	1 00
982. ——— Pink,	Pink,	50
983. ——— Purple,	Rich purple,	50
984. Jessica,	Delicate pink,	62
985. Lovely Rambler,	Brilliant pink,	62
986. Queen of the Belgians, F.	Pure white, very double,	50
987. Rose Angle, F.	Blush roseate, very vigorous habit,	50
988. Ruga, or Tea scented, F.	Pale flesh color,	50
989. Splendens, or Myrrh scented,	Creamy white, globose,	62
990. Variegated leaved,	Single blush, variegated leaves,	50

CLASS XVII.—EVERGREEN ROSES. *Rosa sempervirens.*

The varieties of this class are subevergreen climbers, with neat glossy foliage, which they hold till January. They grow rapidly, forming long shoots which resemble the Ayrshire in their small size and flexile character. Some of the varieties need a slight winter protection of leaves, litter, or earth, when in exposed locations. The flowers are cupped, except those noted.

Name.	Color and Character.	$ cts.
992. Adelaide d'Orleans,	Pink incarnate, in clusters,	50
993. Banksiæflora, F.	White, yellow centre,	1 00
994. Brunoni,	Bright pink,	75
995. Carnea grandiflora, F.	Large, pale flesh color,	1 00
997. Felicité perpetuelle,	White incarnate, compact,	50
998. Jaunatre, F.	Fawn colored rose,	1 00
999. Leopoldine d'Orleans,	Beautiful blush,	50
1000. Madame Plantier,	Rose color, expanded,	50
1001. Melanie de Montjoye, F.	Large, pure white, expanded,	1 00
1002. Minor,	Pale incarnate, autumnal flowering,	75
1003. Myrianthes,	Delicate rose, beautiful form,	50
1004. Odorata, F.	Very large, creamy white, globose,	50
1005. Princess Louise,	Creamy blush,	50
1006. ——— Marie,	Very pale roseate,	50
1007. Rampant, F.	Pure white, blooms in autumn,	62
1008. Reine des Francois,	Bright roseate, full double,	62
1009. Rosea major,	Pale rose color,	62
1010. Spectabile,	Deep lilac rose,	62
Triumph of Bolwiller, same as 1005.	*See Hybrid Climbing Roses.*	
1011. Alba Major, or Plena,	Pure white,	50

CLASS XVIII.—BANKSIAN ROSES. *Rosa Banksiæ.*

This beautiful evergreen family of Roses, is strikingly distinct from all others. All the varieties have fine glossy foliage, and small cupped flowers of neat and beautiful appearance, which are produced in wreaths. Their growth is very rapid, and they form very lengthy shoots in a single season, which are thornless with but two exceptions. This may be deemed the only tender class of Roses, and with the addition of one other variety, comprises all that are really so in this latitude. If trained on the south side of a fence or building, they will only require to be well bound with straw, but when in exposed locations, they must be protected by coiling the branches on the earth and covering them with a frame, or they may be placed in a green-house or cellar, free from extreme frost.

Name.	Color and Character.	$ cts.
1012. Alba grandiflora, F.	Very large, white,	1 00
1013. Blanc double superb,	Fine white,	1 00
1014. Cherokee, Georgia Evergreen, or Lævigata,	Large, single white, spiny,	50
1015. Epineux, a fleur-pleine,	Spiny, neat flowers,	75
1016. Jaune Serin, or Jaune vif,	Bright yellow,	62
1017. Odoratissima, F.	White, odor of orange blossoms,	62
1018. Philadelphica,	Pale yellow, single,	50
1019. Rosea,	Bright roseate,	62
1020. Virginalis,	Pure white, full double,	62
1021. White, F. *White evergreen Multiflora.*	Pure white, pretty,	37 to 50
1022. Yellow, *Yellow evergreen Multiflora.*	Fine yellow, in profusion,	37 to 50

CLASS XIX.— PRAIRIE ROSE, OR WESTERN MULTIFLORA. *Rosa rubifolia,*
vel setigera.

This vigorous native, erroneously named "Michigan Rose," is disseminated over thousands of miles of our mighty western prairies, and
may, in many respects, be deemed a national emblem. Its very robust
and hardy character adapt it even to a Canadian climate. The foliage
is peculiar, and the flowers expand in immediate sequence to the general
flowering of other classes in June. They are produced in profuse clusters or corymbs, many are very changeable, and all remarkably attractive. They are climbers of most rapid growth, often attaining 12 to 20
feet in a season, and the seminal hybrid varieties which will be produced,
and which will, without doubt, combine *perpetual flowering varieties,*
must take precedence over all others, and form a new era in the department of climbers, as they will flourish without care in every region of
our country, and perhaps of the world. The following varieties all have
double flowers of cupped form, except those designated otherwise.

Name.	Color and Character. $ cts.
1023. Altonia,	Rose color, tolerably double, pretty, 75
1023. Anne Maria,	Pale blush, pink centre, full, fine, 1 25
1024. Baltimore Belle,	Pale incarnate, changing to white, full, fragrant, beautiful, large as No. 1042, and in large clusters, 50 to 75
1025. Caradori Allan,	Bright pink, tolerably double, pretty, 50 to 75
1026. Common Michigan,	Single bright pink, changeable, ex., 37
1027. Elegans, *Kennickenick. Chilicothe Multiflora.*	Bright pink, tolerably double, 50
1028. Eva Corinne,	Large light blush, extra double, beautiful, 1 25
1029. Florinda,	Very pale pink, very large, full, showy, 1 50
1030. Gracilis, Prince's,	Roseate changeable, full, extra,
1031. Jane,	Deep rosy lilac, very full, beautiful, 1 25
1032. Kentucky Thornless,	Single, thornless, 75
1033. Linnæan Hill Beauty,	Pale blush, changing to white, very double and fine, 1 00
1034. Milledgeville,*	Brilliant carmine, very splendid, beautiful, glossy foliage, 1 50
1035. Mountjoy,	Pale blush border, deep pink incurved centre, very double, supb., 1 50
1036. Mrs. Henry Clay,	Creamy white, very beautiful, 1 50
1037. —— Hovey,	Large, pale white, beautiful, 2 00
1038. Pallida,	Incarnate changing to white, very fine, 50 to 75
1039. Pride of Washington,	Rose changing to lilac, full double, beautiful, 1 00
1040. Priscilla,	Pale roseate, beautiful, 1 50
1041. Purpurea, or Purple, *Perpetual Pink.*	Purplish violet, full double, rarely blooms in autumn, large as No. 1042, 50 to 75

Name.	Color and Character.	$ cts.
1042. Queen of the Prairies, *Beauty of the Prairies.*	Large, deep pink, often striped, exquisite form, very d'ble, beautiful,	50
1043. Ranunculiflora,	Small, light blush, pink centre, pretty,	1 00
1044. Sappho,	Full double, very pretty, late,	1 50
1045. Seraphine,	Pink with deeper pink centre, very double, late,	1 50
1046. Serena,	Very pretty,	1 50
1047. Spotted,	Single, spotted, prominent petals,	1 00
1048. Superba,	Pale blush, beautiful form, very double,	50 to 75
1049· Triumphant,	Deep Rose, changing to pale violet, full double, extra fine,	1 25
1050. Worthington,	Semi-double.	1 00

CLASS XX.— MOSS ROSES. *Rosa Centifolia Muscosa.*

This class of Roses is greatly esteemed for the extremely beautiful and striking appearance of the flower buds before expansion, which are covered with a most singular mossy appendage. The flowers of most of the varieties are peculiarly beautiful, more especially of the new ones which have been latterly brought to notice. The greater part of them have cupped flowers; those with globose or expanded flowers, are so designated.

Name.	Color and Character.	$ cts.
1061. Agathe leaved, or Feuille Agathe,	Small, pearly blush, nearly white, very double, globose,	1 25
1062. Alice Leroy,	Large, rosy lilac, very good,	1 75
1063. Anemone, or Sanguinea,	Bright, pretty, distinct,	1 75
1064. Angelique Quetier,	Delicate roseate, peculiar foliage,	1 25
1065. Asepala, or Oièllet,	Small, incarnate, rosy border, short singular petals, com.,	1 00
1066. Belle Rosalie,	Very pretty new French variety,	1 75
1067. Blush, or Incarnate,	Delicate blush, large, very fine, globose,	1 00
1068. Brilliant, (Lee,)	Semi-double, bright pink,	1 00
1069· Catharine de Wurtemberg,	Roseate, with stamens, vigorous, distinct, globose,	2 50
1070. Celina, or Gracieuse,	Large, brilliant purplish crimson, lucid foliage, superb,	1 50
1071. Charlotte de Sor,	Blush, Agathe leaved, full, superb,	2 00
1072. Common Red, or Rose color,	Pure rose color, large, globose,	50
Ditto, Extra large plants,		75
1073. Colmar,	Fine new French variety,	2 00
1074. Comtesse de Murinais,	Large, white, vigorous, superb, the first seminal white,	2 50
1075. Condorcet,	Pale roseate, beautiful, globular,	2 00

Name.	Color and Character.	$ cts.
1076. Crested, or Cristata,	Large, roseate, mossy sepals, elegant, globose,	1 00
1077. Crimson, or Damask,	Light crimson, very mossy,	1 00
1078. Crimson Pompone, Oscar Foulard.	Small, purplish crimson, very fine compact,	1 00
1079. Delphinie,	Hybrid, small, bright roseate,	3 00
1080. Diana de Colmar,	New French variety,	2 00
1081. Ecarlate,	Bright rose, fine,	1 00
1082. Eclatante,	Brilliant rose, expanded, robust,	1 00
1083. Emperor,	Bright crimson,	1 75
1084. Etna,	Purplish flame color, superb,	2 00
1085. French crimson,	Large, bright deep rose, distinct,	1 00
1086. Globuleuse,	Light crimson, shaded,	2 00
1087. Grandiflora,	Veined roseate, very large,	1 50
1088. Hardy,	Bright crimson, fine,	1 50
1089. Helene Mauget,	Bright roseate,	1 50
1090. Heloise,	Deep rose, protuberant, globose,	2 00
1091. Hooker's Blush,	Blush, rosy centre, in large clusters,	1 50
1092. Hortensia,	Reddish crimson, fine,	1 50
1093. Indiana,	Rose color,	1 25
1094. Josephine,	Lake, beautiful,	2 00
1095. Juliana,	Rosy pink, semi-double,	1 25
1096. Laffay's Crimson, or Purple,	Purplish crimson, pretty distinct,	1 00
1097. Lansezeur,	Deep crimson, veined with lilac,	2 50
1098. Large Fruited, or A'gros Fruit,	Large roseate, semi-double,	1 25
1099. Lancel,	Deep cherry to pale violet, very mossy, compact,	1 25
1100. Lucid leaved, or A feuilles luisantes,	Delicate blush, with rosette centre, globose,	2 00
1101. Louise Colet,	Delicate roseate, curious leafy calyx,	1 25
1102. Luxembourg Scarlet,	Deep scarlet, purplish tinge, very robust,	75
1103. Malvina,	Lilac roseate, fine, distinct,	1 50
1104. Marbrée,	Semi-double, roseate marbled,	1 50
1105. Maujet,	Bright purplish red, full double, superb,	2 00
1106. Metz,	Brilliant rose color, beautiful,	1 00
1107. Miniature,	Light crimson, semi-double, pretty,	1 25
1108. Mrs. Wood, or Purple Ranunculus,	Small, deep carmine changing to purple, beautiful,	1 50
1109. Moussué partout, or Zoé,	Rose, mossy leaves and flowers, globose,	1 00
1110. Moussué presque partout,	Rose, very double, leaves partially mossed, globose,	1 00
1111. Nivea, or Snowy,	Pure white,	2 00
1112. Orleans,	Purplish flame color,	1 00
1113. Panaget,	Purple striped with red, a novelty,	2 00
1114. Perpetual Red, (Maujet,)	Deep roseate, dwarf, very distinct,	3 00
1115. ———— White, or Four Seasons,	White, large clusters, vigorous growth,	1 00
1116. Pompone, or De Meaux,	Blush, early, dwarf, pretty, com.	1 50

Name.	Color and Character.	$ cts.
1117. Pompone Feu,	Small, deep purplish crimson, full double,	1 75
1117½. Ponctuée, or Spotted,	Rosy red, spotted white, semi-double,	1 25
1118. Précoce,	Deep roseate, sometimes spotted, early,	1 75
1118½. Princess Adelaide,	Hybrid, delicate rose, flowers in corymbs, splendid, vigorous,	2 50
1119. ———— Royal,	Deep purplish crimson, marbled, semi-double, vigorous,	75
1119½. Prolifère, or Mottled,	Roseate mottled, large, globose, robust,	1 00
1120. Prolific, Minor, or Gracilis,	Dwarf, roseate, distinct, globose,	1 00
1120½. Purple leaved, or Feuilles pourpres,	Bright red, young leaves red, pretty,	1 50
1121. Rosinella,	Purplish crimson, expanded,	2 00
1121½. Sage leaved, or Feuille de Sauge,	Bright roseate, distinct, beautiful, vigorous, extra,	1 00
1122. Scarlet, or De la Fleche,	Bright carmine, semi-double, very mossy,	1 00
1123. Scarlet Pompone, or Picciola,	Small, bright red, pretty, distinct,	1 00
1123½. Semi-double roseate,	Large, deep rose,	1 00
1124. ———— purple,	Violet purple,	1 50
1124½. Single Crimson,	Bright purplish crimson, often semi-double, extra,	1 00
1125. ———— Rose,	Roseate, distinct and compact plant,	1 00
1125½. ———— Lilac,	Distinct, curious,	75
1126. Splendens,	Large glossy pink, expanded,	1 00
1127. Unique de Provence,	Pure white, very double, in large clusters, beautiful, globose,	1 75
1128. Varacel,	Dark purple spotted with rose,	2 50
1129. Variegated or striped, Panaché pleine.	New French white, striped with pink, very pretty, full double,	1 75
1130. ———— Semi-double,	Medium size, variegated, semi-double,	1 25
1131. Veillard,	Roseate, very double, globose,	1 00
1132. Velours pourpre,	Light crimson, very double,	1 50
1133. Vesuvius,	Crimson shaded with purple,	2 00
1134. Vilmorin,	Large, deep pink,	1 50
1135. White Bath, or Clifton,	Pure white, sometimes striped, very mossy, globose,	1 25
1136. White French,	Incarnate white, glaucous foliage, globose,	1 00

SUMMER ROSES.

This division of Roses comprises all that are usually known as "June or Hardy Garden Roses," and which produce their flowers during the month of June, with the exception of a few that bloom early in July. Most of the seminal varieties, and particularly those of the Hybrid Classes, that have been brought into notice of late years, are of surpassing beauty, and but few others are deemed worthy of culture in the present improved state of floral taste. We have already referred to the great change in the public taste, adverse to Summer or June Roses, which has arisen, not from any deficiency in the beauty of their flowers, but solely from the short duration of their flowering season, and from the introduction to public notice of hundreds of new varieties of the most splendid description, belonging to those Classes that furnish a profusion of bloom from the opening of spring until the closing of the autumn.

From this consideration we have limited our selections in the eight following Classes, to those only which possess the greatest merit, discarding a large number, more especially of Classes XXIII. and XXIV., which, although still enumerated in many Catalogues, are greatly inferior to the improved varieties which we have retained.

CLASS XXI.—PROVENCE, OR CABBAGE ROSES. *Rosa centifolia var. provincialis.*

Name.	Color and Character.	$ cts.
1137. Anemone,	Rose color,	75
1138. Belgic blush,	Beautiful pale blush, in profuse clusters,	37
1139. —— Minor,	Small, blush, neat, and pretty,	37
1140. Childing's Provence,	Large, light red, fine,	30
1141. Curled,	Veined rose, very distinct,	62
1142. Dianthiflora, or Oiellet,	Small, blush, curious petals resembling a pink,	50
1143. Duc des Centfeuilles,	Handsome, full double,	75
1144. Duchesne,	Very large, roseate,	50
1145. Dutch,	Large, bright red, very fine,	37
1146. Flora's riches,	Violet red, superb form,	50
1147. Glandulosa,	Rose, leaves edged with yellow,	1 00
1148. Imperial blush,	Large, blush, changeable, very showy, tall,	37
1149. King of Holland,	Rose, flower encircled with sepals,	75
1150. Kingston,	Very small, roseate, full,	37
1151. L'aimable de Stors,	Fine red, convex, superb,	50
1152. Lilacina variegata,	Lilac, white stripes, inconstant,	1 00
1153. Old Cabbage Provence,	Large rose, very full,	50
1154. Royal Welsh,	Large blush, beautiful,	50
1155. Striped Unique, or Unique panaché,	White variegated with pink,	75
1156. Superb striped Unique,	White, beautifully striped bright rose,	1 00
1157. Sylvain,	Brilliant rose, superb,	1 00
1158. Unique,	Pure white, very superb,	50
Ditto, Extra large plants,		75
1159. Wellington,	Large, deep rose, very fine,	50

33

CLASS XXII.—DWARF PROVENCE ROSES. *Rosa Provincialis minor.*

These have small neat flowers, and with the exception of No. 1166, are the most dwarf, and the earliest flowering of Summer Roses. All have compact flowers but the one otherwise noted.

Name.	Color and Character.	$ cts.
1160. Burgundy, Button, or Shell,	Deep crimson, very dwarf, suitable for borders.	25
1161. De Meaux,	Pale roseate,	50
1162. Dwarf, or Petite Hundred leaved,	Blush, pretty, very double,	37
1163. Petite Mignone,	Lilac roseate,	75
1164. Pompone, or Dwarf Eglantine,	Blush, neat and pretty,	50
1165. ——— de Bourgogne,	White, pink centre,	75
1166. Rose de Juno,	Blush, very neat and pretty,	37
1167. Spong's,	Light rose, early, cupped,	37

CLASS XXIII.—HYBRID PROVENCE ROSES. *Rosa Provincialis hybridæ.*

Many Roses placed erroneously under this head in other Catalogues, will be found appropriately arranged under Classes XXIV. XXV. and XXVI. All of this class have cupped flowers except where otherwise denoted.

Name.	Color and Character.	$ cts.
1168. Alain Blanchard,	Large, violet spotted, semi-double,	62
1169. Alette,	Large, delicate roseate,	1 25
1170. Anna Czartoryski,	Large, red spotted with purple,	2 00
1171. Aspasie, S.	Delicate incarnate, beautiful,	50
1172. Blanchefleur, S.	French white, beautiful,	50
1173. Blanche de Castille,	Delicate blush, fine,	75
1174. Caroline Walner,	Small, delicate blush, full, beautiful,	1 00
1175. Christine de Pisan,	Rose, marbled with white,	1 00
1176. Coligny,	Large, spotted crimson,	2 00
1177. Donna Sol.	White, tinged with lemon, compact,	50
1178. Dubois Dessauzais,	Large, roseate, superb,	1 25
1179. Duc de Choiseul ponctuée,	Large, roseate spotted,	1 00
1180. Dutchess of Kent,	Light roseate,	1 00
1181. Duchesse d' Orleans,	Large incarnate, fine,	62
1182. Emerance,	Pale lemon, fine,	· 1 00
1183. Eulalie Le Brun,	Variegated rose and lilac, sometimes tricolor, a novelty,	2 00
1184. Foliacée,	Large, rosy incarnate,	1 00
1185. Garnier pages,	Crimson, white border, bud in centre, superb,	1 00
1186. Globe Hip, or Boule de Neige,	Fine white, very fragrant, large,	50
1187. Glory of France, P. S.	Deep shaded rose, superb,	1 00
1188. Hypacia,	Bright red, spotted,	1 00
1189. L'Ingenue,	White, buff centre, compact,	1 00

Name.	Color and Character.	$ cts.
1190. La fille de l'air,	Large, delicate incarnate,	1 50
1191. La ville de Londres, S.	Large, roseate, superb,	62
1192. Madame Labby, P.	Large, bright roseate,	1 50
1193. ———– Huet, P.	Incarnate, very fine,	1 00
1194. Melanie Waldor,	Large, white, beautiful,	75
1195. Margueritte de Valois,	Large, deep rose, spotted,	2 00
1196. Mrs. Rivers,	Pale incarnate, perfect,	62
1197. New Globe Hip,	Creamy white, fine,	62
1198. Odette de Champ divers,	Rose, marbled with white,	62
1199. Panaché, P.	Semi-double, incarnate, striped with red,	2 00
1200. Pauline Garcia,	Large, yellowish white,	1 25
1201. Pompone de la Queue,	Blush, shaded, beautiful,	50
1202. Princess Clementine, P.	Pure white, very large,	1 00
1203. Reine des Belges,	Pure white, fine form,	62
1204. Rosemary,	Large, roseate, spotted, rosette form, with marbled foliage,	1 00
1205. Sombreuil,	Deep rose, white spots,	62
1206. Spotted,	Deep rose, spotted white, large,	75
1207. Theodora,	Pinkish blush, anemone form,	62
1208. Venus,	Large, roseate,	1 50
1209. Wilberforce,	Large, purplish crimson, superb,	1 00

CLASS XXIV.—FRENCH ROSES. *Rosa Gallica.*

1st Division. *Flowers self-colored or shaded.*

The flowers are all of cupped form except those denoted otherwise.

Name.	Color and Character.	$ cts.
1210. Adelaide,	Small, bright crimson, very fine,	75
1210½. Agremont,	Rosy carmine, white border, superb,	1 00
1211. Antoine d'Ormois,	Large, blush, beautiful,	62
1211½. Ardoisée,	Slate color,	62
1212. Assemblage de Beautés,	Brilliant scarlet crimson, very superb,	1 00
1213. Aurelie Lamarc,	Bright roseate, perfect,	1 00
1214. Asmodée,	Large, rosy crimson,	1 00
1215. Belle Esquermoise,	Shaded slate color, very large,	1 00
1216. —— Sylvain,	Pearly white, deeper centre, superb,	1 00
1217. Boula, or Comte de Nauteuil, S.	Crimson purple, large, very superb,	75
1218. Champion,	Dark crimson,	50
1219. Cicero,	Crimson shaded lilac, large,	50
1220. Cochineal,	Bright red,	50
1221. Comte Lacépede,	Large, rosy lilac,	1 00
1222. Cordon bleu,	Shaded, bluish slate color,	37
1223. Crivalis, S.	Purplish blush, compact,	50
1224. Cyrus,	Lilac roseate, large,	62

Name.	Color and Character.	$	cts.
1225. Duc de Guiche,	Large, crimson,		37
1226. Dutchess of Buccleugh, S.	Bright pink, large, splendid,		62
1227. Diadême Superbe,	Small, bright crimson, ranunculus form, beautiful,		50
1228. Enchantress,	Large, roseate,		50
1229. Fanny Parissot,	Pale blush, very large, globular,		50
1230. Feu brilliant,	Very large, brilliant scarlet, compact,		75
1231. Franklin, S.	Large, rich rose, splendid,		50
1232. General Donadieu,	Bright crimson, superb, compact,		75
1233. Grandissima,	Purplish crimson, very large and fine, compact,		75
1234. Groot Voorst,	Large, splendid violet,		75
1235. Guerins Gift, or Guerin de Donai,	Bright rose, full shell, superb, perfect,		62
1236. Heureuse Surprise,	Large, crimson,		75
1237. Jeanne d'Albret,	Very large, bright rose,	1	25
1238. Kean, S.	Bright crimson, shaded shell, large, very splendid,		62
1239. La belle Elize,	Large, blush, fine,		75
1240. La belle Mariée,	Crimson, very full, beautiful,	1	00
1241. La belle Violette,	Dark bluish violet, large, superb,		50
1242. La Muskowa,	Velvety purple, very dark, expanded,		37
1243. La Tour d'Auvergne,	Deep rosy crimson, large, beautiful,		62
1244. La Volupte, or Letitia, S.	Rich deep rose, large, compact, extra,	1	00
1245. Lee,	Large, bright rose, beautiful,	1	00
1246. Le flavia bleuatre,	Bluish marbled, superb,		50
1247. Leon the X.,	Roseate, exceedingly large,	1	00
1248. Ludovicus,	Bluish violet, superb, singular,		37
1249. Ninon de l'Enclos,	Large, deep rose,		75
1250. Nouvelle transparente,	Large, rosy crimson,		75
1251. Ombre Parfaite,	Violet, shaded,		75
1252. Oriflamme,	Deep scarlet, most beautiful, tall,		50
1253. Pierian,	Red, pretty,		37
Pluto,	See Black Roses.		
1255. Rosamonde,	Rosy lilac, fine,	1	00
1256. Sancho Panza,	Large, slate color,	1	00
Superb Tuscany,	See Black Roses.		
1258. Tombeau Napoleon,	Fine red, whitish border, extra,	1	00
1259. Tresarin,	Violet crimson, full, tall,		37
1260. Venustus,	Bright red, handsome,		50
1261. Victoire Bizarre,	Bluish violet, crimson, mottled white, superb,		50
1262. Vidua,	Bright crimson, fine,		75
1263. William, or Guillaume Tell, S.	Large, bright rose, blush border,		75

36

2d Division. Flowers striped, variegated, mottled, or marbled.

All the flowers of this Class are of cupped form unless otherwise denoted. They form a most beautiful and peculiar family, and but one Rose Garden in Europe contains this admirable collection.

Name.	Color and Character.	$ cts.
1264. Abeilard,	Roseate, marbled, tall,	1 50
1265. A fleurs feuilles marbrées,	Purplish crimson, marbled, variegated leaves, compact,	75
1266. Agamede,	Deep rose, spotted white, reflexed,	50
1267. Agar,	Deep rose, spotted, rosette centre,	75
1268. Aglæ Adanson,	Very large rose, spotted white,	75
1269. Aimable Henriette,	Rosy crimson, spotted,	1 50
1270. Andre Thouin,	Brilliant crimson, spotted purple,	50
1271. Antiope,	Purplish crimson, spotted,	62
1272. A rameaux sarmenteux,	Cherry, variegated with lilac,	2 00
1273. Aramis,	White and deep rose, variegated,	2 50
1274. Arethuse,	Pink spotted, pretty,	50
1275. Arlequin,	Light red, marbled,	1 00
1276. Artemise,	Deep roseate, marbled,	1 50
1277. Belle de Fontenay,	Fine red, blush margin, expanded,	50
1278. Belle Herminie, No. 1,	Purple spotted, semi-double,	1 00
1279. ———— No. 2,	Large, deep velvety violet, spotted,	62
1280. ———— No. 3,	Large, violet purple, spotted,	50
1281. ———— No. 4,	Cherry color, marbled,	1 00
1282. ———— No. 5,	Claret, spotted, semi-double,	1 00
1283. ———— No. 6,	Large, crimson mottled white, very pretty,	75
1284. ———— No. 7.	Very large, deep rose, semi-double,	75
1285. Berangère,	Blush border, crimson centre, mottled,	62
1286. Berléze,	Violet crimson, spotted,	50
1287. Bizarre marbrée, S.	Rosy incarnate, often marbled, compact,	50
1288. Catinat,	Violet, spotted with purple,	1 00
1289. Camaieu,	Rosy lilac, striped, often has bud in centre,	62
1290. Charmante Isidore,	Purple, veined with crimson,	37
1291. Comte de Murinais,	Large, slate color, marbled,	1 00
1292. Cosimo Ridolphi,	Purplish crimson, spotted, large,	1 50
1293. Cramoisie picotee, S.	Lilac, finely mottled with purple,	1 00
1294. Cuvier,	Rosy crimson, spotted white, comp.	75
1295. D'Assas,	Deep violet, spotted,	1 25
1296. Donna Sol,	Purplish red, spotted, rosette centre, compact,	1 25
1297. Duc de Nemours,	Violet crimson, mottled with red,	1 00
1297. —— d'Orleans,	Roseate, spotted with white,	62
1299. Esther,	Rose, variegated with claret,	2 00
1300. Euphrasie	Deep rose, finely spotted,	75
1301. Fatime,	Roseate, spotted,	62
1302. Fenelon,	Rosy crimson, spotted,	1 00

Name.	Color and Character.	$ cts.
1303. Fontenelle,	Large, rosy crimson, spotted,	1 00
1304. Fornarina,	Roseate spotted with white,	75
1305. General Foy,	Deep violet crimson, spotted,	1 50
1306 Giselle,	Roseate spotted,	75
1306½. Hersilie,	Roseate spotted,	1 00
1307. Insigne Destekles,	Roseate, marbled,	1 00
1308. Isabelle de Lorraine,	Large rose with pale border, spotted, 1	25
1309. Jean Bart,	Roseate, spotted,	1 50
1310. Jeanne de Laval,	Large, deep rose, spotted,	1 25
1311. —— Hachette,	Large, reddish crimson, spotted,	1 50
1312. Kertly,	Violet, spotted with purple,	1 25
1312½. Lavoisier,	Deep rose, spotted, compact, variegated leaves,	1 00
1313. La Splendeur,	Bright red, motteld, with pure white, 1	00
1314. Le Baron Louis,	Violet crimson, spotted,	1 00
1315. L'Hospital,	Cherry, spotted,	75
1316. Lucille Duplessis,	Deep rose, spotted,	1 00
1317. Lycoris,	Deep pink, spotted white,	50
1318. Madelon Friquet,	Roseate, spotted, expanded, perfect,	1 25
1319. Mazeppa, S.	Red edged and marbled white, superb,	62
1320. Malesherbes,	Purple, spotted,	50
1321. Marceau,	Deep cherry, spotted with rose,	1 50
1322. Mecène,	White variegated with rose, expanded,	2 00
1323. Monime,	Cherry, spotted,	75
1324. Nationale tricolor,	Red, pale centre, edged white, compact,	62
1325. Nelson,	Violet purple, marbled,	1 00
1326. Nero,	Violet crimson, spotted,	62
1327. New Village Maid, Panaché pleine.	White, striped with rosy purple, very double, compact,	1 00
1328. Oeillet flamand,	White, striped with cherry, expanded, superb,	2 00
1329. —— parfait,	Pale rose, striped with bright red, globose, beautiful,	1 00
1330. Omniflore marbrée,	Crimson, dotted with white,	1 00
1331. Omphale,	Roseate, spotted,	1 00
1332. Panaché semi-double,	Variegated, deep rose and lilac, semi-double,	1 00
1333. Perle des panachés,	White, striped with lilac and violet, extra superb,	3 00
1334. Phénice,	Cherry spotted, roseate centre,	1 50
1335. Pourpre strié de blanc,	Purple, striped with white,	1 00
1336. Ranoncule ponctuée,	Red, spotted, compact,	37
1337. Rouget de l'Isle,	Purple, spotted with violet,	75
1338. Royale Marbrée,	Lilac and purple, marbled,	37
1339. Stella,	Pink, shaded with white, pretty,	75
1340. Superb marbled, General Damremont.	Violet purple marbled, variable,	75

Name.	Color and Character.	$ cts.
1341. The Prince, or Le Prince,	Crimson, spotted bright red,	50
1342. Tibulle,	Rosy lilac, spotted,	62
1343. Timarette,	Rosy purple, spotted,	62
1344. Tricolor, or Belle Alliance,	Variegated red, white and purple,	75
1345. ——— d'Orleans,	Red, with white stripes,	75
1346. ——— Superba,	Crimson purple, white stripes, expanded,	75
1347. ——— No. 2,	Deep crimson and purple, veined with white,	1 00
1348. ——— No. 3,	Brownish violet, marbled with red,	75
1349. ——— No. 5,	Violet purple, partially spotted,	1 25
1350. Tricolor de Vazemmes,	Violet purple, veined with white,	1 50
1351. Triomphe de beautè,	Purple striped with violet,	1 00
1352. Tullie,	Large, deep rose, marbled,	50
1353. Uniforme marbrée,	Roseate, marbled,	1 00
1354. Village Maid, *La belle villageoise,*	Rose, striped with lilac,	75

CLASS XXVI.—DAMASK ROSE, AND HYBRIDS. *Rosa Damascena.*

All the following varieties have cupped flowers.

Name.	Color and Character.	$ cts.
1360. Arlinde,	Delicate rosy pink, fine,	50
1361. Blanche d'Avilliers,	Pure white,	1 00
1362. Calypso, S.	Rosy blush, very large,	50
1363. Coralie,	White, rosy centre, beautiful,	62
1364. Déese Flora,	Pearly blush, full double, beautiful,	62
1365. Eliza Voiart,	Bright roseate,	50
1366. Imperatrice, (de France,)	Large, cherry color, beautiful,	75
1367. Ismene,	Large, delicate incarnate,	1 50
1368. Lady Fitzgerald,	Bright crimson, beautiful,	50
1369. La Cherie, La Negresse,	Incarnate, pink centre, superb, *See Black Roses.*	1 00
1371. La Ville de Bruxelles, S.	Large, roseate, glossy foliage,	62
1372. La Fiancée,	Incarnate shaded with rose, beautiful,	50
1373. Leda, or Painted,	White, with rosy margin,	50
1374. Madame de Maintenon,	Rose, edged with white,	75
1375. ——— Hardy,	Large, white, superb,	75
1376. Marc Aurèle,	Large, cherry color, spotted,	1 50
1377. Nereis,	Very delicate roseate,	1 00
1378. Olympe, Pope,	Purplish crimson, *See Black Roses.*	75
1380. Portland Pourpre,	Large, pale purple,	1 00
1381. Pulcherie,	Pure white, distinct, elegant,	1 00
1382. Red, (old variety,)	Rose color, very fragrant,	37
1383. Semiramis,	Large, roseate, fawn centre, superb,	1 50
1384. Veturie,	Roseate, peculiar shoots and foliage,	1 50
1385. Warratah,	Deep purple, splendid,	62
1386. York and Lancaster,	Rose, and white striped, variable,	50

CLASS XXVII.—WHITE ROSE, AND VARIETIES. *Rosa alba.*

The flowers of this class are peculiarly delicate and beautiful, and are all of cupped form, except where otherwise designated.

Name.	Color and Character.	$ cts.
1390. Astrée,	Very large, bright pink,	75
1391. Attila,	Large, brilliant, rosy crimson,	1 00
1392. Belle Clementine,	Roseate mottled,	75
1393. Blush Hip,	Delicate blush incarnate, beautiful,	75
1394. Bouquet blanche,	Pure white, tolerably double,	50
1395. Camelliæ flora,	Small, pure white,	1 00
1396. Camille Boulard,	Bright pink, globular,	75
1397. Celeste,	Incarnate white,	50
1398. Common, or Old White,	Pure white, good old variety,	37
1399. Duc de Luxembourg,	Pale rose, deeper centre, globular,	75
1400. Elize,	Large incarnate, beautiful,	50
1401. Etoile de la Malmaison,	Incarnate, white border, perfect,	1 00
1402. Fanny Somerson,	Rose, very double, compact,	1 00
1403. Felicité, (Parmentier,) S.	Flesh color, convex, very pretty,	50
1404. Ferox,	Incarnate, very spiny,	75
1405. Gracilis,	Small, incarnate, very double,	1 00
1406. Josephine Beauharnois,	White, tinged with rosy buff,	1 00
1407. Lasthénie,	Pale blush, globular,	1 00
1408. La Remarquable,	Beautiful white,	75
1409. La Seduisante,	Rosy incarnate, compact, superb,	1 00
1410. Madam Campan,	Rose, spotted with white,	75
1411. Maiden's Blush,	Pure incarnate, large, beautiful,	50
1412. Marie de Bourgogne,	Roseate spotted, incarnate,	1 00
1413. Naissance de Venus,	Deep pink, beautiful, compact,	50
1414. New Celestial,	Large, bright pink,	75
1415. Petite cuisse de Nymphe,	Small, flesh color,	1 00
1416. Pompon Bazard,	Delicate rose color,	1 00
1417. ———— Carnée, or Blanc.	Incarnate, compact,	50
1418. Princess Lamballe,	Pure white, compact,	1 00
1419. Queen of Denmark,	Large blush, superb, compact,	75
1420. Semi-double White,	Handsome, large,	37
1421. Sophie de Bavière,	Light roseate, full,	75
1422. Sophie de Marsilly,	Pale incarnate, deep rose centre, superb, globose,	1 00
1423. Thornless, or Sans épines,	White, shoots greenish white,	75
1424. Venus,	Pure white,	62
1425. Victoria,	Creamy buff,	50
1426. Viridis, or Rose verte,	White, buds green, curious,	1 00
1427. Vix Bifera,	Roseate,	1 00
1428. Zenobie,	Pale rose,	75

CLASS XXVIII.—DIVERSE, OR UNCERTAIN HYBRIDS.

These are very beautiful French varieties, produced by blending different classes, but whose precise parentage is unknown.

Name.	Color and Character.	$ cts.
1430. Amandine,	Large, delicate roseate,	1 00
1431. Helene Maret,	Large, white, peculiar foliage,	1 00
1432. Joasine,	Purplish red,	1 00
1433. Margarette d'Anjou,	Large, roseate, thornless, foliage and shoots yellowish green,	1 50
1434. Pelletier,	Pale lilac,	1 50
1335. Sextus Pompinius,	Purplish crimson, peculiar shoots and foliage,	1 00
1436. Sydonie,	Roseate, beautiful,	1 00

CLASS XXIX.—BLACK ROSES.

The following varieties have received the above appellation, on account of their very dark shades. They have originated from the classes denominated Provence, Damask and French Roses, and are very splendid varieties.

Name.	Color and Character.	$ cts.
1438. Black Merice,	Velvety black, very large, superb,	50
1439 Chancellor,	Deep crimson, purple marbled, sup.,	75
1440. Cramoisie enflammé,	Dark, extra fine,	50
1441. General Kutusoff,	Very dark, fine,	75
1442. Gloriosa Superba noir,	Very dark, superb, full, tall growth,	50
1443. Grand Czar,	Very dark, extra superb,	1 50
1444. ———— Pandour,	Very large, black, tall growth,	1 00
1445. Imperial,	Very dark, velvety hue,	37
1446. Infernal,	Dark, very fine,	37
1447. Iris noir,	Deep reddish purple,	37
1448. La belle Africaine, *African Black.*	Very dark, extra beautiful,	50
1449. La Cherie,	Small, very dark,	1 00
1450. La Negresse, (Damask,) new,	Small, very deep crimson purple,	1 25
1451. Le Seigneur d'Artzelane,	Very dark, extra,	1 00
1452. L'ombre Superbe,	Dark velvety hue,	37
1453. Lubec,	Dark velvet, very large,	37
1454. Negro, or Negroland,	Dark,	37
1455. Negro Panaché,	Dark violet, mottled,	75
1456. Nigritienne,	Deep purple, very dark,	37
1457. Onispertus,	Very dark, splendid,	50
1458. Pluto, (French,) new,	Deepest violet purple, very dark,	1 50
1459. Pope, (Damask,) new,	Large, deep crimson purple, distinct, inclined to bloom in autumn,	1 50

Name.	Color and Character.	$ cts.
1460. Premier Noble,	Dark, handsome,	37
1461. Rebecca,	Dark, marbled,	37
1462. Regina Nigrorum,	Large bluish black, extra superb,	1 00
1463. Rex Nigrorum,	Small, black marbled, superb, full,	50
1464. Sable,	Very dark, velvety,	37
1465. Sebille Noire,	Purple shaded, fine,	50
1466. Superb Tuscany,	Blackish crimson, large,	50
1467· Tuscany,	Dark velvet, not full double,	37
1468. Ventoris,	Dark, superb,	37
1469. Violacitus,	Very dark, extra superb,	1 00

CLASS XXX.— SCOTCH, OR BURNET ROSES. *Rosa Spinosissima.*

This very distinct class of Roses is of dwarf habit, with small and very delicate foliage. They flower profusely the latter part of May. The flowers are small, globular, and extremely neat and pretty. Above a dozen other varieties can be supplied to those who desire a greater variety of this class.

Name.	Color and Character.	$ cts.
1470. Athol,	Pretty, new,	50
1471. Blush,	Pale blush, beautiful,	25
1472. Cénomane,	Incarnate white, large, beautiful,	75
1473. Cramoisie,	Crimson,	50
1474. Daphne,	Dark, vivid, very pretty,	50
1475. Deep Red, or Atrorubra,	Deep red,	25
1476. Erebus,	Dark red, beautiful,	25
1477. Floribunda,	Pretty blush, delicate foliage, singular,	37
1478. Hardy,	White, shaded with rose,	37
1479. Ianthe,	Very pretty, new,	50
1480. Jugurtha,	Very pretty, new,	50
1481. La Neige,	Pure white, very fine,	50
1482. Marbled,	Neatly mottled,	50
1483. Minerva,	Very pretty, new,	50
Perpetual,	*See Class No. V.*	
1484. Princess,	Violet, curious,	25
1485. Purpurea, or Purple,	Reddish purple,	25
1486. Rœser,	Red and white shaded, singular,	50
1487. Saturnia,	Very pretty, new,	50
1488. Sulphurea,	Pale straw color,	25
1489. Venus,	Dark, distinct, fine,	25
1490. White, or Blanche d'ble,	Pure white, very pretty,	25
1491. William IV.	Pure white, large,	50
1492. Yellow, Double,	Fine yellow,	75
1493. ———, Single,	Bright yellow,	37

4*

CLASS XXXI.—AUSTRIAN BRIAR, OR YELLOW EGLANTINE, &c. *Rosa lutea, &c.*

All the varieties have cupped flowers except those denoted otherwise.

Name.	Color and Character.	$ cts.
1505. Austrian Yellow, or Copper, *Austrian red and yellow.*	Bright lurid red above, yellow beneath, single,	50
1505½. Capucine ponctué,	Yellow beneath and mottled with red above, singular, single,	1 00
1506. Double blush, or Victoria,	Salmon blush, buff centre,	75
1507. Double yellow, *Yellow Provence.* *Sulphurea.*	Globular, large, full double, deep yellow, delicate foliage, blooms rarely,	75
1508. Double yellow, Williams, *Yellow sweet briar.*	Bright yellow,	75
1509. Globe yellow,	Bright lemon yellow, globular,	75
1510. Halrrison's yellow, *Feast's Seedling.* *Hogg's yellow.*	Small, brilliant yellow, blooms profusely,	50 to 75
1511. Harrisonii, No. 1,	Pale yellow, tinged with copper,	1 00
1512. Italian yellow,	Straw yellow centre, very pretty,	1 00
1513. Lutescens, or Siberian yellow,	Small, straw colored, single,	37
1514. Persian yellow,	Deep orange, superb, distinct,	1 00
1515. Pompone yellow,	Globular, small deep yellow, dwarf habit,	1 00
1516. Single orange,	Orange yellow,	1 00
1617. Single yellow,	Brilliant yellow,	50
1518. Superb yellow, Williams,	Pale yellow, tinged with red,	1 00
1519. La bien trouvé,	Pure white, highly fragrant, globose,	75

CLASS XXXII.—SWEET BRIARS AND HYBRIDS. *Rosa rubiginosa.*

All are cupped flowers except Nos. 1541 and 1549, which are globular; and all are double of course unless stated as single.

Name.	Color and Character.	$ cts.
1525. Apple bearing, or Malifera,	Early, blush, very fragrant,	37
1526. Carmine,	Bright carmine,	1 00
1527. Carnation,	Beautiful blush,	75
1528. Celestial,	Pale blush,	50
1529. Chinese,	Deep rose,	1 00
1530. Clementine,	Rosy blush, pretty, distinct,	75
1531. Cluster,	Lilac rose,	50
1532. Dog, or Hip, single, *Rosa canina.*	Red, hedge rose of England,	37
1533. Ditto, double,	Red, fragrant,	50
1534. Iver cottage,	Pale rose,	62

Name.	Color and Character.	$ cts.
1535. Maiden's blush,	Pale blush,	
1536. Margined Hip, double, *Emmeline. Madeline.*	White, shaded pink, violet edge, superb,	1 00
1537. Margined Hip, single, *Hebe's lip.*	Creamy white, pink margin, single,	37
1538. Monstrous,	Single, pale red,	25
1539. Montezuma, weeping,	Single, pale rose,	50
1540. Mossy,	Light pink, mossy buds,	75
1541. Riego,	Rose, raspberry odor,	1 00
1542. Rose angle,	Deep lilac rose,	50
1543. Roseate, American,	Bright rose, pretty,	75
1444. Royal,	Pale rose,	75
1545. Scarlet, European,	Bright red, small,	75
1546. Splendid,	Bright brilliant crimson,	75
1547. Superb,	Rose, robust habit,	1 00
1548. Victoria,	Roseate,	50
1549. White American,	White, superb form, extra,	1 00
1550. White European,	White,	75

CLASS XXXIII.—FRANKFORT OR TURBAN ROSE. *Rosa turbinata.*

Name.	Color and Character.	$ cts.
1550. Ancelin,	Very large, deep rose, elegant,	75
1551. Aristote,	Large rose, with white border,	1 00
1552. Frankfort, (old variety,)	Very large, blush,	37
1553. Freelate,	Red, monstrous size,	75

CLASS XXXIV.—TREE, OR STANDARD ROSES.

This fancy class of Roses, although an improvement of modern date, has now become one of the most striking and beautiful appendages of the Flower Garden. It is comprised of the finest varieties, budded on strong stocks three to five feet from the ground, which form handsome heads, and present the appearance of miniature trees. In this manner they bloom more profusely and produce larger flowers ; and nothing can be more ornamental than an avenue of these trees, or groups of the different varieties, placed at suitable distances in a parterre. The Hybrid Chinese, the different classes of Perpetuals, the Bourbon, Hybrid Bourbon, Moss, Noisette, Chinese Ever-Blooming, and Tea-Scented, are the classes that are usually selected for this object, and above 400 varieties of these Tree Roses can now be supplied. All the classes enumerated are perfectly hardy except the three last named, and they require to have the heads bound in dry moss or straw, or to have some other casual protection, during the severe winter weather. The different varieties of Perpetuals and Bourbon, all of which bloom throughout the entire summer and autumn, are among the most admirable in point of ornament, and are perfectly hardy. The usual price for this class of Roses is $1 50 to $2 each, but we now offer them for $1 each, and some extra large sized plants at $1 25 to $1 50 each, and as we cultivate only a portion of the most desirable varieties of each class as Tree Roses, the selection of the varieties must necessarily be left to us. Purchasers can, however, name the classes from which they desire the selections to be made, and even the varieties, if they think proper, and we will conform thereto as far as possible. When the selection is left to us, the purchaser will be sure to receive choice varieties only.

When any of the varieties that are priced at $1 00 to $1 50 in the Catalogue for plants of the ordinary character, are desired to be of the Tree or Standard Class, an addition of fifty cents each will be made to the prices designated; but where the Catalogue price exceeds $1 50, no addition will be made, and it will be perfectly convenient to supply many of the higher priced varieties as Tree Roses. Half Standards can be supplied of a few varieties, which are budded 1¼ to 2 feet in height.

Standard Climbing Roses.—Price $2 00 each.

The vigorous varieties of Climbing Roses, may be rendered peculiarly ornamental when budded on strong stocks 6 to 8 feet in height, as they then form beautiful pendulous trees, their flexible branches drooping quite to the earth, and at the season of bloom, they present a most unique and imposing appearance. On some of the stocks we have budded two varieties, of dissimilar colors; the price of these is $2 50 each.

CLASS XXXV.—PROMISCUOUS SUMMER OR JUNE ROSES, USUALLY DENOMINATED HARDY GARDEN ROSES.

These, with a few exceptions to which an asterisk is attached, are the older varieties of Roses, the asterisk designating the new varieties. Many of this class are exceedingly beautiful, and it is only to be regretted that their period of bloom comprises but a few days.

Name.	Color and Character.	cts.
1560. Bright Crimson,	Brilliant hue,	50
1561. Brunette Superbe,	Dark marbled, extra,	37
1562. Burning Coal,	Small, flame red, shaded, superb,	37
1563. Carmine Brilliante,	Fine carmine,	50
1564. *Champion,	Dark mottled, superb,	50
1566. Couleur de Cendre,	Blush, deep pink centre, singular,	37
1567. Crimson Velvet, or Double Velvet.	Brilliant crimson, marbled,	25
1568. Dark Marbled,	Purple mottled, superb,	25
1569. Dark Violet. *Violet foncé*,	Splendid violet, mottled,	50
1570. Dazzling Red,	Bright red, very fine,	50
1571. *Duc de Cornuaille, (*Hybrid*,)		75
1572. Early Blush,	Shell form,	37
1573. Edemberger,	Crimson, marbled with violet,	50
1574. Fashionable,	Superb, deep crimson,	30
1575. Favorite Agate,	Very delicate blush,	37
1576. Flanders,		50
1577. *Fleur d'Amour,	Reddish violet, large, splendid,	75
1578. Geuconditus,	Blush, splendid,	50

Name.	Color and Character.	$ cts.
1579. Glittering Red,	Bright red, beautiful,	37
1580. Gloria Mundi,	Elegant, full double,	37
1581. Goliah, or Giant,	Light roseate, large,	25
1582. Grand Agathe,	White shell, pearl centre, very double,	
1583. ——— Alexander,	Dark violet, red centre, splendid,	50
1584. ——— *Duc,	Light crimson, round protuberant centre, superb,	1 00
1585. ——— Pompadour,	Very dark purple, extra,	25
1586. ——— Purple,	Deep purple, large,	37
1587. Great Crimson,	Vivid crimson, large, fine,	37
1588. Grand Montreuse,	Brilliant red, splendid,	75
1589. Great Red Mogul,	Large, red, handsome,	37
1590. Hay's Early Blush,	Light red,	50
1591. Hedgehog, or Ferox, single,	Purple, early, shoots clad in spines, curious,	25
1592. *Henard, (Hybrid,)		75
1593. *Imperiale,		50
1594. Imperial, Purple,	Fine purple,	37
1595. ——— Beauty,	Dark violet, superb,	37
1596. Incomparable Purple,	Dark mottled, very fine,	37
1597. ——— Violet,	Violet shell, tall, superb,	50
1598. King of the Purples,	Small, flame-color, shaded, superb,	1 00
1599. —— of Rome,	Large, crimson, very double,	50
1600. La Cerise,	Beautiful red,	75
1601. LaMajestueuse,(French)	Bright crimson,	50
1602. Le Deuil,	Small, dark violet purple, fine,	37
1603. Lovely Violet,	Violet, mottled and edged with white,	50
1604. *Louis le Roi, (Hybrid,)		75
1605. Marie Louise,	Velvety crimson,	30
1609. *Madame Ohl, (Hybrid,)	Red,	50
1610. *Morin,		75
1611. Ornement de parade,	Fine violet, grows tall,	25
1612. Perfect bouquet or Fringed,	Blush, full double, superb,	37
1613. Petite blush,	Small, neat blush,	50
1614. Petit panaché,	Variegated, small size,	30
1615. *Pourpre elegans,	Reddish violet, fine,	75
1616. Predominant,	Fine purple,	37
1617. *Professor Reinworth,	New and beautiful,	1 00
1618. Prolific Agate,	Blush shell, very full, fine,	37
1619. *Rose virginale,	Delicate, pale rose,	75
1820. *Sanspareille,	Purple and crimson,	75
1621. Septhun,	Red, variegated,	37
1722. Striking red,	Violet mottled, superb,	50
1623. Superb red,	Beautiful red,	75
1624. Transparent,	Peculiar shade, handsome,	37
1625. Triompheronde,	Purple, large, convex centre,	37
1626. Unrivalled purple,	Fine purple, convex centre,	37
1627. *Venustus vigo,	Extra fine,	50
1628. Violet a cœur rouge,	Fine violet, red centre, singular,	50
1629. Violet marbled,	Fine violet, mottled,	37
1630. Volidatum,	Fine violet, edged with white,	50

SMALL SELECTIONS OF ROSES.
To be be made by us, each plant of a distinct variety, with names.

A Splendid Collection,		of 12 Summer or June Roses,	$7 00
A fine	do	of 12 do do do	5 00
A good	do	of 12 do do do	4 00
A splendid	do	of 12 Hybrid Perpetuals,	7 00
Do	do	of 12 Damask Perpetuals,	8 00
Do	do	of 12 Bourbons,	6 00
Do	do	of 12 Hybrid Bourbons,	7 50
Do	do	of 12 Hybrid China,	5 00
Do	do	of 12 Noisette,	4 00
Do	do	of 12 Chinese Daily,	4 00
Do	do	of 12 Tea-Scented,	5 00
Do	do	of 12 Black,	6 00
Do	do	of 12 Ayrshire, 2 of each variety,	4 50
Do	do	of 12 Scotch, 2 of each do.	3 00
Do	do	of 12 Hybrid Climbing, 2 of each variety,	5 00

A collection of 12 Bourbon, China, Tea and Noisette varieties,   4 00

A collection of 12 varieties of Tree Roses, according to size of the plants, and splendor of the varieties, $10 to 15 00

A collection of 100 Roses of 50 varieties, 2 each, comprised of the various classes,   25 00

The following, per dozen.

Red Moss,	$5 00
Ditto, large size,	7 50
Crimson, or Damask Moss,	9 00
Luxembourg Scarlet Moss,	8 00
Unique White Provence,	5 to 7 00
Cabbage Rose,	4 00
Boursault, Maheka, and Indica Major, for Stocks, each,	2 00
Sweet Briar, for stocks,	1 50
Manetti,	3 00
Common Michigan, single,	2 50
Queen of the Prairies,	4 50
Champney's Pink Cluster,	3 00
Blush Noisette,	3 00
Red Damask Monthly, or Four Seasons,	5 00
Harrison double Yellow,	5 00
Red and Yellow Austrian,	5 00
La Reine Perpetual,	9 00
Cloth of Gold, or Chromatella Noisette,	9 00
Solfatare Noisette,	8 00
Russelliana, or Cottage Rose,	4 00
Greville, or Seven Sisters,	3 50

All hardy Trees, Shrubs and Plants, Green-House Plants, Bulbous Flower Roots, Seeds, &c., enumerated in any American Catalogues, can be supplied at least as low, and in most cases lower, than they can be obtained elsewhere in the Union. The orders will be executed with a degree of precision that cannot be surpassed, and in but few cases equalled, as this establishment is the only one that concentrates all the articles offered for sale within itself; and we are, therefore, under no necessity, as is too commonly the case, of purchasing from different persons, (often ignorant and irresponsible,) the requisite supplies, but supply hundreds of other Nurseries throughout Europe and America.

REJECTED AND SUPERSEDED ROSES,

Being inferior and some being synonymes.

Those who desire these kinds, can have them at 18 to 25 cents each during the present season, after which they will be entirely thrown aside.

Summer, June, or Hardy Garden Roses.

Admirable.
Adonis.
Albo novo pleno.
Athalie.
Belle aurore.
Bicolor.
Bijou.
Bijou royal.
Bijou de parade.
Bizard royal.
Bizar triomphant.
Blanda, or Labradore.
Blush,or False Unique.
—— damask.
—— thornless.
Bordeaux.
Bright purple.
—— superb.
Brigitte.
Brilliant crimson.
—— violet.
Brown Superb.
Brune brilliante.
Brunette aimable.
Cardinal.
Carmine.
Carmine superb.
Carnation.
Celestial.
Charming beauty.
Cinnamon, or May.
Colvill's Provence.
Coquette.
Couleur excellente.
Coupée.
Couronne Imperiale.
Cramoisie faveur.
Cramoisie flamme.
Crimson variegated.
Crowned rose.
Cupid.
Damask Provence.
Dark damask.
—— shell.
—— velvet.
Delicatesse.
Delicieuse.
Despong.

Double blush Burnet leaved.
Dutch blush.
—— cinnamon.
—— red musk.
—— tree.
Dwarf proliferous.
Early hundred-leaved.
Eclatante superbe.
Elysian.
Emperor.
Evratina.
Ex albo violaceo crispa.
Faultless purple.
Favaricus.
Félicité.
Fiery.
Fine purple.
Finest purple.
Fleur de parade.
Flora.
Flora nigricante.
Florentine.
Flore rubro.
Formidable red.
Fudide Lisky.
Garnet.
Glory of the reds.
Grand monarch.
—— pivoine.
—— sultan.
—— triomphant.
—— Turkey.
Great blush Mogul.
Great Royal.
Greatness.
Great purple.
Grisdeline.
Guerin.
Hyacinth.
Incomparable.
Insurmountable beauty
Interesting.
Invincible.
Isabelle.
King.
King of the reds.
La belle distinctive.

La grandesse.
Ladies' favorite.
Lancaster damask.
Lancaster changeable.
La palée.
La Zulmée.
Lisbon.
L'ombre panaché.
Louis XVIII.
Majestic.
Marbled.
Marbled apple bearing.
Marvellous.
Mere Cigogne.
Miniata.
Minor hundred-leaved.
Montpelier.
Napoleon.
New Dutch virgin blush
Nonesuch.
Nonpareil.
Nosegay.
Oriental beauty.
Ornament of the reds.
Pæstina.
Pale violet.
Paragon.
Parisian.
Pearl of Weisenstein.
Perfect ranunculus.
Perruque.
Plicate.
Polivites.
Pomona.
Poppy.
Porcelain à bordre blanc.
Precieuse.
Predestina.
Princess Charlotte,
Proliferous carmine.
Provence comprimée.
Purple mignone.
—— velvet.
—— violet.
—— royal.
—— triumphant.
Pyramidal.

Queen.
Queen of Hungary.
Queen of roses.
Ranunculus.
Red agate,
Red Belgic.
Reddish violet.
Red and violet.
Red mignone.
Red unique.
Red variegated.
Red velvet.
Rosa pumila.
—— Teneriffe.

Rose à mille fleurs.
Rose tendre incarnata.
Royal agate.
—— blush.
—— bouquet.
—— crimson.
—— purple.
—— virgin.
Rudicanlis.
Saint Francis.
Sans rival.
Scarlet Brabant.
Small mignone.
Sombre agréable.

Splendid beauty.
Stadtholder.
Steban.
Striped velvet.
Superior.
Surpassing.
Syren.
Tall climbing Provence.
Theophanie.
Variegated beauty.
————— crimson.
Vergrandus.
Virgin blush.
Watson's blush.

Black Roses.

Black Mogul.
——— Damask.
——— Prince.

Brussels.
Dark Mottled.

L'Obscurité.
L'Ombre Agréable.

Scotch Roses.

Alloa.
Banff.
Benlomond.
Bicolor.
Campsey.
Dalkeith.

Dalrymple.
Dunbarton blush.
Greenock.
Harrison's white.
Lady Montgomery.
Maiden's blush.

Pale colored.
Pentland.
Red prolific.
Single variegated.
—— white.

China Roses.

Aglæ Loth.
Animated.
Barclay's scarlet,
—————— purple.
Belle Chinoise.
—— Isidore.
—— Clarissima.
Bisson à odeur d'Anisette.

Camellia rouge.
Centifolia.
Chaussée.
Clintonia.
Double dark velvet, or Otaheite.
Dutchess of Kent.
Grenadier.
Gigantea.

Paris.
Purpurea.
Ronald's China.
—— white.
Seneca.
Theresa Stravius.
Undulata.
Vanilla.
Washington.

Tea-Scented China.

Adelaide.
Belle Traversi.
Chevalier d'Amour.

Etienie.
Kurtzii.
Lilacina.

Pœonia flora.
Thebe.
William Wallace.

Hybrid China Roses.

Belle Ecossoise.
—— et mince.
—— Thérèse.
Bizarre de la Chine.
Carré de Boisgeloup.
Celicel.
Cerisette.
Cesonie.
Columbienne.
Coulure.
D'Audigné de la Blanchaie.

Eynard.
Helvetius.
Holmes' Mandarin.
La Naiade.
Naide.
Lansezeur.
Lilac Queen?
L'Ingenue.
Louis Philippe.
Marechal Mortier,
Marie de Nerrea.

Mantault, or Manteau.
Narcisse Desportes.
Natalie.
Ponceau capiamont.
Princess.
Prolifère.
Promethée.
Stadtholder.
Thurette.
Tuscany.
Wellington.

Noisette Roses.

Ainé.
Alzand.
Amenia.
Amelie.
Anatolie.
Andreselle.
Belle Noisette.
Bougainville.
Blush Bengal.
Cadot.
Cerise.
Charles X.
Charmante.
Chrystalline cluster.

Countess of Crillon.
Countess of Fresnel.
Demetrius.
Dufrenoye.
Duchess of Orleans.
Duchess of Parma.
French pure white
Herbemont's Caroline.
Jane.
Julia, or Julia Dante.
Lafayette.
Lady Byron.
Landreth's   Carmine
cluster.

La Nymphe.
La Brilliante.
La Cherie.
Maria.
Mignon.
Orloff.
Pompone.
Pourpre.
Princesse Clementine.
Pulchella.
Sarmenteuse.
Sultana.
Superba.
Victoria.

Bourbon and other Perpetual Roses.

Alzais.
Alzina.
Augustine Lelieur.
Celimene.
Couronne des pourpres.

Couvrier.
Damask, flesh colored.
De Trianon.
Gen. Dubourg.
Isle Bourbon carnée,

Lee's blush perpetual.
Powellii.
Pulcherie.
Theresita.

Ayrshire Roses.

Blush favorite,
Blush virgin,

Red marbled.

Ayrshire Creeper, or
Rosa Arvensis.

Diverse Roses.

Frazer's blush, or Pink Musk.
Brooke's climbing China.

New Hybrid, climbing.
Red Boursault.

Single Roses.

Nivea.
Procera.

Red leaved.
Rosa capreolata.

Single red thornless.
—— Sweet brier.

GENERAL PRICES OF FRUIT TREES, &c.

Comprising only the most choice which Europe, Asia and America, have yet presented to the world.

	Each. Cents.	per hun'd. Dollars.
Apples, 350 select varieties,	30 to 37	25 to 30
Pears, 300 do. do.	37 to 50	35 to 45
Cherries, 120 do. do.	50	37½ to 45
Plums, 200 do. do.	50	37½ to 45
Peaches, 160 do. do.	25	20
Do. Assorted, fine kinds,		15
Do. Of 15 to 20 fine market kinds,		10 to 12½
Apricots, Nectarines and Almonds,	37	30 to 34
Quinces, Orange and Portugal, 5 to 5½ feet,	37	30
Do. do. do. 4 to 5 feet,	30	25
Do. do. do. 3 to 4 feet,	25	20
Currants of different kinds,		8 to 15
Raspberries, do.		5 to 10
Gooseberries, do.		12 to 15

Paulownia Imperialis, the most splendid Ornamental Tree ever introduced, and perfectly hardy, $6 per doz.

N. B.   A few very rare varieties of Fruit Trees are higher priced.

Extra large sized Fruit Trees can be supplied of many kinds suitable for immediate bearing, of which a distinct Catalogue will be furnished.

Ornamental Trees, Flowering Shrubs, Roses of every description, Bulbous Flower Roots, splendid Dahlias, Herbaceous Flowering Plants, Green-House Plants, Garden and Flower Seeds, &c., will be supplied at prices as low or lower than genuine articles can be elsewhere obtained. A liberal discount to wholesale purchasers.

WM. R. PRINCE & CO.'S
NEW CATALOGUES,

With reduced prices, which are distributed gratis, on application per mail, post paid, or of their Agents, Clark & Austin, Fulton-st., N. Y.

No. 1. Descriptive Catalogue of Fruit Trees, Shrubs and Plants.
" 2. Descriptive Catalogue of Hardy Ornamental Trees, Shrubs and Plants.
" 3. Bulbous and Tuberous rooted Flowering Plants, Double Dahlias, &c.
" 4. Green-House Trees, Shrubs and Plants.
" 5. American Indigenous Trees, Shrubs and Plants, and their Seeds.
" 6. Garden, Agricultural and Flower Seeds, with reduced wholesale prices.
" 7.   Do.   do.   do. in French.
" 8. Wholesale Catalogue for Nurseries only, with prices of Trees, &c., of different sizes by the quantity.
" 9. Catalogue of Fruit Trees, and of some rare Ornamental Trees, &c., of extra large size.

N. B. During the present summer, (1846,) we will publish the 35*th edition* of our Catalogues on an enlarged scale, with several hundred additional varieties of the most estimable Fruits, accompanied by very precise descriptions, and a greatly increased assortment of Ornamental Trees, Flowering Shrubs, splendid Roses, Herbaceous Plants, &c. They will form the most comprehensive and perfect works of the kind ever yet published, and replete with information. Price $1, to be remitted, post paid, with the application.

BOOKS.

Prince's Treatise on Horticulture,	-	-	-	-	$ 75
———— Treatise on Fruits, 2 vols.,		-	-	-	2 00
———— Treatise on the Vine,	-	-	-	-	1 50
———— Manual of Roses,	-	-	-	-	50

PRINCE'S MANUAL OF ROSES.—*Price* 50 *cts.*

This work has just been issued from the press. It comprises the most complete history of "The Rose," including every class of this interesting family, that has ever appeared in this country or in Europe. Every variety that is comprised in any English, French or American work on the same subject, is fully described in this, together with an immense number of new and splendid varieties that have not been noticed in any previous publication. The most ample information is also given as to the culture and propagation of all classes of "The Rose." Published, by the author, William R. Prince, and by Clark & Austin, Saxton & Miles, Wiley & Putnam, and Stanford & Swords, Booksellers, New-York.